ANGELS

ANGELS

KNOFEL STATON

COLLEGE PRESS PUBLISHING COMPANY· JOPLIN, MISSOURI

Library of Congress Cataloging-in-Publication Data

Staton, Knofel.
  Angels/by Knofel Staton. Demons/Leonard W. Thompson.
      p.   cm.
  Includes bibliographical references and index.
  ISBN 0-89900-939-5 (softback : alk. paper)
  1. Angels.   2. Devil--Christianity.   I. Thompson, Leonard W., 1941–
Demons.   II. Title: Demons.   III. Title.
  BT966.3.S72 2005
  235—dc22
                                                                    2005009876

To

Cathryn Comeaux

who patiently and lovingly

represents God

by helping

functionally impaired people

regain their abilities

so they can better enjoy a full life

CONTENTS

Foreword		**9**
Author's Preface		**10**
1. The Reality of Angels: Yes or No?		**13**
The Paradox	13	
Angelology: A Vacuum	13	
Angels: Universally Believed	15	
The Authoritative Source	16	
One Source, Many Opinions	17	
The Historical Decline of Belief	18	
The Resurgence of Belief	20	
Belief in the Unseen	21	
Our Cultural Problems	23	
2. The Present Popularity of Angels		**25**
Existence of Angels on the "Religious Hit Parade"	25	
Evidences of the Rise in Popularity	27	
Explanations of the Popularity Rise	29	
Examples of Interpreting Angel Activity	32	
The Essential Source	34	
Extricating Fact from Fantasy	36	
3. Angels: Their Biblical I.D.		**38**
Angels and People: A Community from God's Creation	38	
Linking Heavenly Angelic Beings to Earthly Human Beings	39	
As Messengers	41	
As Spirits	42	
Multiple Functional Terms	43	
Seraphim and Cherubim	47	
Principalities and Powers	48	
The "Angel of the Lord"	48	
Angels as Dead Saints?	51	

4. **Angels: Their Nature**   **54**
    Not Comprehensively Described   54
    Their Basic Nature   54
    Their Source   56
    Like Humans   56
    Unlike Humans   57
    Their Language: Communication Skills   58
    Their Number   59
    Their Organization   59
    Their Names   61
    Their Habitation   61
    Their Appearances   61
    Their Manifestations on Earth   62
5. **Angels: Their Relationships and Biblical Work**   **64**
    Relationship with God   64
    Relationship with Jesus   65
    Relationship with the Holy Spirit   66
    Relationship with the Church/Saints   67
    Their Work on Earth for Heaven's Sake   69
    Their Work in Heaven for Earth's Sake   74
6. **Angels Today: Yes or No?**   **77**
    Cessation of Believing   77
    Continuation of Believing   79
    Consistency in Serving   81
    Commitment to Openness   85
7. **Guardian Angels: God's Idea or Ours?**   **90**
    Looking at Various Positions   90
    Looking at Two Passages   93
    Noninclusive Evidence   95
    Complex Questions   96
    A Human Idea or God's   97
8. **Experiencing the Unexplainable**   **99**
    Living with Incomplete Knowledge   99
    Living with Faith, Hope, and Love   99
    The Finite Living with the Infinite   100
    The Infinite Reaching the Finite   101
    Living with the Realities beyond Us   101
    Living with Angels among Us   102
    Living with God for Us   103

7

Practicing the Presence of God   104
Living with the Unbelievable   105
Living with Openness and Caution   106
Living with Scripture and Experiences   106
Experiencing Authentic Angels   107
Intimate Living with God   109
Living with God Who Is Bigger Than We Thought   110
Living with the Unexplainable   111
Works Cited   **113**

FOREWORD

I suspect that there are many of you who, like me, have not given a lot of thought to the topic of angels. You might believe they exist because you recall familiar episodes that are recorded in Scripture. The top angel incidents that come to my mind are when the angel spoke to Mary about how she would conceive and bear a son, the heavenly hosts who announced Jesus' birth, and the ones who interacted with the women at the empty tomb after Jesus' resurrection. Beyond some of these examples, I am hard-pressed to recite very much more about their purpose or their involvement during biblical times, let alone their continued activity in modern days.

You may be surprised, as I was, to find that the Bible is full of references to angels. In writing his book Dr. Staton has done what many of the rest of us have not taken the time or effort to do. He has researched hundreds of references, condensed concepts from them, combined that information together with his expert knowledge of Scripture, and then created a readable study on angels. He examines angels from several different perspectives and guides the reader to assess who or what they are, what they do and do not do, and what God's purpose is in using them. The underlying current that courses through the book's chapters is the author's commitment to the authority of Scripture in determining his beliefs and conclusions about the role and pertinence of angels, both in the past and today.

Dr. Staton's ability to take what he knows from academia and Scripture, and then to present it in a readable, understandable, and helpful way is exceptional. I am delighted to recommend this book, and I trust that you will find it challenges your thinking and expands your consideration of the unexplainable things of God, including angels.

Cathryn Comeaux, O.T.
Rochester, Minnesota

AUTHOR'S PREFACE

I was surprised when Mark Moore called to inform me that College Press planned to publish two books to be bound as one on the topic of demons and angels and requested that I do the research and writing on angels. I was initially surprised because I had written a series of published articles on demons, but nothing on angels.

I was asked to balance the book with positions and teachings from both scholars and Scriptures, along with the pertinence of angels today. As I began the biblical research, I was subsequently surprised to discover the pervasiveness of angels throughout both Testaments. It is sometimes easy to read through Scriptures and miss the obvious.

It is sometimes easy to read through Scriptures and miss the obvious.

I was also surprised to see the pervasiveness of angels in non-biblical literature. For instance, the Library of Congress lists over 9,000 angel-related sources from diverse traditions and positions. During the past fifteen years, hundreds of nonreligious books have been published about angels, and major journals, periodicals, magazines, and newspapers have published numerous angelic-related articles, while biblical and theological scholars have been slower to do the same. A couple of helpful exceptions are Wayne Grudem's *Systematic Theology* and Stephen Noll's *Angels of Light, Powers of Darkness: Thinking Biblically about Angels, Satan & Principalities*, which is the most detailed biblical study published in recent years.

As I studied and meditated on this topic, I uncovered something others have not shared in their writings: that is, the close relationship of God's angels (His *heavenly* representatives and servants) with God's people (His *earthly* representatives and servants). I am convinced we need to seriously explore and apply that connection lest we become more focused on angels coming to earth than upon God's people staying on earth.

11   From this study, I am also con- **Preface**
vinced the Bible does not develop a systematic angelology (theology of angels), so there
is much about angels that is unexplainable. Moreover, I am convinced
that God never intended to stop using His angels for ministries on
earth. If so, He never shared that plan in Scripture. So we need to be
open to experience the unexplainable.

Nonbiblical teachers and writers should neither set the agenda nor define the nature and function of angels for Christians.

Nonbiblical teachers and writers should neither set the agenda
nor define the nature and function of angels for Christians. A person
believing they have experienced angelic appearances does not automatically guarantee the authenticity of those appearances nor that
God's heavenly angels are/were in those appearances.

Our positions about the reality, identity, nature, relationships, characteristics, works/ministries, and the ongoing relevance of angels must
be rooted in Scripture. God knows more about His angels than any biblical or nonbiblical teacher and author, and He revealed their presence
and practices from Genesis through Revelation. Scripture has a significant practice of shedding light on positions, teachings, and writings.

We must be careful not to allow our traditions, beliefs, feelings,
convictions, church affiliations, positions, and experiences to construct
theological or experiential boxes in which we think God remains. We
need to be willing to be uncomfortable with not knowing when and
how God may intervene in earthly affairs. Our God is in heaven and He
does whatever *He* pleases, not whatever *we* please. And we should not
replace the "He" with the "we" (Ps. 115:3; 135:6). All that God pleases
to do is for our benefit whether or not we recognize it at the time. He is
God-for-us, and His pleasure relates not only to *what* He does for us, but
also to *how* He does it, including sending His angels on any day to anyone for any reason, because His angels are *His* "ministering spirits sent
to serve those who will inherit salvation" (Heb. 1:14).

For too long I ignored the biblically pervasive topic of angels.
And perhaps some of the readers of this book have also neglected the
possibility of the reality of angels functioning throughout both biblical
and modern history. My quest for truth has taken me into different
directions from some of my teachers, colleagues, and traditions of my
church affiliation. As soccer players are encouraged to "go where the

Preface

ball is," so my theological methodology is to "go where the Bible is," not "where the crowd is," not "where the congregations are," and not "where the culture is."

I am deeply indebted to Cathryn Comeaux, an occupational therapist at Mayo Clinic in Rochester, Minnesota, for she was an "operational therapist" for this book. Cathryn squeezed into her crowded responsibilities the tasks of reading and revising the draft. She contributed hundreds of suggestions and fulfilled the biblical truth, "As iron sharpens iron, so one man sharpens another" (Prov. 27:17). Cathryn touched one of my gifts with the "iron" of one of hers and significantly sharpened mine. Because of her, the results of the research are now much more readable. Consequently, this is not just my book but also hers. And we hope you, the reader, will be open to God's angels and to experience the unexplainable of what the God-for-us does. And in so doing you will please God who does what He does and how He does it to serve and to please you whom He loves so dearly.

Knofel Staton
Hope International University
Fullerton, California
Knofelee@earthlink.net

CHAPTER 1

THE REALITY OF ANGELS: YES OR NO?

The Paradox

Billy Graham began his book about angels with a text and a question. The text he used revealed that God would command His angels to guard and protect someone in danger.[1] Graham then asked the question, "Are there supernatural beings today who are able to influence the affairs of men and nations?" He could have added "nature," because his text and question came after he wrote about a non-Christian Chinese woman who was being attacked by a tiger. When the woman cried out, "Oh Jesus, help me," the tiger immediately stopped and fled away.[2] Can God give orders to nature including sending angels to scare off wild animals? Psalm 147:15-18 answers with a resounding yes, "He sends his command to the earth; his word runs swiftly. He spreads the snow like wool and scatters the frost like ashes. He hurls down his hail like pebbles. Who can withstand his icy blast? He sends his word and melts them; he stirs up his breezes, and the waters flow." Once God sent an angel to change a donkey's bray to human words (Num. 22:26-30). Why would we believe that an angel shut the mouth of lions in Daniel's day, but would not shut the mouth of a tiger in our day (Dan. 6:21)? That would be a paradox at best.

Angelology: A Vacuum

The study of angels (angelology) is rather recent among Christians as well as connecting angelophany (the appearance of an angel) with theophany (the appearance of God). I never had a class about angels in any of the five different religious institutions of higher education I attended, nor have I yet to hear one sermon or lesson about

---

[1] Billy Graham, *Angels: God's Secret Agents* (Garden City, NY: Doubleday, 1975) 1.
[2] Ibid., 1-2.

Angels 1

angels in the church. That kind of neglect from class lecterns and church pulpits helps to maintain a vacuum into which many diverse concepts about angels have been conceived, born, and grown to a full-fledged system of beliefs. One scholar wrote, "No other theological subject has been so much the victim of so much unbridled imagination of generations of teachers and preachers."[3]

There are many questions to ponder about angels such as the following: (1) Do they exist? (2) If they do exist, what is their source? (3) When and how did they begin? (4) What do they look like? (5) What do they do? (6) How many are there? (7) Can we communicate with them? (8) Can we tell them what to do or not do? (9) Does everyone have a guardian angel? (10) If they are protectors, why do so many bad things happen to people? (11) If they guide us, how, why, and when? (12) Do they have a language of their own? (13) Are they organized? (14) Were angels sent from heaven in the past but not today? (15) Is it possible to develop a systematic angelology? (16) Why are angels so popular today? (17) Why do some Christians not believe in angels? (18) Who are they? (19) What are their basic characteristics? (20) From what source do we draw for correct information about angels?

The last question is the most essential one to answer because of two extreme positions. One extreme position is to reject any interest in angels. The other extreme position is to inject angels into every endeavor. This latter position is increasingly appearing in popular writings even within Christian literature such as *Guideposts,* its web site, and its published book, *Angels among Us.* As we read various and diverse stories of angelic appearances and ministries, do we automatically link them to either Divine Providence or to Devilish Paganism? An April 7, 2003, History Channel special, "Angels: Good or Evil?" outsourced the original idea of angels to pagan practices and art.

Two extreme positions are to reject any interest in angels and to inject angels into every endeavor.

How will we work through the complex issues related to believing or not believing, accepting or not accepting? We could tap into one or more various approaches such as the following: (1) Accepting what was taught in church tradition. Many follow the Nicene Creed of A.D. 325 which included, "I believe in one God, Father Almighty, maker of

---

[3] Rob van der Hart, *The Theology of Angels and Devils* (Notre Dame, IN: Fides Publishers, 1972) 18.

heaven and earth. And of all things visible and invisible," with angels being among the things invisible. However, others were taught that appearances and ministries of angels ended with the close of the New Testament era. (2) The evidence from personal experiences. (3) Believing in the reality of all angelic appearances that are reported in magazines and books without having personally experienced one. (4) Automatically denying the reality of past or present angels. (5) Labeling the idea of angels as a gimmick for solving problems or having problems solved. (6) Affirming the reality of angels because all religions report some interaction with heavenly beings.[4] (7) Affirming the reality of angels because of the evidence in the Old and New Testaments.

Angels: Universally Believed

Angels continue to be universally accepted across diverse religions and cultures both in past and the present times. Babylonians believed angels were gods. Roman mythology viewed them as being semigods. Greek poets wrote about millions of spiritual creatures walking on earth. Egyptian and Eastern cultures produced legions of art depicting supernatural creatures.[5] Today, members in the three major world religions—Islam, Judaism, and Christianity—believe in angels. Biblically, angels appeared across the history of both Old and New Testament periods. Angels were involved in the ministry of Jesus and the early Church. After the first century, early Christian leaders such as Ambrose, Jerome, and Augustine accepted the reality of angels. Later, scholars such as John Calvin wrote about biblical angels, "For if we desire to recognize God from his works, we ought by no means overlook such an illustrious and noble example."[6]

Angels continue to be universally accepted across diverse religions and cultures.

More recently, Karl Barth believed the Church had no right to consider angels in songs, prayers, and pictures if it does not deal with biblical revelations about angels.[7] One contemporary scholar argues

---

[4] William Riordan, "The Interaction between Heaven and Earth: An Interview with Brother Donald Mansir, F.S.C." *The Catholic World* 238, no. 1424 (March 1995) 74-79.
[5] A.C. Gaebelein, *The Angels of God* (reprint, Grand Rapids: Baker, 1969) 14.
[6] John Calvin, *Institutes of the Christian Religion*, I.14.3, 162.
[7] Karl Barth, *Church Dogmatics*, ed. by G.W. Bromily and T.F. Torrance (Edinburgh, Scotland: T&T Clark, 1960), III.3, 373.

Angels 1

that angels served God's people well in the past, and "it may now be time to experience that service again."[8] Rory Fox developed five reasons for believing in angels and challenged theologians who do not believe to provide an acceptable interpretative principle that deletes angelic reality.[9] Fox's five reasons are natural phenomena, personal experiences, biblical authority, ecclesiastical authority, and *a priori* considerations. While *a priori* is one reason listed for *believing*, Bernard Ramm wrote that *a priori* considerations cannot be used for *not believing*; "Modern man can have no *a priori* objection to the experiences of angels."[10]

The Authoritative Source

Upon hearing I was writing on angels, a friend of mine remarked, "For me to believe in angels would be like believing in ghosts." That person had never seen either an angel or a ghost, and thus would not believe in the unseen.

On one hand, not to believe in what cannot be seen would result in not accepting the existence of the Holy Spirit or God who is Spirit (John 4:4). Barth contended that to deny angels is to deny God.[11]

On the other hand, angel popularity is increasing at breakneck speed, with no unified authoritative source for evaluating their nature, their services, and appearances. Consequently, some rest their position on subjective feelings and speculations. In contrast to subjectivity Calvin wrote, "We should not indulge in speculations concerning the angels, but search out the witness of Scripture."[12] Because God has revealed what is profitable for us to know about angels in the Bible, there is no need to depend upon creative speculations and curious feelings. Thus empty speculation is fruitless.[13]

While Scripture is our authoritative source, it may not be desirable nor helpful to develop an ironclad systematic theology about angels. For angels, in the Scripture, arrived and left on varied missions with diverse

---

[8] David Fass, "How the Angels Do Serve," *Judaism* 40, no. 3 ((Summer 1991) 281-289.

[9] Rory Fox, "Can There Be a Reason to Believe in Angels and Demons?" *The Downside Review* 115, no. 399 (April 1997) 112-138.

[10] Bernard Ramm, "Angels," in *Basic Christian Doctrines*, ed. by Carl F.H. Henry (rep., Grand Rapids: Baker, 1971) 63.

[11] Barth, *Dogmatics*, III.3, 486.

[12] Calvin, *Institutes*, I.14.4, 163.

[13] Ibid., 163-164.

activities, appearances, and messages with no clear pattern. What is clear, however, is that they are God's ministering spirits (Heb. 1:14) and that God's ways are not our ways; He does whatever pleases Him (Ps. 115:3). But angelic diversity is no reason to circumnavigate the Bible as our unified and only authoritative source. Barth reminds us,

> The biblical witness to the revelation and works of God includes the witness to angels. . . . This is the fact which forms our starting point. The Dogmatics of the Christian Church has no other reason or cause to enter the sphere [of angelology] apart from this fact, which is not merely indisputable, but springs at once to our notice and demands. And we must stick with the Bible's witness.[14]

Our primary source is not the testimony of people, but the two testimonies of Scripture—the Old Testament and the New Testament.

The scriptural witness to angels is pervasive.

The scriptural witness to angels is pervasive. The Greek word for an angel or angels (*angelos*) appears 428 times—251 times in the Greek translation of the Old Testament (The Septuagint), and 177 times in the New Testament. Angels appeared at the beginning of the Old Testament and arrived and left through the Prophetic books. They arrived in Jesus' ministry (51 times in the Gospels), served throughout the history of the Church in Acts, and their existence saturates the last book in the New Testament (67 times—at least once in every chapter, but one).

One Source, Many Opinions

There are diverse opinions about angels from respected students of the Bible. Consequently, Stephen Noll calls for a revival of "serious exegetical examination of the vast references in both Testaments."[15] Barth called for discipline to counter the nonbiblical and contradictory positions of early Christian scholars. The differences are varied. For instance, Origen believed there were different angels assigned to different plants, animals, stars, and other aspects of nature. Thomas Aquinas thought angels existed all over corporeal things. Clement of Alexandria believed the entire Old Testament was communicated

---

[14] Bart, *Dogmatics*, III.3, 412.
[15] Stephen Noll, "Thinking about Angels," in *The Unseen World: Christian Reflections of Angels, Demons and the Heavenly Realm*, ed. by Anthony Lane (Grand Rapids: Baker, 1997) 1-27.

Angels 1

through angels. Hillary believed angels delivered the daily manna, protected the temple, flogged pagans who tried to enter the temple, and split the curtain at the death of Jesus. Gregory of Naziansen taught that angels looked for the prodigal son, are heads of local congregations, purify water at baptism, and judge every sermon preached.[16] Much of the above came from popular philosophical ideas. No wonder Barth warned that we should limit our knowledge to biblical revelation, and not mix philosophical thinking with biblical revelation.[17]

There are diverse opinions about angels from respected students of the Bible.

As Claus Westermann noted, the theology of angels can get out of hand.[18] This is easily seen from the pen of Thomas Aquinas, who was considered to be the ancient "angelic doctor." Aquinas wrote a comprehensive theology of angels in his *Summa Theologica*, but cited only one Scripture. Consequently, Barth wrote a stinging criticism that Aquinas's theology "has nothing whatever to do with the knowledge of . . . or fidelity to the biblical witness . . ." and that Aquinas's eight reasons for the existence of angels were purely philosophical.[19]

The Historical Decline of Belief

Since angels were active during the Old Testament, Jesus' life, the history of the early Church in Acts, and believed by Christian leaders throughout the early centuries of Christianity, the Middle Ages, and the Reformation era, why is there today a vacuum of belief among many individual Christians and among corporate denominations and congregations? The answer lies partly, if not largely, in the shift of many beliefs during the 17th to 19th centuries—the period of the Age of Enlightenment (also referred to as the Age of Reason, the Age of Rationalism, and the Age of Naturalism). During that era, the popular belief in angels declined steadily. That decline was the result of "scientific" and philosophical thinking (at times it is not easy to separate the two) that influenced theological thinking.

---

[16] Jean Danielou, *The Angels and Their Mission: According to the Church Fathers,* trans. by David Heimann (Westminster, MD: Christian Classics, 1976) 4-51.

[17] Barth, *Dogmatics,* III.3, 369-418.

[18] Claus Westermann, *God's Angels Need No Wings,* trans. by David Scheidt (Philadelphia: Fortress Press, 1979) 76.

[19] Barth, *Dogmatics,* III.3, 392-393.

Naturalism emerged from scientists who concluded that every event or result on earth was caused by a source that existed *within* the boundaries of this universe—a closed system. Thus every effect must have a *natural* cause at its root. Philosophers picked up on that idea, and developed the concept that every happening had to have a *rational* cause. Thus the Age of Reason—Rationalism. Francis Bacon (1561–1623) maintained that all reality must be affirmed by only the *empirical* method. René Descartes (1596–1650) popularized the view that everything had to be *reasonable.* He affirmed the idea of a "God of the gaps." That is, he viewed God as a possible cause for what could not be explained, but when a reasonable cause was discovered the "God of the gap" was eliminated. Given enough time there would be no gap, and thus no room for God. Spinoza (1632–1677) taught that revelation could not transcend reason, for reason is the only source of knowledge about reality. John Locke (1634–1704) advanced that concept with his view that revelation is just natural reasoning, thus no supernatural involvement. David Hume (1663–1727) insisted there is nothing supernatural beyond reason. In the mid-18th century J.J. Wettstein debunked revelation by collecting pagan parallels to the New Testament.

Naturalism and Rationalism infiltrated theological thinking and teaching. If there is only the natural and not the supernatural, and the only causes come from within the universe (closed system) with none coming from outside or above the universe (open system), then centuries of traditional theological thinking and teaching begin to unravel. For instance, Samuel Reimarus (1694–1768) wrote that the apostles invented Jesus' resurrection. F.K. Bahndt wrote eleven volumes developing the position that all miracles were nonhistorical. That position helped drive G.H. Lessing's position that all events must be repeatable to be historical. K.H. Venturini wrote four volumes developing his thesis that all miracles can be explained with natural reasoning. David Strauss's *Life of Jesus* (1835–36) dropped the theological bomb by writing that the early Church used creative imagination for supernatural sayings and acts of Jesus. That triggered several major bomb blasts that made direct hits against the historical Jesus. Thus it became popular to dissect and separate Jesus' life from the Jesus of fact (what really happened) to the Jesus of faith (what people inserted because that's the kind of Jesus they wanted). Albert Schweitzer pretty well defused the bombs by labeling those attempts to dehistorize Jesus as being no more

than scholars creating a Jesus after their   **20**
own image, which revealed more about
their theologies than about Jesus.

Because of the above kind of thinking that spread across the educational world like a Southern California brushfire with a 50-mph wind, by the beginning of the 20th century many theologians and churchmen concluded that "angels" were nothing more than pure fantasy, "belonging to a culture of the past that was not overly precise about truth and reality."[20]

Putting angels in the same category as Mickey Mouse and Winnie the Pooh continues. Since Schweitzer's "silencer," others picked up the Age of Enlightenment kind of thinking and conclusions. Rudolf Bultmann influenced contemporary liberal theology more than any theologian. Bultmann was adamant in arguing that it is not possible for a modern person to believe in the advances of modern technology on the one hand and to believe in the New Testament on the other hand.[21] Bultmann wrote a massive New Testament Theology in which he relegated most of the New Testament to myth.[22] The Jesus Seminar today keeps that kind of thinking before the public.

The Resurgence of Belief

While the belief in angels took a gigantic hit by the start of the 20th century, the writings of major Reformation leaders such as Calvin, Wesley, and Luther kept the reality of and the belief in angels alive for a remnant of Christianity. However, Barth deserves the most credit for the resurgence of belief among Christians. He devoted more pages to affirming the reality of angels than any other theologian up to his time. Barth maintained that angels are true even if they cannot be historically proven.[23] He wrote, "to deny angels, to limit them, or reduce them to any kind of immobility is to tilt against windmills. It is like trying to limit the sea with a handful of sand."[24] For Barth, Christians must discuss angels in relation to God and His kingdom with all discussions

---

[20] Michael Welker, "Angels in the Biblical Tradition: An Impressive Logic and the Imposing Problem of Their Hypercomplex Reality," *Theology Today* 51, no. 3 (October 1994) 357-380.

[21] Rudolf Bultmann, "New Testament and My Theology," in *Kerygma and Myth*, ed. by Bartsch (London: SPCK, 1964) 1:5.

[22] Rudolf Bultmann, *Theology of the New Testament*, trans. by Kendrick Grobel (New York: Charles Scribner's Sons, 1955) vols. 1 & 2.

[23] Barth. *Dogmatics*, III.3, 374-375.

[24] Ibid., 450.

tied to the Old and New Testaments while accepting no other authority or traditions.[25] The Roman Catholic Church also deserves credit for not allowing the positions popularized during the Age of Enlightenment to dilute its two-century-old faith-stance about angels as codified in the *Catechism of the Catholic Church.*

In spite of the belief decline during the Age of Enlightenment, there has never been a total break in the ongoing belief in angels by everyone in every place. The earliest art that included angels dates to around 2500 B.C. in Egypt and is located in Walters Museum.[26] Angels have always been a part of Jewish belief and teaching; however, in Jesus' day, the Jewish Sadducees did not believe in them. Their unbelief is connected to their not accepting the unseen world including life after death.

There has never been a total break in the ongoing belief in angels by everyone in every place.

Belief in the Unseen

While one contemporary philosopher believes it is as impossible to believe in the unseen world as it is to believe in a flat earth, and so relegates the reality of angels to our inner thoughts—the spiritual reality within us,[27] another keen philosopher notes there is nothing in philosophical thinking that deletes the belief in the unseen nonmaterial spirits. To discard angels because they are not materially seen is to discard other nonmaterial realities such as thoughts.[28] We need to put a curb on not believing what we do not see or experience, for as Alexander Whyte wrote, "Only God knows what awaits us beyond the curtain of the seen."[29]

To discard angels because they are not materially seen is to discard other nonmaterial realities.

Do not the appearances of angels coming to earth as reported in the Bible affirm the reality of the unseen world in heaven where God, Jesus, and our deceased loved ones live? Science is increasingly affirm-

[25] Ibid., 371-372.

[26] "Angels: Good or Bad," History Channel, two-hour special (April 7, 2003).

[27] Walter Wink, *Naming the Powers: The Language of Powers in the New Testament* (Philadelphia: Fortress Press, 1987) 4-6.

[28] Mortimer Adler, *The Angels and Us* (New York, Macmillan, 1982) 107.

[29] Alexander Whyte, *The Nature of Angels* (Grand Rapids: Baker, 1976) 127-128.

Angels 1

ing the reality of the unseen with nothing in scientific research that disproves the reality of the unseen.

Christ was able to see the Kingdom of God within an individual, the Father to whom we pray, and the Holy Spirit descending on Him. Christ, who knew the value of seeing the unseen, declared to His apostles, "Because you have seen me, you have believed; blessed are those who have not seen and yet have believed" (John 20:29; see also 1 Pet. 1:8). And could not He have also said something similar about affirming angels we do not see? And does not the inspired Scripture communicate that with, "Do not forget to entertain strangers, for by so doing some people have entertained angels without knowing it" (Heb. 13:2). That Hebrews verse stands between two verses about humans—love each other as brothers (verse 1), and "Remember those in prison . . . and those who are mistreated" (verse 3). It is possible that angels may materialize and approach us as needy people to evaluate and perhaps enhance our passion, compassion, consideration, care, and hospitality. Abraham and Lot certainly entertained angels without knowing it until later (Gen. 18:1-33; 19:1-3).

To not believe because we do not see is to functionally oppose Christianity, for Christians live by faith, not by sight (2 Cor. 4:18; 5:7; Heb. 11:1-6). Perhaps keeping some angels unseen is one of God's ways to emancipate us from our addiction to the material world—to only what is physical and seen. Perhaps some of us need the enlightenment of the inward eyes of the heart to affect the outer eyes of the head. Paul understood that, as seen in the content of some of his prayers, "I pray that the eyes of your heart may be enlightened in order that you may know the hope to which he called you . . . and his incomparably great power for us who believe" (Eph. 1:18-19). This particular Greek word for "know" (*eido*) emphasizes knowing by experience, and could be translated "experience." God wants us to experience what we may not physically see. Our God is above and beyond the materials of the physical.

Our God is above and beyond the materials of the physical.

Perhaps no one is as blind as the person who can see outwardly, but refuses to see inwardly. Consequently, we must be cautious about not believing what we have not seen or have not experienced, for it is "by faith we understand that the universe was formed at God's command, so that what is seen was not made out of what was visible"

23   (Heb. 11:3). By engaging an imagination of the unseen, scientists have discovered many marvels in the unseen such as electricity, gravity, atoms, germs, bacteria, viruses, genes, blockages in arteries, cancer, and so on. Because of belief in the unseen, Columbus started the trip that discovered this country. Reality is *never* restricted to the seen, to the believable, or to the explainable.

Angels 1

We must be cautious about not believing what we have not seen or have not experienced.

Our Cultural Problems

Van der Hart understands our reluctance to believe when he observes, "people in the sophisticated West are simply unfortunate, insofar as our understanding of nature makes it impossible for us to think of angels as moving about in the skies, and so we are tempted to assume that we cannot believe in them anymore."[30] However, angels appeared in the Bible from Genesis through Revelation. It is puzzling for us to believe that the world began the way the Bible describes and not to believe in angels who are reported to have witnessed the creation.

What rationale allows us to believe in the reality of biblical people, but not in the reality of angels who served them? What rationale supports our nonbelief in angels when the top leaders of God's people in the Old Testament, Jesus, and His apostles believed in them? What rationale feeds our lack of belief in angels if we believe that Jesus existed and that angels appeared to Him at pivotal times in His life such as making the announcement of His conception, warning about Herod's attempt to kill Him, strengthening Him after His wilderness temptations, ministering to Him in Gethsemane, rolling back the stone at His tomb, accompanying Him to heaven, and returning with Him? And what rationale allows us to anticipate heaven and life after death, which are described in the book of Revelation in which angels are mentioned more often than in any other biblical book, yet not believe in angels? Will those who do not believe in angels be embarrassed when Jesus comes with them and takes us to live forever with them?

There is no objective reason to think that angels are not still present and serving when they were consistently present and serving in the beginning and the middle of earthly history, and will be present and

---

[30] Van der Hart, *Theology*, 17.

Angels 1

serving at the end of earthly history. They are probably involved on earth far more than we think, and certainly than we see. There is not a hint in the Bible that the earthly service of angels will cease. Van der Hart advises if we accept the Bible as authoritative, "we would do well to pay serious attention to the whole problem of angelology."[31] Westermann keenly observed, "These messengers of God cannot be eliminated, symbolized, spiritualized, or demythologized by some exegetical method or other without losing a major part of the Bible."[32]

To not believe in angels may border on trying to limit God by restricting His power to our experiences and His will to our wishes. It may be our attempt to keep God inside the box we construct so He will be where we want Him to be and do what we want Him to do and not to do. To do that is to close us off from experiencing the unexplainable. Christians can create a closed system that honors the one designed by pagans. And this is one way we can do it. Sticking with the Bible is to affirm a totally open system created by God for our good.

Truth is often stranger than fiction. However, fiction can saturate thinking and teaching about angels. Lots of fiction has spread through numerous reports of angel appearances and interpretations about those appearances. Much of the proliferation is not supported by biblical evidence and does not agree with the biblically described nature, character, characteristics, and ministry of angels. Patrick Miller noted, "conjuring up angels and devils is the result of imagination that has worked over time and has dug a rut between fantasy and reality."

But how has that proliferation developed? We turn to that in the next chapter.

[31] Ibid., 16.
[32] Westermann, *God's Angels*, 72.

CHAPTER 2

THE PRESENT POPULARITY
OF ANGELS

Existence of Angels on the "Religious Hit Parade"

During the decades of the fifties and sixties "Hit Parade" was one of the most popular weekly radio programs among both adults and teens, because the top songs on the chart for that week were played. Teenagers who missed the program would surely know which songs made it to the top 3 or 4 before the next school day. Today, angels are among the top 4 or 5 on the Christian's popularity chart along with contemporary worship services, church growth through the seeker movement, mega congregations, gifts of the Holy Spirit (especially speaking in tongues), and nondenominational congregations. Were a survey of religious-related topics taken that targeted not only Christians, but also those who were not connected to any congregation and those who have no interest in Christianity, angels would no doubt quickly rise to the top of the religious "Hit Parade" chart.

Angels were included in Christian liturgy in every century since Christ.

A *Wall Street Journal* article reported, "After a hiatus of maybe 300 years and much skepticism, angels are making a comeback."[1] The interruption of angelic popularity was not total, because angels were included in Christian liturgy in every century since Christ.[2] But by the close of the 20th century angel popularity soared according to the findings from several different polls. The Chrysler Corporation's poll reported that 75% of Americans believe in angels, 65% have an angel decoration in their homes, and 55% believe every person has a personal

---

[1] Gustav Niebuhr, "After a Hiatus of Maybe 300 Years and Much Skepticism, Angels Are Making a Comeback," *Wall Street Journal* (May 12, 1992) 7.
[2] Nathan Mitchell, "Negotiatin Rapture: Rumors of Angels," *Worship* 71, no. 4 (July 1997) 350-357.

Angels 2

guardian angel. A study supervised by **26** Professors Tom Hodges and Robert Owen at Ohio University reported that one out of every five people surveyed believed he/she has seen an angel or knows someone who has; 77% believe angels are heavenly beings; 73% believe angels visit our world. Their study broke down the percentage of believers by the following categories: Men 72%; Women, 81%; Teens, 83%; African Americans, 87%; Hispanics, 76%; Whites, 76 %; Asian Ameicans, 57%; Northeast Region, 71%; West Region, 73%; Midwest Region, 77%; South Region, 83%; Without any religion, 47%. Those least likely to believe held postgraduate degrees and had a combined household income of $80,000 or more.[3] A *Time* magazine poll reported that 69% of American adults believe in angels with 46% believing they have a guardian angel. The Gallup poll reports the number of adults believing in angels increased from 68% in 1978 to 76% in 1994. Timothy Jones surveyed teenagers, and reported the number of teenagers who believe in angels increased from 64% in 1978 to 76% in 1992. The polls reveal that a transgenerational belief in angels increases at about the same rate.

Several people admit believing in angels who do not believe in God.

Several people admit believing in angels who do not believe in God. That may be due to the fact that over the past decades, many confirmed skeptics became believers in angels. One such example is Sidney Callahan who retracted his previous article in *Commonweal* in which he dismissed the existence of angels, but later accepted the reality of angels as one element of the "Mysterious Reality of God's Plenitude."[4]

"Angelphiles" (affection with angels) is a new descriptive word for those who keep a high and consistent interest in and an involvement with angels. Americans are fascinated with angels as seen by angels on greeting cards, bumper stickers, license plate frames, household decorations, books about angels, angel book stores, songs, movies, TV programs, jewelry, web sites about angels, the number of

---

[3] Tom Hodges and Robert Owen, "Do you believe angels, that is, some kind of heavenly beings who visit Earth, in fact exist?" a survey conducted and published in *Skeptic* 9, no. 3 (2002) 14.

[4] Sidney Callahan, "The Trouble with Angels: My Conversion Experience," *Commonweal* 122, no. 21 (December 1, 1995) 7.

Evidences of the Rise in Popularity

Philosopher, Mortimer Adler, the past Chairman of the Board of Editors of the *Encyclopedia Britannica* and Director of the Institute for Philosophical Research in Chicago, shared one of the most interesting evidences of the shift in popularity. Adler is the author of many books including *Aristotle for Everyone, How to Think about God,* and *Six Great Ideas.* In 1943, he and Robert Hutchins agreed to edit *Great Books of the Western World.* Their first task was to choose over 100 great ideas to consider for selecting Great books. Adler wanted to include angels as one of the great ideas but was sharply criticized not only by his coproject partner, but also by the then President of the University of Chicago, and by William Benton, the Publisher of the *Encyclopedia Britannica.* Those critics argued that angels would not be accepted as a great idea by potential readers since angels were neither relevant nor beneficial, and thus would not be interesting to people. However, Adler persisted and won. The supposed "irrelevancy of angels" as evaluated by his critics changed between the 1940s and 1980s when overflowing crowds packed large auditoriums every time Adler lectured about angels.[5] After 1990, the interest in angels in American culture and literature shifted quickly and significantly.

Malcolm Godwin's 1990 book, *Angels, An Endangered Species* (NY: Simon and Schuster), did not do well. But two years later Joan Anderson's book, *Where Angels Walk,* sold over a million copies and remained on the *New York Times'* best-seller list for over a year. Writings about angels appeared in some of the nation's most accepted publications. In 1993, *Time* magazine devoted its cover to angels. *Guideposts* developed a series on angels, "His Mysterious Ways," and opened a popular web site devoted to the topic of angels. Articles about angels appeared in the *New York Times Magazine* (April 1996), *The Wall Street Journal* (May 1992), the *Atlantic Monthly* (July 1996), *Newsweek* (December 1993), *Redbook* and *Ladies Home Journal* (both December 1993). Major newspapers carried angelic articles, such as the *People Weekly* (May 1993), *Longmont Daily News* (May 1981), *Buffalo News* (January 1993), *Los Angeles Times* (September 1992), *Detroit Free Press* (December 1993), *The Orange County Register* (December 1992

---

[5] Adler, *Angels and Us,* x-xiii.

Angels 2   and 1993), *The Washington Post,* and *The Chicago Tribune.*

The topic of angels pops up in many different aspects of our culture that includes a Church of Angels in Carmel, California; popular songs, such as "Angels Watching over Me," "Teen Angel," "Earth Angel," "Angel Eyes," "Where Angels Fear to Tread," "You Are My Special Angel," and many more; in TV specials (May 1994 and April 2003); in movies such as "Angel on My Shoulder," "The Bishop's Wife," "Michael," "Field of Dreams," "Wings of Desire," "Following So Close," and others. For several years the TV show "Touched by an Angel" topped the ratings with 20 million viewers each week. Others include "Highway to Heaven," "Angel Fire," and more recently, "Joan of Arcadia." A Broadway play, "Angels in America" received the 1993 Pulitzer Prize in Drama and was described as the most important theatrical event of the latter part of the 20th century.[6]

Book publishers entered the angelic market with over 300 books published about angels since 1990. Some of the angelic books have been on best-seller lists for many consecutive months. In 1993, the *Publishers Weekly* included several pages of books on angels from New Agers on the left to fundamental Christians on the right. Ballantine Books in Anderson, New York, is a major contributor to the increase of angel books. Their best sellers include Terry Taylor's *Answers from the Angels*, Eileen Freeman's *Touched by Angels,* Karen Goldman's *Angel Encounters,* Sophy Burnham's *A Book of Angels*, Rosemary Guiley's *Angels of Mercy*, and *Ask Your Angel* by Alma Daniel, Timothy Wylie, and Andrew Ramer. Ballantine Books published other popular angelic books including Joan Webster Anderson's, *Where Miracles Happen: True Stories of Heavenly Encounters* and *Where Angels Walk: True Stories of Heavenly Visitors.* James Redfield and Betty Eadie's book, *Embraced by Light* was listed number one on *New York Times's* best-seller list for more than 30 months. James Redfield's *The Celestine Prophecy* was listed for nearly two years. Dan Brown's *Angels and Demons* is number eight as I write this in the fall of 2003. Besides Ballantine Books, other companies that have published books on angels include Fortress Press, Zondervan, Westminster/John Knox Press, Mamre Press, Harper San Francisco, and many others, with publishing rights sold to outlets such as *Literary Guide, Thorndike, Catholic Digest, Guideposts, Reader's Digest,* and *National Enquirer.*

These books are quite significant for shaping diverse beliefs

---

[6] Bruce Weber, "Angels Angels," *New York Times* Magazine (April 25, 1993) 29-30.

29   about the identity, nature, appearances, and works of angels. The most popular

books give examples of people ordering angels who obey, talking back and forth to angels, using magic incantations to attract angels, seeing angels in all kinds of forms, and receiving all kinds of messages and services from angels—nearly all of which are self-centered and seldom, if ever, God-centered. Some explain detailed systematic steps for contacting angels. Many of the printed stories encourage people to insert angels into situations, and then report their presence in all kinds of coincidences.

Experiential teachings about angels are gleaned from over 5,000 reported annual appearances of angels to people. Who among those who credit angels for every minute detail in their lives would not want their angels to match or surpass the appearance and services of other angels for other people? If an angel does not match or surpass it when expected to do so, does that lack contribute to a person's sense of lessened self-worth? And do many appearances and sensational services inflate a person's ego? Could 1 Corinthians 8:1 be augmented by the Spirit today to also read, "Angel appearances puff up, but agape-love builds up"?

Explanations of the Popularity Rise

The most effective source for increasing the popularity of angels is not the Bible but the New Age movement to which many of the above authors are related in one way or another. This movement has over 1500 sites on the Internet with one site, "Angel Ring," receiving nearly half a million hits daily.

The most effective source for increasing the popularity of angels is the New Age movement.

But what factors trigger such an interest that the media continue to connect with that interest? It is difficult to determine where the line is drawn between the media reflecting the culture or fueling the interest into an inferno for the media's own profit as suggested by Trudy Bush.[7] There are many related "winds" that merge to conjure up the "perfect storm" of angelology. Gabriel Fackre suggests one catalyst is the kind of culture that is empty of piety. That sets up openness to

---

[7] Trudy Bush, "On the Tide of Angels," *Christian Century* 112, no. 8 (March 1, 1995) 236-238.

Angels 2

claims of other "supernatural encoun- **30** ters."[8] Dennis McManus believes one influential source is the expanding popularity of Spiritualism enhanced by the International General Assembly of Spirituality and The National Spiritual Alliance.

Spiritualism seems to spread faster where negativism, dissatis-factions, and disappointments abound.[9] Amy Schindler believes angels are created by people to fill their unmet needs and their inability to either solve their problems or to find an existing source for dealing with some of the complex problems that come with a complex culture.[10] Wendy Kaminer sees the popularity coming from people who cannot do critical thinking, and so are in need of some kind of codependent relationship. Kaminer also believes authors and publishing companies who feed this "psychological nonsense" engage in moral vanity.[11] Ron Rhodes ties the escalating angelic popularity to peoples' realized need for protection in a threatening and insecure world.[12] Wink ties it to the collapse of materialism, which opens people to spiritual realities in order to gain a sense of more stability in life.[13]

I suspect the rise in desiring, anticipating, and interpreting the presence of angels in all kinds of situations is related to the self-per-ceived and God-created need for human connectedness in the midst of a very disconnected culture. Relational disconnectedness is related to many different factors: (1) our highly mobile society that disconnects family members from one another; (2) our highly independent thinking that claims we can pull ourselves up by our own bootstraps; (3) our superficial relationships that are empty of continuous mutual consider-ations, respect, honor, attention, sacrifice, and close companionship in the dark tunnels of life; (4) the saturation of machines to which we relate instead of people—ATM machines, automatic computerized

---

[8] Gabriel Fackre, "Angels Heard and Demons Seen," *Theology Today* 51, no. 3 (October 1994) 345-358.

[9] Dennis McManus, "Angels: Their Importance in Our Lives," *Catholic World* 238, no. 1424 (March 1995) 69.

[10] Amy Schindler, "Angels and the AIDS Epidemic: The Resurgent Popularity of Angel Imagery in the United States of America," *Journal of American Culture* 22, no. 3 (Fall 1999) 49-61.

[11] Wendy Kaminer, "The Latest Fashion in Irrationality: When the Inner Child Finds a Guardian Angel, Publishers Are in Heaven," *Atlantic Monthly* 278, no. 1 (July 1996) 103-106.

[12] Ron Rhodes, *Angels among Us* (Eugene, OR: Harvest House, 1994) 33.

[13] Walter Wink, *Unmasking the Powers: The Invisible Forces That Determine Human Existence* (Philadelphia: Fortress, 1986) 2.

"communication" over the phone and
Internet, self-serve and pay-at-the-pump
gas stations, answering machines, and so on;
(5) privacy fences that keep us from seeing and connecting with neigh-
bors; (6) corporations that view profit as their most valuable asset and
employees as tools. This list can easily be much longer.

The multiple and diverse dysfunctional and noncaring relationships with people, hooked up with the ever increasing interaction with
nonpersonal machines, leave an emptiness inside of us because we
were created to be relational beings who need community and close
companionships. Add to that the information age that demands a reasonable answer or explanation for events, experiences, and surprises in
life, and we have the perfect recipients for regular real or unreal angelic visitations. When people-companions are not meeting God-created
desires, and when natural explanations do not unlock mysteries in life,
it is easy to plant an "Angel in the Gap." The New Age Movement
moves in on this and fills the gap for many people, because it is rooted in ancient Hinduism that views everything as divine. Thus the
Christian's One God as The Eternal Being above us and around us and
for us and in us by His Holy Spirit is not unique and not needed. But
without *the personal God* who created us, there is a vacuum both within us individually, and among us corporately that something, someone,
or some idea will fill whether or not it is linked to a real fact or to an
unreal fantasy.

It is easy to plant an "Angel in the Gap."

The corporate Church and individual Christians should not
ignore the above issues and needs in our complex culture, nor stand
idly criticizing and condemning the attempts people use to fill those
needs while not relating to those needs with the good news of God's
love channeled through the presence and practices of Christians reaching and serving the hurting and broken. These people desperately need
to experientially know that God loves them and desires to be their
companion through the live-in Holy Spirit and through His people,
who exist on earth to be His representatives, His stand-ins, His ambassadors, His visible servants with skin on. Christians are the extension of
God's love, acceptance, compassion, and ever-present help in the
midst of the dark tunnels and the deep pits of life. Christians united
together with other Christians are the continuing presence of the Body
of Christ, which might lessen the necessity of angelic ministries, but not
eliminate them.

Angels 2

If people do not experience the love of God through Christians, they can more easily fill the love-vacuum, the companion-vacuum, and the help-vacuum by inventing angelic visitations for all kinds of situations without relating to God. Doing so becomes an experience of cheap grace as a God-substitute. Rhodes picks up on this, "Angels are popular today because they are allegedly a means of attaining God's help without having to deal directly with God."[14] I would add to that, "and without having to deal directly with God's people when they are unattainable, unapproachable, uncaring, unloving, unwilling to help, unwilling to be friendly with outsiders, unwilling to get along with other members in the same congregation and with members in other congregations and denominations." So in the absence of the lovely presence of God in His people, many are open to shout, "Come, lord angels!"

Examples of Interpreting Angel Activity

It is possible that emptiness and aloneness may motivate some people to believe angels are directly involved in situations. However, we must not conclude that any fictional or nonfictional experience with angels is due to the recipient being empty or lonely. Here is a sampling of situations in which people believed angels were active. These are gleaned from a variety of sources from New Agers to Conservative Christians:

1. A little girl knocked on a physician's door at night to report her mother was very sick. The doctor followed the girl to the mother's house and the girl disappeared without going inside. Once inside the house, the doctor discovered that the little girl that came to his door and led him to her mother's house died a month earlier; the coat she wore when she came to the doctor's house was hanging in the closet at the mother's house.[15]
2. Hostile natives were turned back from destroying the house of missionary, John Paton, because they saw hundreds of men dressed in shining garments who circled the house with drawn swords.[16]
3. Japanese rebels in Africa were turned back several days in a row from killing missionary children because they saw soldiers dressed in white guarding the school.[17]

---

[14] Rhodes, *Angels among Us*, 31.
[15] Graham, *Angels*, 2-3.
[16] Ibid.
[17] Corrie ten Boom, *Marching Order for the End Battle* (Fort Washington, PA: Christian Literature Crusade, 1969) 89-90.

Angels 2

4. Captain Eddie Rickenbaker believed angels sent the sea gull to him and his crew that were in life rafts hundreds of miles from where any sea gull could have been. Eating the bird and using its inner parts to catch fish saved their lives. This incident is recorded in the Air Force Museum at Wright-Patterson Air Force Base near Dayton, Ohio.

5. Nelson Sousa dove into ice-covered water looking for a boy who had fallen through the ice; he found the boy and believed the man on the ice above him that pointed to the boy was an angel.[18]

6. Attorney Richard Whally believed an angel led him to disregard a false witness in a murder trial.[19]

7. Mary Krupicka believed an angel guided her out of a burning house.[20]

8. Charles Leggett believed an angel saved him from a fall because of the way he landed.[21]

9. Jerry Bond entered a burning house to find a little girl and felt a hand, which he believed belonged to an angel, pushing and leading him to her room.

10. A woman believed a man who helped her work with her stalled car for six hours was an angel. A woman who was ticked off at her mother in a hospital believed the Jamaican cleaning lady who stopped and spoke about her own need for mother-talk was an angel, because it caused the angry daughter to settle down; her mother died one week later. A couple who needed a new tire believed it was an angel who rolled a tire and wheel down the street, then into a creek, and abandoned it.[22]

11. A person who saw her dead mother's ghost believed it was her mother's angel.[23]

12. An Israeli officer believed an angel kept 120,000 Syrians with 1,400 tanks from advancing on Israel's army of 12,000.[24]

---

[18] *Angels among Us*, compiled by the editors of *Guideposts* (Carmel, NY: Guideposts, 1993) 13-18.

[19] Ibid., 19-22.

[20] Ibid., 45.

[21] Ibid., 58.

[22] Sophy Burnham, *A Book of Angels: Reflections on Angels Past and Present and True Stories of How They Touch Our Lives* (New York: Ballantine Books: 1995) 39-59.

[23] Ibid., 17.

[24] H.C. Moolenbaugh, *Meeting with Angels: One Hundred and One Real Life Encounters* (New York: Barnes & Noble, 1995) 149-153.

13. Howard Storm fell deathly sick, went into unconsciousness, and saw his life leave his body. Then he believed a group of angels gave his life back to him and told him to live differently in order to be fit for heaven.[25]

14. Angels helped people get their cars started, a tired mother change the sheets on her child's bed, and gave directions to people disoriented in strange places.[26]

15. Joe Stevenson believed an angel saved his house from catching on fire when a fast-moving brush fire was approaching.[27]

16. Don Boso believed an angel was transformed into a dog and growled madly to keep him from leaving home. Later it was discovered a murderer was hiding nearby at that exact time to kill Boso as soon as he would have left the house.

Similar experiences, and many which are more bizarre than any of the above, are countless with over 5,000 people a year reporting angelic appearances and services. Joan Anderson records over 100 "miracles" attributed to angels.[28] Allison Fabian shared several different ways angels are materialized into earthly beings for service, such as in a black poodle dog, a stranger, a woman, a weathered-looking man, a skier, the reappearance of a dead man now living, a scruffy bearded man, and an invisible force taking control of an out-of-control car.[29]

The Essential Source

Even though many connect the increase of interest in and experiences of angels to felt-needs, Ramm correctly notes, "Whether there shall be angels or not cannot be determined by any concept of necessity. . . . The existence of angels . . . is known and determined by divine majesty."[30] Without biblical revelation as *the only* essential and irreplaceable source, the popularity of angels makes it difficult for many to tell the difference between fiction and nonfiction—between fact and fantasy. The many different directions from teachings in the mass media

---

[25] "Angels," History Channel, April 7, 2003.

[26] Bush, *Tide of Angels*, 238.

[27] *Angels among Us, Guideposts*, 23-27.

[28] Joan Webster Anderson, *Where Angels Walk: True Stories of Heavenly Visitors* (New York: Ballantine Books, 1992).

[29] Allison Fabian, "Readers Swear: Angels Are Out There," *Cosmopolitan* 223, no. 5 (November 1997) 174-176.

[30] Ramm, "Angels," 63.

of books, magazine articles, television, music, Internet, and movies add to that difficulty. Below are some of the different directions into which the media pulls people:

1. Angels will always give us what we want.[31]
2. Angels will answer our prayers.[32]
3. We all need to know how to communicate with angels.[33]
4. Angels long for *us* to assign them tasks and projects.[34]
5. Everyone is meant to enjoy and share the unconditional love of the nine choirs of angels.[35]
6. Angels usually communicate with us in the silence of our interior understanding. We hear them with our hearts.[36]
7. Angels are citizens of our inner space.[37]
8. Angels are our invisible friends.[38]
9. Talking with angels is the most natural thing in the world and everyone can do it.[39]
10. Angels exist to be our guardian companions.[40]
11. Angels are our "radar of luck." They will keep a person aware of unfortunate opportunities and guide them to fortunate ones.[41]
12. Angels are probably the UFOs people report seeing.[42]
13. Angels will pop ideas into our minds.[43]
14. Angels can let us know who is calling before the phone rings.[44]
15. Angels come as people who died to talk with us.[45]

And that list can go on nearly endlessly. The above is only a very small sampling of teachings coming from the above sources that

---

[31] Burnham, *Book of Angels*, 51-57.
[32] Ibid., 50-51.
[33] Janice Connell, *Angel Power* (New York: Ballantine Books, 1995), xiii-xiv.
[34] Ibid., xvi.
[35] Ibid., xv-xvi.
[36] Ibid., xvii.
[37] Alma Daniel, Timothy Wyllie, and Andrew Ramer, *Ask Your Angels* (New York: Ballantine Books, 1992).
[38] Ibid.
[39] Ibid.
[40] McManus, *Angels*, 68-70.
[41] Merrill Markoe, "I Network with Angels," *New Woman* 7, no. 4 (April 1997) 58-61.
[42] Riordan, "Interaction," quoting Mansir, 75.
[43] Burnham, *Book of Angels*, in most of the experiences she cites.
[44] Ibid., 76.
[45] Ibid., 77.

Extricating Fact from Fantasy

Is the popularity of angels an aspect of awesome angelology or of awful angel mania? The positive side of the popularity is that it directly opposes the philosophical and theological positions developed and popularized during the Age of Enlightenment that imprisoned us inside the concept of a closed system (see chapter 2). Angelic popularity is evidence of a heightened awareness of transcendence—that there *is* reality beyond our universe that can and does infiltrate this planet for our good.

Angelic popularity is evidence of a heightened awareness of transcendence.

However, the negative side of angelic popularity is that it may feed a false need to have an explanation for every event. Such a need can nudge people into reading angels into every event or the results of every event that is unexplainable. Or if it is explainable, people may choose not to accept the less sensational natural explanation for a more sensational one, as if God did not create a world in which surprises can happen without His direct input, but certainly not without His direct interest. Some people habitually prefer subjectivity to objectivity, the unreal to the real. Thus emotionalism of situations can easily take precedence over exegesis of Scriptures. While accepting the reality of the supernatural, some have neglected the value of the natural. Without realizing it, we may actually substitute our superstitions and desires for real supernatural encounters and not know the difference and not recognize the real when it does come. To impose unreal angels into surprising events may deaden us to the real angels. Then eventually we do not need the real supernatural as long as we can insert the virtual supernatural into anything natural.

Without realizing it, we may actually substitute our superstitions and desires for real encounters.

To insert supernatural beings into circumstances can open us up to influences that are antiscriptural and antigodly. Mansir makes a keen analytical observation about the New Age religion being "little more than a cover for confused Satanic worship expressed in books and

music which has shaped the younger gen-
      erations to have a tolerance for an infatu-
ation with the devil."[46]

Daniel traced an interesting shift. In biblical times angels were servants of God. By medieval times, they were servants of anyone who knew their names and requested them to do various services. Today, angels are beyond the context of religion and will speak to anyone who will silence the mind long enough to listen.[47]

The task placed before Christians is to analyze the vast reported experiences of and teachings about angels from God's only written source of authority, the Bible. Shedd suggests we measure the validity of angel stories with two questions: Do they have verification in biblical accounts? And, was the outcome helpful to at least one person? The second question is too broad and can be misleading. The second question would be better stated, "Was the outcome beneficial to God's mission on earth?"

That requires us to turn to the biblical revelation about angels, which will be addressed in the next chapter.

---

[46] As reported in Riordan, "Interaction," 78.
[47] Daniel et al., *Ask Your Angels*, 44.

CHAPTER 3

ANGELS: THEIR BIBLICAL I.D.

Angels and People:
A Community from God's Creation

The first word for "God" in the Bible is the plural Hebrew word, *Elohim* (Gen. 1:1). The first reality about God revealed in that plural word is that God has always existed within a community—the Father, Son, and Holy Spirit. The biblical God is relational. John spotlighted that when he wrote, "God is love" (1 John 4:16). Agape love is God's basic relational characteristic.

The dominant attribute of God's agape love is unselfish sharing.

The dominant attribute of God's agape love is unselfish sharing: authentic love does not hoard; it does not insist upon its own way; it does not take freedom away from the loved one; it woos and waits; it is open to and for the loved one; it seeks to please the loved one, and is pleased when it does; it is not self-seeking, but other-serving; it always protects; it always wants to close the gap between the lover and the loved one; it always protects the loved one; it is always willing to stand up for the loved one; it prioritizes the loved one; it rejoices in the loved one; it gives freedom to the loved one; it outlasts all other characteristics. God is all of that and more, for all His other attitudes are relational and flow from love. He is our model of what love is and what love does.

God shared Himself when He created people, "Let us make man in our image, in our likeness . . ." (Gen. 1:26a). The "us" and "our" refer not only to the reality of the Father, Son, and Holy Spirit, but also to the kind of relationship the three have among themselves; they are so close that the three are one. God shared His relational nature when He put his own breath (Spirit) of life in people (Gen. 2:7). The word "breath" is from *neshamah,* one of the two Hebrew words for Spirit—God's Holy Spirit as seen in Job 33:4, "The Spirit of God has made me; the breath of the Almighty gives me life." (See also Job 34:14.) Paul used the Genesis term when he wrote about the Holy Spirit in Romans 8:2—Spirit (or breath) of life.

God not only shared the nature of His kind of relationship with people, but also the nature of His kind of functions which include the following: (1) The creative God shared that function when He said, "Be fruitful and increase in number; fill the earth . . ." (Gen. 1:28). People can and hopefully do conceive others out of love as God created the first people out of love. We are not to conceive like barnyard animals without love, feelings, purpose, joy, etc. (2) The caring God also shared that function, "The LORD God took the man and put him in the Garden of Eden to work it and take care of it" (Gen. 2:15). (3) The ruling God also shared that function, ". . . let them rule over the fish of the sea and the birds of the air, over the livestock, over all the earth, and over all the creatures that move along the ground . . . fill the earth and subdue it . . ." (Gen. 1:26b,28).

God is able to meet all needs of this world and of all beings within this world without the partnership of others. After all, He is God *Almighty*; however, authentic love never exists in isolation. So God created others and shared His kind of "ministries" with them, so they could and would participate in His kind of merriment as they reach out in unselfish service to others as God does.

Both people and angels are God's representative ministers to and for others.

God not only created people, but also angels, "For by him all things were created: things in heaven and on earth, visible and invisible, whether thrones or powers or rulers or authorities; all things were created by him and for him " (Col. 1:16; see also John 1:3). Both people and angels are God's representative ministers to and for others. Angels are "sent to serve those who will inherit salvation" (Heb. 1:14); and God's people are "Christ's ambassadors . . ." (2 Cor. 5:20).

Linking Heavenly Angelic Beings to Earthly Human Beings

Angels were created before people were, for they witnessed God creating the world (Job 38:4-7). Although humans are not called

Angels 3

"angels" in the Bible, they share some commonality with angels, such as the following: (1) God created both. That contradicts the notion that angels are really some kind of subjective feeling or a subconscious concept as Wink suggests.[1] (2) Both share many of the same functions. (3) Angels can appear in human form, although not being human. (4) Both received messages from God to share with others. (5) Both are to be God's servants. (6) God prepared heaven to be the eternal home for both. As angels reside in heaven, the Christian's citizenship is also in heaven (Phil. 3:20). Thus Peter refers to Christians as aliens on earth (1 Pet. 1:1). (7) Rebellious angels and rebellious people will inherit the same eternal destiny (Matt. 25:41).

Linking heavenly beings with human beings is not to downgrade angels who live in heaven and visit the earth. They are God's special envoys who, when sent to earth, represent Him. God's people on earth are also His envoys who are on earth to represent Him. Perhaps seeing the link between God's heavenly and earthly representatives might help God's people value our responsibilities more, and help others value the role of God's people more.

God gave angels freedom to obey or disobey.

Out of His love, God gave heavenly angels freedom to obey or disobey; to be selfless or selfish; to be His companions or His competitors; to represent Him or to rebel against Him. Many used that freedom against God. The obedient and disobedient angels battled each other in heaven. Those that rebelled lost the battle, their status with Him, and their residence in Heaven (Rev. 12:7-9; see also 2 Pet. 2:4-9 and Jude 6). After that battle, it is even more amazing that God would create people and give them the same kind of freedom He gave angels—the freedom to obey or disobey; to represent Him or rebel against Him; to be His companions or competitors; to accept their citizenship in Heaven or to live as if earth is the final home; and to share with others or to selfishly hoard as much of our belongings as possible. The consequences will be the same as for the rebellious angels, "Depart from me, you who are cursed, into the eternal fire prepared for the devil and his angels" (Matt. 25:41; see also verse 46).

But if we do God's unselfish ministry as the obedient angels do, we will receive the same permanent dwelling place as they, "Come, you who are blessed by my Father; take your inheritance, the kingdom

---

[1] Wink, *Unmasking*, 71.

prepared for you since the creation of the world" (Matt. 25:34). Both God's people and His angels will dwell together in heaven (Rev. 7:9-11).

We can give too much attention to God's heavenly representatives and not enough to His earthly ones—and vice versa.

It is possible to give too much attention to God's heavenly representatives—angels—and not enough to His earthly ones—individual Christians and the corporate Church. But it is also possible to give too much attention to God's earthly representatives and not enough to His heavenly ones—individual angels and the corporate host of angels. Both God's people and God's angels originated from the same source, God, and share many of the same descriptions and corresponding deeds that follow.

As Messengers

Both the Old Testament Hebrew word for "angel" (*malak*) and the New Testament Greek word (*angelos*) literally mean "messenger." But *malak* is also translated as "messenger" over 100 times in the Old Testament, and *angelos* is translated as "messenger" in Matthew 11:10; Mark 1:2; Luke 7:24,27; 9:52; 2 Corinthians 8:23; 12:7; and James 2:25. John the Baptist was prophesied to come as a *malak* in Malachi 3:1 and then functioned as an *angelos* in Mark 1:2.

The primary function of heavenly angels is to deliver a message from God in one way or another.

The primary function of heavenly angels is to deliver a message from God in one way or another. People who heard the heavenly angels felt they were hearing the words of God. But angels are not God's only chosen messengers for earth. Each Christian is a living message from God as Paul reminded the Corinthians, "You yourselves are our letter, written on our hearts, known and read by everybody. You show that you are a letter from Christ, the result of our ministry, written not with ink but with the Spirit of the living God, not on tablets of stone but on tablets of human hearts" (2 Cor. 3:2-3). As God sent angels to earth with His messages, so God keeps His people on earth with His messages. Many people either *cannot* read God's written word (foundationally illiterate) or *will not* read it (functionally illiterate when it

Angels 3

As Spirits

The heavenly angels are those who did not fall from their original service and status as reported in Revelation 12:7-9, "And there was war in heaven. Michael and his angels fought against the dragon, and the dragon and his angels fought back. But he was not strong enough, and they lost their place in heaven. The great dragon was hurled down—that ancient serpent called the devil, or Satan, who leads the whole world astray. He was hurled to the earth, and his angels with him" (see also 2 Pet. 2:4 and Jude 6).

Heavenly angels are "ministering spirits sent to serve those who will inherit salvation" (Heb. 1:14). Pharisees equated an angel with a spirit at one of Paul's trials when they agreed, "We find nothing wrong with this man. . . . What if a spirit or an angel has spoken to him?" (Acts 23:9). By saying "a spirit or an angel," the Pharisees constructed a literary parallel that identifies one as being the same as the other one.

As a ministering spirit, no heavenly angel is inferior or superior to any other ministering spirit, for each is an obedient servant. Jesus equated greatness with selfless service: "whoever wants to become great among you must be your servant . . . just as the Son of Man did not come to be served, but to serve . . ."; and, "For who is greater, the one who is at the table or the one who serves? Is it not the one who is at the table? But I am among you as one who serves" (Matt. 20:26,28; Luke 22:27). It seems likely that the measurement of greatness would be the same for God's heavenly representatives as for His earthly ones—unselfish service.

We Christians should not follow the example of the rebellious angels but the obedient ones.

As God's representatives living on earth, we Christians should not follow the example of the rebellious angels who lived in heaven, but the obedient ones who still serve God. No one is to feed self a dose of inferiority or superiority complex as Paul reminded the Corinthians, "Now the body is not made up of one part but of many." The foot should not feel it is not as important as the hand. ". . . The eye cannot say to the hand, 'I don't need you!'" (1 Cor. 12:14-21). Paul helped the Corinthians understand that about himself, "What, after all, is Apollos? And what is Paul? Only servants, through whom you came to believe—

as the Lord has assigned to each his task" (1 Cor. 3:5).

Multiple Functional Terms

"Messengers" and "ministering spirits" are the foundational terms upon which all others rest. But there are several other functionally descriptive terms that help us grasp the diversity of angelic services including the following:

1. **God**. This description is not suggesting that an angel is actually God. The term is functional (their external deeds), not ontological (their internal nature). An angel's mission and manner so represents God that it is as if God is present. After all, to represent God is to "re-present" Him. The term "angel" and "God" were interchangeable in several places such as in Moses' burning bush experience (Exod. 3:2-4). The actions of angels were actions that God would have done and did do through them. Calvin believed this "God" description of angels heightened the fact that they display God's presence as in a mirror. That is, God's brightness shines through them.[2] As it is with angels so it is to be with Christians. Paul gave us a needed reminder, "It is God who works in you to will and to act according to his good purpose" (Phil. 2:13). Thus the transcendent God continues to incarnate Himself in His heavenly and earthly servants. But why does He do that? Donald Bloesch is helpful by noting that God in Himself is "radically independent of all creaturely power. Nevertheless has the freedom to make him dependent on those whom he has created. He exists by his own power, but he seeks to fulfill his plan and purpose in cooperation with his people whom he empowers by his Spirit."[3]

2. **Mediators**. Job 33:23 reported, "There is an angel on his side as a mediator, one out of a thousand, to tell a man what is right for him. . . ." Angels are God's mediators with His message. Although there is only one salvation mediator between God and humans—Jesus Christ (1 Tim. 2:5), God uses both His heavenly and earthly beings as "paramediators." For instance, see Moses' mediating ministry with the Pharaoh (Exod. 7–11) and Peter's with Cornelius (Acts 10). Jesus clarified this when He said, "As

[2] Calvin, *Institutes*, 1.14.5, 165-166.
[3] Donald G. Bloesch, *God the Almighty* (Downers Grove, IL: InterVarsity, 1995) 88.

Angels 3

the Father has sent Me, I also send you" (John 20:21, NASB). Perhaps some can be so engrossed with the idea that an angel is sent from God that they are not as equally excited about a person also sharing a mediating ministry and message from God. Some may desire to become an angel when getting to heaven, but not want to become God's mediating kind of servant on earth. Why would a person consider the mission of God's heavenly angels to be more essential to the mission of God than the mission of His earthly servants? Perhaps we need to look not only through a window to see the possibility of a heavenly angel on the other side with a mission from heaven for earth's sake, but also to look into a mirror to see the earthly person on this side of the mirror with a mission on earth for heaven's sake.

3. **Watchers**. Daniel saw an angelic "watcher" descend from heaven (Dan. 4:13,17, NASB). God uses angels as watchers, not because He cannot see, because He sees it all, "The eyes of the LORD are everywhere, keeping watch on the wicked and the good" (Prov. 15:3). Then why the need for angels as His partnered watchers? Perhaps it is to help them understand the rationale behind God's actions and reactions and to encourage them to be involved with broader and deeper perspectives. Angels desire to see and grasp what God has done, is doing, and will do as recorded in 1 Peter 1:12, "Even angels long to look into these things." God's people on earth were also referred to as His watchers (Ezek. 33:2-20, NASB). Human watchers are to be as zealous and responsible as the angelic ones. Why would we feel either privileged or perplexed knowing heavenly angels may be watching us, but not concerned that some fellow Christians may also be watching us in order to serve us? Why would we be more responsive to God's angelic heavenly watchers than to His human earthly watchers? It is possible that God sent and continues to send heavenly watchers as sort of a last resort, for we may be too independent from each other to be responsible to and for each other.

4. **Sons of God**. Angels are identified as angels in many places (such as Job 1:6; 2:1; 36:3; Ps. 89:6, NASB). At times, the NIV translates "sons of God" as "angels" and by doing so camouflages the significance of the *functional* term of "sons." To refer to angels as "sons of God" does not mean they are literally "born" of God; but it does mean they are part of God's family,

and their attributes, principles, priorities, and practices characterize God. In Bible days a person was referred to as "a son of" what was being characterized by that person. Thus Jesus labeled James and John "sons of thunder" (Mark 3:17), and the apostles labeled Joseph, the Cyprian, "son of encouragement" (Acts 4:36). Christians are also referred to as God's sons (and daughters), because we have His *sperma*, seed in us, which is His Holy Spirit (1 John 3:9,24). God's Spirit equips us to participate in His divine nature in such a way that we are able to mirror and mimic God (2 Pet. 1:4; John 5:16; Eph. 5:1). If we want others to view us as "sons and daughters" of God, we need to manifest God's character—particularly His foundational character of love, as clearly stated by Jesus, "But I tell you: Love your enemies and pray for those who persecute you, that you may be sons of your Father in heaven" (Matt. 5:44-45). This does not mean that we "may be" who we already are (1 John 3:1-2), but that others who experience us may be able to link us to God. Angels and Christians share that distinction and responsibility.

5. **Holy Ones**. This was a common term for angels. For instance, see Job 5:1; Daniel 8:13; Deuteronomy 33:2. Jesus will return with the "holy ones" with Him (Zech. 14:5), which refers to the angels as announced by Jesus in Matthew 25:31. The terms "holy ones" and "saints" are from the same root word, which describes a person being dedicated. In Greek culture the words were used to identify two people who were married to each other. Each one was the other's "saint." That meant the woman was set apart from all other women to belong to her man, and the man was set apart from all other men to belong to his woman. Both were to be committed to care for the other one, to be closely bonded companions with the other one, and to meet the needs of the other one. "Saints" is the most common New Testament word that identified Christians, and is connected to the Church being the Bride of Christ. It is possible for two people to be married to each other and not function as saints with and for each other. When that happens, a gap exists between the two who need to work at building a bridge to span that gap. That is difficult to do, and sometimes impossible, when the other person may not see the gap or does not want it bridged. There can also be a gap between Christians and God that needs bridge

Angels 3

building. James put it this way, "Come near to God and he will come near to you" (Jas. 4:8). That does not mean God has moved away from us and is purposely keeping His distance, but it does mean that we have moved away from God. Some heavenly angels did that, and God gave them up to their freedom-of-choice decisions. Paul affirms that God will also give people up to their decisions (Rom. 1:24-28, "God gave them over").

6. **Heavenly Host**. Angels were often referred to as "hosts" in the Bible (see Deut. 4:19; 17:3; Josh. 5:14; Luke 2:14; Acts 7:42, and over a hundred other places). The word "host" stresses a large gathering and described angels as members in God's heavenly court (Dan. 7:10). "Hosts" was also a military term, and thus identified angels as members in God's army. With military kinds of functions, angels were ready for any command of God to protect His people, even if that meant entering into the battle, which they did on more than one occasion. Calvin described angelic hosts "like soldiers maintaining their leader's standard and ready to carry out his commands. As soon as God beckons, they gird themselves for the work."[4] (*Institutes* 1.14.5, 165). While we might think that kind of designation and work belongs only to angels, Paul reminds us that Christians are in a battle as soldiers to please our Commander-in-Chief and are equipped for spiritual battles against principalities and powers and the "god of this world," Satan (2 Tim. 2:3-4 and Eph. 6:10-18; 2 Cor. 4:4). We are to fight the good fight against the devil and his troops, fellow rebellious angels, but not the bad fight against God and His troops, fellow redeemed Christians.

7. **Mighty Ones**. The Psalmist understood that angels are powerful, "Praise the LORD, you his angels, you mighty ones who do his bidding" (Ps. 103:20). Michael Welker is helpful with his comment that a serving angel is an example of God's power.[5] Christians are also recipients of God's power for His purposes as affirmed by Paul, "I pray also that the eyes of your heart may be enlightened in order that you may know the hope to which he has called you, the riches of his glorious inheritance in the saints, and his incomparably great power for us who believe. That power is the working of his mighty strength" (Eph. 1:18-19). Paul

---

[4] Calvin, *Institutes*, 1.14.5, 165.
[5] Welker, "Biblical Traditions," 370.

acknowledged that power in his own life, "To this end I labor, struggling with all his energy, which so powerfully works in me" (Col. 1:29). Each congregation is to tap the power, which glorifies (characterizes) God as Paul declared, "Now to Him who is able to do exceeding abundantly beyond all that we ask or think, according to the power that works within us, to Him be the glory in the church and in Christ Jesus to all generations forever and ever. Amen" (Eph. 3:20-21, NASB).

Seraphim and Cherubim

Although we do not know with certainty the meaning of the word "seraphim" (plural for seraph), many believe it refers to a burning glow. The seraphim were positioned around the throne of God. As we do not know the meaning of the word, we also do not know the precise identity of the seraphim. However, it seems likely they are angels because they functioned as angels did.

It is possible that seraphim are not a special separate category of angels, but rather a term referring to all angels who are around the throne at any given time. Perhaps that accounts for the word having something to do with a burning glow which would come from God on the throne.

As we do not know the exact identity of the seraphim, we also do not know the precise identity of the cherubim (plural for cherub). Many believe the word refers to being an intercessor. However, biblically cherubim usually functioned as literal guards. For instance they were posted to keep Adam and Eve out of the Garden of Eden (Gen. 3:24). Many of the 91 times they are mentioned in the Old Testament it seems like they are decorative ornaments symbolizing God guarding places, such as watching over the Ark of the Covenant in the Holy of Holies and watching the entrance to the Holy of Holies by being on the ten curtains of the tabernacle and later of the temple. One word-picture of God reveals Him sitting on the outstretched arms of cherubim that appear to be like a throne-chariot (1 Chr. 28:18; Ezek. 1:4-28). They were described as being in a human form with wings (Ezek. 1:5-14).

Like seraphim, the cherubim function as angels do, although not directly called angels. Barth believed both seraphim and cherubim are holistic terms referring to angels as a whole.[6] But Welker, drawing from

---

[6] Barth, *Dogmatics*, III.3, 455.

Angels 3

Westermann, believes they are two different entities.[7] My position is that it is not
helpful to identify them more specifically than
what they are biblically reported as doing, which is quite sparse.

Principalities and Powers

It is possible that "principalities and powers" when linked
together refer to angels. The NIV does not retain these two terms, but
uses other terms such as power, rulers, and authorities with rather
inconsistent translations. Principalities and powers were created with
Christ being Lord over them as He is Lord over all created reality (Col.
1:16; 2:10). At times the terms refer to heavenly beings (Eph. 1:20-21;
3:10); at other times to beings opposed to God and His representatives
(Rom. 8:38; Eph. 6:12); at other times the terms refer to people on earth
who hold authoritative positions, such as government officials (Titus
3:10). Principalities and powers may be a literary parallelism that does
not identify two separate entities, but one.

Because of the diverse references about them, it seems likely
they refer to some kind of authoritative power—heavenly or earthly,
good or bad. There is no evidence to suggest they refer to some sort of
chain of command or to some kind of spiritual order within the organization of angels as Noll does.[8]

The "Angel of the Lord"

The term "angel of the Lord" (or "of God") appears 48 times in
the Old Testament in 14 different books and 19 times in the New
Testament in 3 books. What that description means is not clearly
known. Ramm is helpful in his statement, "There is some obscurity . . .
which an honest exegesis will not overlook."[9] Following are several different suggestions for the meaning of "angel of the Lord":

1. A representation and a type of God.[10]
2. God himself. This suggestion is gleaned from the fact that "angel of
the Lord" is interchanged many times with "the Lord" or "God."[11]

[7] Welker, "Biblical Traditions," 378.
[8] Stephen Noll, *Angels of Light, Powers of Darkness: Thinking Biblically about Angels,
Satan, and Principalities* (Downers Grove, IL: InterVarsity, 1998) 124-153.
[9] Ramm, "Angels," 68.
[10] Ibid., 69.
[11] Wayne Grudem, *Systematic Theology: An Introduction to Biblical Doctrine* (Grand
Rapids: Zondervan, 1994) 40; Welker, "Biblical Traditions," 370.

3. A manifestation of Christ prior to His incarnation on earth.[12] This suggestion relates to the fact that the term, "angel of
the Lord" is interchanged with only "the Lord" in a few places.
4. A special servant of God.[13]
5. An angel of higher stature than others with special ministries for Yahweh.[14]
6. The voice of God—the voice of the sender in the voice of the one sent.[15]
7. The Holy Spirit of God.[16]
8. The "angel of God's presence" referred to in Isaiah 63:9.[17]

The specific identity of the "angel of the Lord" is related to what this angel did, which includes the following:

1. Contradicted what an "angel" sent by Moab said to Elijah.
2. Spoke directly to various people including Abraham, Balaam, Daniel, David, Deborah, Gideon, Hagar, Haggai, Hezekiah, Jacob, and Joshua in the Old Testament; and to Joseph, the shepherds, Peter, and Philip in the New Testament.
3. Opened eyes to see the unseen—eyes of a donkey and Balaam.
4. Engaged in two-way communications with people (throughout most of Zechariah).
5. Protected and guided the Hebrews through their wilderness wanderings.
6. Rescued Peter from prison.
7. Appeared in human form.
8. Protected people.
9. Threatened people.
10. Destroyed cities and people.

---

[12] John MacArthur, Jr., *God, Satan, and Angels: Selected Notes, Selected Scriptures*, ed. by Mark Hall (Panorama City, CA: Word of Grace Communications, 1983) 60-63.
[13] Maxwell J. Davidson, "Angels," *Dictionary of Jesus and the Gospels*, ed. by Joel B. Green and Scot McKnight (Downers Grove, IL: InterVarsity, 1992) 9.
[14] Daniel G. Reid, "Angels, Archangels," *Dictionary of Paul and His Letters*, ed. by Gerald F. Hawthorne and Ralph P. Martin (Downers Grove, IL: InterVarsity, 1993) 20; Hans Bietenhard, "Angel, Messenger, Gabriel, Michael," *New International Dictionary of New Testament Theology*, ed. by Colin Brown (Grand Rapids: Zondervan, 1975) 101.
[15] John Cunningham, "Christology and the Angel of the Lord," *Journal from the Radical Reformation: A Testimony of Biblical Unitarianism* 6, no. 2 (Winter 1997) 3-15.
[16] John R. Levison, "The Prophetic Spirit As an Angel according to Philo," *Harvard Theological Review* 88 (April 1995) 189-207.
[17] A. Cohen, *The Psalms* (London: Soncino Press, 1974) 100.

Angels 3

The "angel of the Lord" is interchanged with "God" and with the "Lord" in several passages, and the words of this angel were referred to as being the words of the Lord and of God, but it never announced, "I am God." The grammatical structure of the term can mean one of the following: (1) one who is the Lord; (2) one who is sent from the Lord; (3) one who shares such a close relationship with the Lord that the Lord Himself is characterized by what this angel did or said.

Even though some people saw an "angel of the Lord" and thought they had actually seen God, there is no conclusive evidence that the "angel of the Lord" is a theophany—an appearance of God Himself, or is a Christophany—a pre-incarnation appearance of Christ Himself. The idea that this angel was Christ is unlikely for many reasons, which include the following:

(1) God never said to any angel (including the "angel of the Lord") "you are my son" (Heb. 1:5).

(2) Christ is superior to all angels including the "angel of the Lord" (Heb. 1:4).

(3) All angels, including the "angel of the Lord," are to worship Christ (Heb. 1:6).

(4) It is unlikely that while in Mary's womb, Christ would appear to Joseph as an "out-of-the-womb" experience (Matt. 1:20).

(5) It is unlikely that Christ appeared to the shepherds in an "out of the infant body/manger" experience to see "me" (Luke 2:9).

(6) It seems unlikely that Christ would have appeared in an "out of the body" experience when He was about two years old to warn Joseph to escape to Egypt (Matt. 2:13).

(7) Nowhere in the New Testament is Christ ever identified as being that angel of the Lord throughout the Old Testament; although He is identified as being the Rock that provided water for the Hebrew people (1 Cor. 10:4).

While it is possible the "angel of the Lord" was a theophany, it is more likely this description is a general term referring to any angel on a mission for God. Rabbi Hirsch is beneficial. He believes the "angel of the Lord" is an angel without any special identity except being sent by the Lord/God as are all angels.[18]

---

[18] Samson Raphael Hirsch, *The Pentateuch: Genesis*, rendered into English by Isaac Levy, 2nd ed., rev. (Gateshead, NY: Judaica Press, 1989) 1:547.

Perhaps this angel refers to God's **Angels 3** own personal angel (sort of like an executive assistant), for it is possible that both God and Jesus had *their* angel (for God's angel see Gen. 24:7; Dan. 6:22, and several other places; for Jesus' angel see Rev. 1:1; 3:5; 22:6; 22:16).

There may be more ink spilled trying to nail down the specific identity than is either necessary or helpful since all heavenly angels are God's ministering spirits and since the presence of God's Spirit is the presence of God (Ps. 51:11; 139:7; Eph. 2:22; 1 John 3:24). However, any angel is either God's or Jesus', and is thus the extended presence of God or Jesus. Thus the description, "angel of His presence," can fit any angelic visitation to earth with God's mission and message (Isa. 63:9).

Angels as Dead Saints?

One of the most popular questions people ask about angels is whether or not their loved ones who died became angels in heaven. The idea that loved ones are angels watching over us is comforting to some. If that thought comforts people, there is no harm in thinking it regardless of whether or not our loved ones are or are not angels. However, it might be more comforting to know they are not seeing the problems that stress us, the wrong decisions we make, the suffering we may experience, and so on. Few of us would want to know everything our children and grandchildren are going through every moment of every day.

The idea that loved ones are angels watching over us is comforting to some.

Perhaps it would be more comforting to know that when our loved ones die they are immediately in the presence of God, for to be absent from the body is to be at home with the Lord (2 Cor. 5:8); they were transformed into Christ's likeness (1 John 3:2-3; 1 Cor. 15:50-58) and will return with Him when He comes back (1 Thess. 4:16-18). Perhaps it might be more comforting to know they are not watching the stuff we go through and how we do or do not handle it well. Perhaps it comforts us more to know they are in heaven and not engaged with the crud on earth, but are full of joy and celebration as recorded in the book of Revelation:

> After these things I looked, and behold, a great multitude, which
> no one could count, from every nation and all tribes and peoples and
> tongues, standing before the throne and before the Lamb, clothed in

white robes, and palm branches were in their **52** hands; and they cry out with a loud voice, saying,

"Salvation to our God who sits on the throne, and to the Lamb." And all the angels were standing around the throne. . . . And one of the elders answered, saying to me, "These who are clothed in the white robes, who are they, and from where have they come?"

And I said to him, "My lord, you know." And he said to me, "These are the ones who come out of the great tribulation, and they have washed their robes and made them white in the blood of the Lamb. For this reason, they are before the throne of God; and they serve Him day and night in His temple; and He who sits on the throne shall spread His tabernacle over them. They shall hunger no more, neither thirst anymore; neither shall the sun beat down on them, nor any heat; for the Lamb in the center of the throne shall be their shepherd, and shall guide them to springs of the water of life; and God shall wipe every tear from their eyes" (Rev. 7:9-17, NASB).

Knowing our loved ones are experiencing the above may be more comforting than thinking they are watching our experiences—tears, hunger, thirst, and problems caused by circumstances, calamities, and climate.

There is not enough biblical evidence to conclude that angels are dead saints.

While some believe angels are dead saints, there is not enough biblical evidence for that conclusion. Only two biblical passages suggest the possibility. One passage comes from those who mistook Peter's presence following his prison break to be "his angel" (Acts 12:15); however, that probably only reflects their own belief. At that time Jews commonly believed dead saints became angels. The second passage is 1 Thessalonians 4:14 which reports that Jesus will bring with him those who have died. Some identify those who have died with the angels who will accompany Jesus on His return as reported in Matthew 25:31. However, those who have died and the angels are more likely to be two different beings when factoring in several considerations including the following:

1. Those who die in Christ will be transformed with different bodies, not into angelic beings (1 Cor. 15:35-58).
2. The dead saints will be like Christ (1 John 3:2). However, after His resurrection Christ did not appear as an angel and will not return as one.

3. Moses and Elijah appeared to Jesus, but not as angels (Luke 9:28-36).

4. Some attempt to validate the idea that dead people are angels because they have spoken to them; however, God condemned the practice of communicating with the dead. So it would be wrong for dead saints to communicate with people who live on earth. Talking with the dead was the downfall of Saul (1 Sam. 28; 1 Chr. 10:13; see the law in Lev. 19:31).

5. The Israelites never asked their dead saints to help them, nor for God to send them.

6. Nowhere does any text clearly link dead saints to angels. In fact, a careful reading of the book of Revelation eliminates that connection, for there is a clear distinction between dead saints who are in heaven and angels who are in heaven. Heaven will be populated by both angels (mentioned 64 times in the book of Revelation) and by people (see both people and angels in the same scene in Rev. 7:9-11): "A great multitude that no one could count, from every nation, tribe, people and language . . . and . . . the angels. . . ."

Calvin's thought is probably accurate—confusing dead saints with angels is preposterous.[19]

In summary, we should appreciate these clear statements about angels may be more than some apprehend or appreciate: (1) angels are ministering spirits sent to serve those who will inherit salvation (Heb. 1:14); (2) Jesus is superior to them all; (3) all angels are to worship Him (Heb. 1:4,6); (4) we are not to worship angels (Rev. 19:9-10).

Identity cannot be separated from nature. We will explore angelic nature next.

---

[19] Calvin, *Institutes,* III.20-23, 881-884.

CHAPTER 4

ANGELS: THEIR NATURE

Not Comprehensively Described

The Bible does not go into depth about the nature of angels. Barth suggests we should not try to define or describe them beyond the biblical characterizations. For Barth, this is *the* error those make who develop a systematic angelology.[1] However, Barth may be too skimpy by stating that we know nothing beyond the fact that angels do not marry.[2]

John Milton in *Paradise Lost* developed a theology of angels that included much more than their marital status. However, he challenged rejecting the reality of angels because they cannot be seen (materialism), or because they do not fit a person's perception of reality (rationalism). Barth believed angels are distinct from both God and mankind; however, they share some similarities and dissimilarities with both.[3] Augustine believed the term "angels" identifies their office but not their nature.[4]

Their Basic Nature

What It Does Not Include

There are several aspects which are not part of angels' basic nature. For instance, there is no biblical evidence they were created in the image of God as Dickason maintains.[5] They are not just internal feelings of people as Wink believes.[6] One of Wink's problems is that he "winks" at heaven being a reality, saying it is just a term describing a

---

[1] Barth, *Dogmatics,* III.3, 450.
[2] Ibid., 451.
[3] Ibid., 371.
[4] *Catechism of the Catholic Church,* 2nd ed., rev. and promulgated by Pope John Paul II (Rome: Liberia Editrice Vaticana, 1997) 85:329.
[5] Fred C. Dickason, *Angels: Elect and Evil* (Chicago: Moody Press, 1975), 32.
[6] Wink, *Unmasking,* 71; *Naming,* 105-113.

person's spirituality.[7] That position relegates any heavenly entity or being, such
as an angel, to a psychological concept—the
creation of God in our image rather than us in His.

According to Hebrews 1 and 2 the basic nature of angels does *not include*:

(1) created in God's image
(2) sons or children of God
(3) kings
(4) saviors or priests
(5) forgivers of our sins
(6) living in us
(7) Christ's substitutes
(8) on the throne
(9) to be worshiped
(10) members of the Godhead
(11) servants for us to order around
(12) all-knowing
(13) just a psychological phenomenon
(14) the dwelling place for the incarnated holistic God—Father, Son, and Holy Spirit. On earth, the trinity dwells only in people—God in us (Eph. 2:22); the Spirit in us (1 John 3:24); and Christ in us (Col. 1:27).

What It Does Include

Basically angels are spirits and servants (Heb. 1:14). As spirits, angels do not have bodies as we understand bodies, for Jesus declared, ". . . a spirit does not have flesh and bones as you see that I have" (Luke 24:39, NASB). The NIV translation of "spirit" as "ghost" in a few places is misleading. As bodiless spirits, angels are invisible to us unless they are transfigured into some kind of material form (Num. 22:31; 2 Kgs. 6:17; 9:11). Many times in the Bible materialization accompanied their visits to earth.

We do not know precisely what all angels look like in heaven. Calvin thought they have "celestial bodies."[8] Mansir views them as "minds without bodies."[9] The *Catholic Catechism* teaches they have "spiritual, non-corporeal bodies."[10] Augustine confusingly believed these

---

[7] Wink, *Unmasking*, 91.
[8] Calvin, *Institutes*, 1.14.5, 165.
[9] Riordan quoting Mansir, "Interaction," 77.
[10] *Catechism*, 85:328.

Angels 4

spirits are not angels until they are sent on a mission; but are pure spiritual creatures whose perfection surpasses all visible creatures.[11]

Their Source

The nature of angels is directly related to and determined by their source/origin. The Father in tandem with the Son and the Holy Spirit created angels, "All things came into being by Him, and apart from Him nothing came into being that has come into being" (John 1:3, NASB). The "Him" in John 1:3 refers to Jesus through whom God made the world (see also Col. 1:16 and Heb. 1:2). The Spirit was active in the creation of this universe (and no doubt in all of God's creative activities) as revealed in Scripture, "and the Spirit of God was moving over the surface of the waters. Then God said . . ." (Gen. 1:2-3, NASB). God did not create without the movement of the Spirit. The members of the trinity work in unison as eternal partners.

Aquinas believed angels were created along with the material universe;[12] however, angels witnessed the creation and thus evidently existed prior to Genesis 1:1 (Job 38:7). So the *Catholic Catechism* errs by teaching that angels appeared after the creation.[13] It seems likely that God would have created angels according to their own kind—a unique category of life, because He created every other life-form (except humans) "according to its (or their) kind" (See Gen. 1:11-12,21,24-25). Angels were no doubt created to be naturally good (as stated in the *Catechism,* 98:391). There is no evidence to support Westermann's position that angels were created to no longer exist when their assigned tasks are finished.[14]

Like Humans

While angels are distinct from humans, they share many likenesses including the following:

1. Can speak (Matt. 28:5; Acts 12:6-12)
2. Can sing (Rev. 4:11; 5:11)
3. Worship God (Heb. 1:6)
4. Do not know everything (Matt. 24:36)

---

[11] Ibid., 85:330.
[12] Pascal P. Parente, *The Angels* (St. Meinard, IN: Grail Publications, 1957) 3-4.
[13] *Catechism*, 86:332.
[14] Westermann, *God's Angels*, 11.

5. Desire to look into the meaning and application of God's work (1 Pet. 1:12)

Angels 4

6. Can be taught (Eph. 3:10)
7. Have free will, for some sinned (2 Pet. 2:4; Jude 6; Rev. 12:9)
8. Eat (Gen. 18:2; 19:3; Ps. 78:25)
9. Rejoice (Luke 15:10)
10. Serve (Heb. 1:7,14)
11. Can perform assigned tasks (Heb. 1:14)
12. Have intellect to receive assignments and understand them (inferred from the above)

Unlike Humans

While angels share some similarities with humans, their holistic characteristics are unlike humans in the following ways:

1. Created above humans (Ps. 8:5; Heb. 2:7)
2. Usually invisible
3. Can affect nature in miraculous ways (John 5:4)
4. Can be transfigured into various forms, such as animal and human form
5. Not flesh and blood
6. Do not experience death (Luke 20:36; although some rabbis wrongly taught that angels perish after serving their tasks.[15])
7. Do not marry (Matt. 22:30). However, some teach this passage refers to only those angels that did not fall. But there is no evidence that Satan's angels are capable of having sex with women. Adler believes they may have gender, but without sex, which for him represents the highest expression of love;[16] but God who created gender did not negatively view sexual intimacy between a husband and a wife.
8. Can move with speed from heaven to earth and vice versa (the significance of the metaphor "wings")
9. Not created in the image and likeness of God; although some Rabbis teach they were[17]
10. Are spirits (Heb. 1:4; 12:22-23)
11. Not limited to living in a restricted form
12. Not to be redeemed from their sins

---

[15] Fass, "How Angels Serve," 2.
[16] Adler, *Angels and Us*, 138.
[17] Parente, *Angels*, 204.

Angels 4

13. Not recipients of benefits from Christ's death and resurrection
14. Cannot be a "new creation" in Christ
15. Not objects of salvation
16. Excel in strength. One killed 185,000 soldiers on one night.
17. Not "born" from sexual intercourse and conception
18. Not to be evangelized
19. Some have wings (however, it is rare to encounter angels in the Bible with wings). The number of winged angels in art is grossly exaggerated.
20. Do not reproduce

Their Language: Communication Skills

Angels appear to know and understand all languages and can speak to anyone to whom they are called to minister. They certainly communicate with God and may communicate with each other (Zech. 1:9-11; 2:3-5).

We have no objective evidence that angels' natural language is some kind of heavenly dialect.

We have no objective evidence that angels' natural language is some kind of heavenly dialect. The reference in 1 Corinthians 13:1, "If I speak in the tongues of men and of angels . . ." is not automatically introducing the existence of an actual secret kind of language. First of all, "of angels" can be translated "of messengers" and may be a literary parallel with "tongues of men" equating men with messengers. This could suggest how human messengers without love can use language to please or emotionally stimulate their hearers as musicians do with musical instruments, thus "I am only a resounding gong or a clanging cymbal." This is more likely the meaning than the idea that angels have some kind of ecstatic language that belongs to the angelic world, because of several following factors:

(1) Every other example in the next three verses involves people, not angels.
(2) People, not angels, do the speaking gifts in the preceding and following chapter (12 and 14).
(3) Every time an angel spoke in the Bible, it was in a known human language.
(4) The word "tongues" is from the Greek word *glossa*. Every other time it is biblically used, it refers to either the physical tongue

in the mouth or to a known human language.

(5) The book of Revelation, which gives us the most comprehensive look at the verbalization of angels in heaven, does not even hint that angels are using an unfamiliar language.

(6) All those in heaven understand what is being spoken.

(7) This squares with Paul's use of language, and his criticism of how some others use language (see Gal. 1:10; 1 Thess. 2:13; 2 Tim. 4:3).

It is possible that there will be a universal language in heaven as there was on earth when Jesus came.

Their Number

At one time scholars debated how many angels could stand on the point of a needle, which Parente correctly notes is a useless exercise without divine revelation.[18] Jesus said He could draft 72,000 angels to help him (Matt. 26:53; one legion has 6,000 members). No one but God knows the actual number, and He did not choose to reveal it. It is, however, described as being innumerable; thousands upon thousands; and ten thousand times ten thousand (Deut. 33:2; Ps. 68:17; Dan. 7:10; Rev. 5:11).

Lightner believes the number is the same today as it was when they were created; since there is no evidence angels experience either death or reproduction.[19] However, God can create more angels if he desires, for "our God is in heaven; he does whatever pleases him" (Ps. 115:3; 135:6).

Their Organization

Some divide angels into a chain-of-command kind of order. MacArthur thinks they are organized as thrones, dominions, principalities, powers, and authorities with the angel, Michael, being the leader over other angels.[20] Others believe they are organized into three different levels.

Level one: seraphim, cherubim, and thrones;
Level two: dominions, virtues, and powers;
Level three: principalities, archangels, and angels.

[18] Ibid., 6-7.
[19] Robert Lightner, *Angels, Satan, and Demons: Invisible Beings That Inhabit the Spiritual World* (Nashville: Word, 1998) 25.
[20] MacArthur, *God, Satan and Angels*, 135.

Angels 4

The angels in level one are closest **60** to God with the first one mentioned being even closer than the others. Those in the lower levels are closer to earth.[21] Parente's three-tiered organization varies from the above,[22] and Billy Graham suggested an organization of ten orders.[23] Some try to pinpoint a specific function for each different organizational category.[24]

Dionysius first devised this three-tiered organization in his, *The Celestial Hierarchy*. Barth believed Dionysius' work was one of the greatest frauds in church history.[25] Calvin thought Dionysius' work was nothing but talk and foolish chatter.[26] Westermann rejects the idea of separate classes of angels. Those organizational ideas were invented in postbiblical days without biblical support.[27]

Barth thinks those who devised a ranking among angels were trying to relate it to "host," which was a military term with ranking among soldiers;[28] but Barth maintains that any "order" of angels relates to their function and service and not to ranks.[29] Van der Hart thinks angels needed to be organized in order to be accepted by a culture that depended upon and trusted structure, and would have considered any unstructured reality to be irrelevant.[30] But that is mere speculation, for we do not know what various cultures would or would not accept. Linking various terms to angels which are not directly linked in the Bible is dubious. Some descriptions include the following: power, principalities, authorities, dominions, and virtues.

Since there is no systematization of angels in Scripture, there is no need to construct one or to accept someone else's creation of one.

Since there is no systematization of angels in Scripture, there is no need to construct one or to accept someone else's creation of one.

---

[21] See Daniel et al., *Ask Your Angels*, 15.

[22] Parente, *Angels*, 41.

[23] Graham, *Angels*, 49.

[24] See some suggested functions in Daniel et al., *Ask Your Angels*,17ff; Noll, *Angels of Light*, 15ff; Parente, *Angels*, 63-74; Rhodes, *Angels among Us*, 89-90.

[25] Barth, *Dogmatics*, III.3, 385.

[26] Calvin, *Institutes*, 1.14.4.

[27] Westermann, *God's Angels*, 23.

[28] Barth, *Dogmatics*, III.3, 456.

[29] Ibid., 459.

[30] Van der Hart, *Theology*, 27.

Dickason rightly notes that creating orga- **Angels 4**
nizational charts for angels is more eisegesis—reading into the text what is not there—
than exegesis—drawing from the text what is there.[31] Barth believed it
is a mistake to organize angels schematically.

Their Names

The Protestant Bible includes names of only two angels, Michael
and Gabriel (Dan. 10:13,21; Luke 1:19,26-27; Jude 9; Rev. 12:7-8).
The Roman Catholic Bible names a third one, Raphael (Tobit 2:15).

Gabriel means, "Mighty one of God," who revealed the meaning
of visions, brought good news, appeared once as a human, and functioned as a teaching angel (Dan. 8:15; 9:21; Luke 1:11-12,19,30-34).

Michael means, "Who is like God," and was called the archangel, a "great prince," and an angel who guarded Israel (Dan.
10:13,21; 12:1; and Jude 7-9). Since God named two of them, He may
have named all the others since He evidently summoned them and sent
them on assignments. However, we do not know that with certainty.

Their Habitation

God's angels' permanent residence is heaven (the book of
Revelation); the fallen angels' is Hell (Matt. 25:46). However, New
Agers believe angels live everywhere, "in rocks and stone; on trees and
in rivers; on animals and deserts and in human minds."[32] Because of
this belief, New Agers prioritize and insert the presence of angels into
all kinds of activities, plans, and feelings.

The number of terms for angels and their functions cannot fully
capture the reality of angels.[33] While heaven is their home, it is not
their "hold." Under orders, they come and go to serve those for whom
they are sent.

Their Appearances

There is no biblically definitive description of how all angels
look, but there are diverse "looks," including the following:

1. Dressed in white robes; perhaps communicating purity (Mark
   16:4)

---

[31] Dickason, *Angels*, 87.
[32] Burnham, *Book of Angels*, 243.
[33] Barth, *Dogmatics*, III.3, 450.

2. Carrying harps; perhaps communicat- **62**
ing a relaxing stress-free mood and/or a
love of music (Rev. 15:1-2)

3. Standing around the throne; perhaps communicating respect and honor (Rev. 7:11)

4. In a cloud with a rainbow above the head, and legs like fiery pillars; perhaps communicating a guiding function as a cloud did for the wandering Hebrews; and with the rainbow communicating that their presence affirms that God is the promise keeper (Rev. 10:1)

5. Flying; perhaps communicating they are on the move for God (Rev. 14:6)

6. Clean with shiny linen and golden sashes around the chest; perhaps communicating the sin-free environment with valuable and beautiful hearts (Rev. 15:5-6)

7. Wings. Only seraphim and cherubim were described as having wings; perhaps communicating both mobility and a temporary stay on earth. Westermann notes that angels do not need wings to bridge the distance between heaven and earth.[34]

There is not enough consistency in the descriptions to ensure their identity by how all angels look. Perhaps that is one reason we might entertain angels without knowing it (Heb. 13:2).

Their Manifestations on Earth

While angels are usually invisible because they are spirits, at times they visited the earth in various forms and ways. However, their visible manifestations are not often described. Hunter believes angels did not visit in identical or repeated forms.[35] Biblical angels do not fit our popular ideas of angelic manifestations. The New Age movement believes they appear in unlimited forms; however, the following limited number of biblically revealed forms might disappoint New Agers:

1. Through an animal's voice (Num. 22:28-30)
2. Through a human form (Gen. 18-19; Gen. 32:22-30)
3. Through a dream (Gen. 28:12; Matt. 1:20; 2:13)
4. Through a voice without the speaker being seen (Gen. 16:7; 21:17; Luke 1:11-20; John 12:29)

---

[34] Westermann, *God's Angels*, 23-26.
[35] Charles and Frances Hunter, *Angels on Assignment* (New Kensington, PA: Whitaker House, 2001) 45.

63 Of course God can send His angels with any form He deems essential to the assigned mission/task. But since it is rare for the Bible to specifically describe the appearance of angels, we must be careful not to nail down how all angels look.

We do not know how many people visibly saw angels in the Bible.

We do not know how many people visibly saw angels in the Bible. Westermann notes that many visitations were visible only to the persons to whom the angels were sent, and not by others.[36] At times some of those to whom angels were sent did not know their visitors were angels until after the visitation was over (Genesis 18 and 19). Their "unrecognizableness" seems to be a common pattern in the Bible, which accounts for the relevance of the following instruction, "Do not forget to entertain strangers, for by so doing some people have entertained angels without knowing it" (Heb. 13:2).

We do not have to know we are entertaining angels, but the angels know and God knows them and us. And that is enough. There is little reason we should develop heads bigger than our hearts because angels visited us. Ego can hinder enlightenment.

Although angelic appearances were not easily recognized, their relationships and ministries were. To that we now turn.

---

[36] Westermann, *God's Angels*, 19.

CHAPTER 5

ANGELS: THEIR RELATIONSHIPS AND BIBLICAL WORK

Relationship with God

Angels are not independent "lone ranger" beings on the loose. God created angels to participate in community relationships—with one another, with God, and with God's creation. As servants of God, angels are at His disposal to serve others in specific ways. In a sense, angels function as God's apostles (from a Greek word that means one sent out from a higher source), and as ambassadors of the "government" from heaven to the culture on earth.

Because angels function directly from heaven (Gen. 22:11; Rev. 15:5), they bring God's transcendence to our temporary earthly experiences. To be in the presence of angels is to be in God's vicarious presence. God declared that His authority is with His angels who do His work and speak His words (Exod. 23:20-21). In many biblical texts, the presence of angels is interchangeable with the presence of God (Gen. 3:11,13; Exod. 3:2,6,14; Judg. 6:11-24; 13:2-23; Luke 12:8; 15:10; Acts 7:30-32).

To be in the presence of angels is to be in God's vicarious presence.

Barth believed this interchange reveals the close relationship between God and His angels. "It means the presence and operation of God Himself in a heavenly creaturely form."[1] When angels acted, it was God acting through them; when angels spoke, it was God speaking through them; to obey angels is to obey God. The transcendent becomes immanent through the angels.[2] Welker noted, "As humans become multi-present by sending messengers, so God relatively fini-

---

[1] Barth, *Dogmatics*, III.3, 478.
[2] John Shea, "Angels We Have Heard on Low," *U.S. Catholic* 6, no. 12 (December 1995) 38.

tizes Himself through angels."[3] Barth makes a summary kind of statement, "In a sense God throws a bridge across the space between heaven and earth."[4]

Jewish scholars believed God consulted with angels before creating the earth.[5] While angels populate heaven, surround the throne, accompany God, and are subject to Him, there is no indication God consulted with them before or during His creative activities. They are his ministering spirits, mediators, assistants, envoys, and deputies, but not his advisers.

God did not create angels (or people) because He was lonely as some teach, but because He is relational and loves community for the sake of those in the community. Noll notes, "While God's Lordship is Supreme it is not *totalitarian* . . . but is carried out partly through spiritual intermediaries. . . ."[6] Augustine believed in its beginning heaven was the heavenly city of angels.[7]

Relationship with Jesus

As angels have a close relationship with the Father, so they enjoy one with Jesus. The *Catholic Catechism* states, "Christ is the center of the angelic world. They are *His* angels . . . because they were created through Him and for Him."[8]

Angels related to the Messiah prior to Jesus' conception, with the announcement to Mary, His earthly birth via the announcement to the shepherds, his early life by warning Joseph to leave Judea, His temptations in the wilderness, His sorrow in the Garden of Gethsemane, His resurrection by being at the tomb, and will return with Him. Jesus affirmed the reality and existence of angels by speaking about them (Matt. 13:39-49; 18:10; 22:30; 24:31; 25:31; 26:27; and other places in Mark, Luke, and John).

Jesus was superior to angels as Hebrews 1:5-13 revealed in the following ways:

[3] Welker, "Biblical Traditions," 369.
[4] Barth, *Dogmatics*, III.3, 494.
[5] Meir Zlotowitz, *Bereishis: Genesis: A New Translation with a Commentary Anthologized from Talmudic, Midrashic, and Rabbinic Sources* (Brooklyn: Mesorah Publications, 1986) 1a:68.
[6] Noll, *Angels of Light*, 47.
[7] Ibid., 5.
[8] *Catechism*, 86:331.

Angels 5

1. God never addressed angels as His son and He their father.
2. Angels are to worship Jesus, not vice versa.
3. Angels are servants, while Jesus is the King of the kingdom.
4. Jesus was at the beginning of all created things, but angels were created.
5. Earth and heaven are the work of Jesus' activity, not of angelic activity.
6. Angels can perish (such as the fallen ones who will), but Jesus will not.
7. Jesus is at the right hand of the Father, which is the place of highest honor, while angels stand around the throne.
8. Angels are servants of the saints, while Jesus is savior of and Lord over the saints.

While the New Age movement does not accept Jesus being over angels, there are many New Testament teachings and experiences of angels with Jesus that support His superiority, such as the following:

1. Jesus sent angels on missions (Mark 13:2-7; Rev. 22:16).
2. God left nothing that is not subject to Jesus including angels (Heb. 2:8; Matt. 28:18).
3. Jesus was cocreator of things including angels (John 1:2; Col. 1:16).
4. Angels served Jesus (Matt. 4:11).
5. Angels would have come to rescue Jesus from being executed had Jesus ordered them to do so (Matt. 26:53).
6. Angels will accompany Jesus' return (Matt. 16:27; 25:31; Mark 8:38; 13:27; 2 Thess. 1:7).
7. Angels will assist Jesus in separating the wicked from the righteous after His return (Matt. 13:49; 25:32).
8. Angels worship Jesus (Heb. 1:6; Rev. 5:11-12).

It is antibiblical to think the superiority of Jesus is false Christology as the New Agers teach.

Relationship with the Holy Spirit

Although the Bible reveals little about angels' relationship with the Holy Spirit, it is inappropriate to eliminate one while affirming their relationship with the other two persons of the trinity. It is safe to conclude that angels' relationship with the Holy Spirit parallels their connection with the Father and the Son.

The "angel of God's presence" (Isa. 63:9) certainly links angels to the Holy Spirit who is *the* presence of God (Ps. 51:11; 139:7; Eph. 2:22; 1 John 3:24). In a few places angel and Holy Spirit are interchangeable (Acts 8:26 with verse 39). Noll views the relationship as an inner and outer reality. The Holy Spirit is the inner (or invisible) voice and appearance of God, and an angel is the outer (or visible) voice and appearance of God.[9]

Relationship with the Church/Saints

Angels function on earth to serve saints, were active in the life of the early Church, and were mentioned in letters to churches in Rome, Corinth, Galatia, Colosse, Thessalonica, and the Christian recipients of Hebrews, 1 & 2 Peter, James, and 1 Timothy. Angels will also serve the Church at the end of the age by leading us in worship in heaven. In the meantime, "the whole life of the church benefits from the mysterious and powerful help of the angels."[10] The Church is not on her earthly journey without angels.[11]

There are several different opinions about what the phrase "to the angel of the church" means in the seven times used in the second and third chapters of Revelation. The issues rotate around whether the "angel" or "messenger" has a heavenly or earthly identity. The conclusion is not easy, and we may not know the correct identity this side of heaven.

There are two popularly held views as to whom or what is the angel of the church in Ephesus, in Smyrna, in Pergamum, in Thyatira, in Sardis, in Philadelphia, and in Laodicea. The first popular view is that "to the angel of the church" indicates every congregation has a specific heavenly being assigned to it. The second popular view is that the angel of the church refers to the lead human messenger in each congregation such as an evangelist, pastor, elder, or teacher.

While both of those interpretations are quite possible, I opt for a third view. The Greek construction of the words "To the angel of the church" allows for the "angel" and the "church" to be appositional, which identifies the two as one = "To the messenger *which is* the church." In each situation "to the angel of the church" is tied to "hear what the Spirit says *to the churches*" (see Rev. 2:1 linked with 2:7; 2:8

[9] Noll, *Angels of Light*, 87-91.
[10] *Catechism*, 87:334.
[11] Ibid., 90:352.

with 2:11; 2:12 with 2:17; 2:18 with 2:29; **68**
3:1 with 3:6; 3:7 with 3:13; and 3:14 with
3:22). That "to the angel of the church" means "to the messenger which is the church" squares with the fact that all the instructions given to the "angel/messenger" are in the second person plural—"you all." The plural "you" is certainly not addressing a single angel for an angel is not the one being evaluated, but the churches as seen by what is linked to them, such as declarations, deeds, perseverance, hardships, energy, affections, sins, services, immorality, reputation, patience, and so on. All but two recipients of the messages are to repent or face consequences such as, God will fight against them; He holds their rebellion against them; He will remove their lampstand; He will come like a thief; He will spit them out of His mouth. But those who repent will participate in the tree of life; will receive a new name; will be given authority over nations; will never be blotted out of the book of life; will be kept from the hour of trial; will have God's name written on them; God will come to them; and all will be overcomers.

It is my belief that the congregations that were reprimanded were not being God's correct representatives while the two that were complimented were representing God well with His message. I see no reason to shift the direct object of these instructions to a literal angel or to one leader in the church, especially when every commendation and condemnation is addressed to recipients in the plural—you plural—thus "all of you." The seven messages given to the seven churches were probably not given to seven different intermediaries to deliver, but to the entire congregation as delivered from the Holy Spirit through John as were most other church letters in the New Testament. In a sense these seven congregations foreshadow all congregations today. Each congregation today must take seriously its responsibility to repent when needed, and to be faithful, to please God, to protect, and to share the message of God locally and globally.

Since angels are "ministering spirits sent to serve those who will inherit salvation" (Heb. 1:14), we will not know until we get to heaven all the various ways during all the various times in all the various places where angels served the Church at large by ministering to her members. Perhaps not knowing is a gift from God to keep us from expecting or demanding identical services, to keep us humble, and to keep us from judging the status of churches by angelic visitations to them.

Needs differ from culture to culture and from one time period to another time period. Consequently, we must not box God in or box Him out by our comparisons and expectations. Perhaps the biggest vacuum in the modern church is to not believe any service by any angel has ever happened or will happen.

Their Work on Earth for Heaven's Sake

Contrary to the thinking of some, the word "angel" was not a metaphor, which was added to the Bible from pagan influences. While metaphors never materialize and cannot be seen or heard, angels who put on material forms were visibly seen, and when speaking were audibly heard.

Their General Work

Angels in the Bible were always pointing beyond themselves to God, and never jockeyed for popularity. Barth wrote, "They always look away from themselves and they invite and command others to look away from every creature, themselves included, to the One who alone is worthy. . . ."[12] They never cease glorifying God.[13]

Angels in the Bible were always pointing beyond themselves and never jockeyed for popularity.

Contrary to the popular "Touched by an Angel" show, they seldom gave their names or revealed their identities up front because they were more interested in revealing their involvements than their identity. They were friends to God's friends and foes to God's foes. This is one way God kept His promise to His people, "I will bless those who bless you, and whoever curses you I will curse" (Gen. 12:3). Biblical evidence contradicts Schenck's suggestion that angels ministered only to those in the Old Covenant.[14]

One of God's consistent characteristics is to show others what He is like.

One of God's consistent characteristics is to show others what He is like (See Ps. 19:1-4; Rom. 1:10-20). He is the self-disclosing God while remaining quite transcendent—the Totally Other One. As one means of communicating Himself, He used angels to bridge His transcendence from heaven to earth. Thus one description of God is simply

---

[12] Barth, *Dogmatics*, III.3, 460.
[13] *Catechism*, 90:350.
[14] Kenneth L. Schenck, "A Celebration of the Enthroned Son: The Catena of Hebrews," *Journal of Biblical Literature* 20, no. 3 (2001) 467-481.

Angels 5

"Word"—communication—"In the beginning was the Word, and the Word was
with God, and the Word was God" (John 1:1).
Calvin correctly believed that an appearance of an angel discloses
God's divine majesty.[15] Forrester Church put it this way, "Their presence is witness to the presence of God among us 'to eternity in time'
with their traces among us daily."[16]

Barth believed angels who visit earth are separated from the other
ones to do a special work that contributes to the earthly history of salvation; after the assignment is finished, those angels disappear again into
the general body of angels to do what they do in heaven and to wait for
another summons for a mission to earth.[17] Angels always praise the Lord
by pleasing Him through obeying and doing His bidding (Ps. 103:20). In
that regard, they are heavenly models for the kind of representatives
God's people are to be on earth, as we are to also praise and please God
by doing His bidding. As angels understand what pleases God, so His
people are to "find out what pleases the Lord" (Eph. 5:10; 1 Thess. 4:1);
obeying his commands pleases Him (1 John 3:22). Jesus revealed the reason of His effective life when, speaking about His relationship with God,
He said, "I always do what pleases him" (John 8:29).

The holistic general work of angels can be described by one
word, "correspondence." That is, what they do corresponds with God's
commitment, concerns, character, conduct, and compassion. And so it
should be with God's people on earth, "We are therefore Christ's
ambassadors, as though God were making his appeal through us"
(2 Cor. 5:20). We are never not God's ambassadors regardless of what
we are doing in labor or leisure, in fights or fun, in plans or prayers, in
thinking or talking, in recreation or rest, in driving or riding, in waiting
or going, in receiving or giving, in serving or being served, and in loving or being loved. Even when Paul was in prison and in chains, he was
God's ambassador (Eph. 6:20).

Their Specific Work

All that angels do and how they do it are indeed mysterious and
powerful.[18] The primary specific work is to be messengers as both the

---

[15] Calvin, *Institutes*, 1.14.5, 165.

[16] Forrester Church, *Entertaining Angels: A Guide to Heaven for Atheists and True Believers* (San Francisco: Harper & Row, 1987) 35.

[17] Barth, *Dogmatics*, III.3, 455.

[18] *Catechism*, 87:334, 268:1028.

Hebrew (*malak*) and Greek (*angelos*) words mean. At least once people linked Paul's ministry of messages to being an angel, "Instead you welcomed me as if I were an angel of God, as if I were Christ Jesus himself" (Gal. 4:14). That one statement clearly revealed that people considered the presence of God's people to be as significant as the presence of angels. And the presence of angels was viewed as the extended presence of God or Christ. That is one significance of the Church functioning as the Body of Christ. And to do so is to be effective representatives of God. Do outsiders sense that from the way God's people act and react today?

As messengers, angels were agents of revelation as reported in Hebrews 2:2, "For if the message spoken by angels was binding, and every violation and disobedience received its just punishment. . . ." God wants His angels' message and His peoples' message to be His (Acts 7:30-35; 2 Kgs. 1:3-4; 2 Thess. 2:13). And that can happen as we allow God who is at work in us to actually work through us to do His good purpose (Phil. 2:13). Angels do not have a corner on mirroring God, for we are to "be imitators of God, therefore, as dearly loved children and live a life of love" (Eph. 5:1). And we can, because the Spirit of God lives in us; the same Spirit in the same percentage that lived in Jesus.

While being a messenger seems so ordinary to us, it was not so in biblical days. Van der Hart notes that a messenger was a very important person who represented the sender, so much so that to hear the messenger was received as hearing the person who originated the message. The messenger was actually a window through whom people viewed the sender.[19] Thus the message of angels paralleled that of prophets, which may account for why so few angels appeared in the writings of Old Testament Prophets with the exception of Zechariah. (20 times in Zechariah; twice in Isaiah; once in Daniel; and once in Hosea. For a comprehensive development of this see Edgar Conrad, "The End of Prophecy and the Appearance of Angels/Messengers in the Book of the Twelve."[20])

Another specific angelic ministry was to set up a set of circumstances for God to meet certain needs such as the connection of Rebekah to become Isaac's wife (Gen. 24:1-7,40-66). Many incidences may have

---

[19] Van der Hart, *Theology*, 23-24.
[20] Edgar W. Conrad, "The End of Prophecy and the Appearance of Angels/Messengers in the Book of the Twelve," *Journal for the Study of the Old Testament* 73, no. 1 (1997) 65-79.

Angels 5

really been "**God**cidences" even without mentioning the activity of angels. As it was in biblical days, so it surely is today. Barth notes that the significance of mentioning angels in various situations proves those events were not the result of fate, chance, human self-help, or the assistance from others, but were interventions from God.[21]

Angels certainly intervened in events on several occasions (Gen. 19:11; 22:11-17; Exod. 3:1-5; Matt. 2:13,19,22; Acts 5:19-20; 8:26; 12:6-11; 22:10-11; 27:23-24, and many other places). We have no idea of the millions of other times God intervened without revealing the presence and influence of His angels. Perhaps one way we entertain angels without knowing it is by experiencing those *in*cidences that later we discovered were "**God**cidences." One day God may replay the video of our lives to reveal those times to us.

Several times angels protected God's people by intercepting events such as stopping the lion's mouth (Dan. 6:22), stopping Abraham from killing Isaac (Gen. 22:11), sending Hagar back home (Gen. 16:7-16), keeping flames from burning those three chaps (Dan. 3:28). leading Peter's prison break (Acts 5:19), and many other times. (For examples see Exod. 14:19-20; 32:34; 1 Kgs. 19:5-7; Ps. 91:11-12; Ezek. 9:1-10; Zech. 12:8; Matt. 2:12; Luke 4:10-12). Perhaps that explains how some people conquered kingdoms, escaped the edge of the sword, women received back their dead, and other experiences.

It is interesting to note that the above list started with two situations in which angels were reported as being interceptors—shutting the lion's mouth and quenching the flames (Heb. 11:32-35). Thus it is not unlikely that angels were also involved in all the other events as well without having been revealed or reported as such. Surely those same phenomena continue throughout history including that slice of history we are now living. Of course it is difficult for us to understand why angels do not protect all God's people in all situations, for many were flogged, tortured, stoned, sawed in two, put to death by the sword, persecuted, mistreated, and kept on the run living and hiding in caves and holes in the ground (Heb. 11:36-38). While we cannot explain that because of our limited rationale, we can get excited when we read that the "world was not worthy of them. . . .These were all commended for their faith, yet none of them received what had been promised. God had planned something better for us so that only together with us would they be made perfect" (Heb. 11:38-40).

---

[21] Barth, *Dogmatics*, III.3, 496-497.

73   At times angels were active interceptors who brought destruction to things
and death to people who threatened and/or **Angels 5**
hurt God's people. At times God "unleashed against them his hot
anger, his wrath, indignation and hostility—a band of destroying
angels" (Ps. 78:49). Sometimes militant angels were sent to outsiders
who were enemies against God's people; but sometimes they were
sent to insiders—members of God's people—who were spreading dissension among His people (Ps. 78:49). God hates those who do that
(Prov. 6:16-19).

Each congregation today needs to take notice that God will pun-
ish even those within the church who intentionally weaken the congregation's witness by spreading bitterness, control, and disunity.
Church leaders should disfellowship such people in order to stop the
spread of spiritual gangrene. Titus 3:10-11 is one of the instructions that
hurts the church when neglected, "Warn a divisive person once, and
then warn him a second time. After that, have nothing to do with him.
You may be sure that such a man is warped and sinful; he is self-con-
demned." In our desire to be liked by everyone, we may ignore that
admonition without realizing that Christ died for the Church and loves
the Church for whom He died (Eph. 5:25).

To review what angels did against enemies of God's people should be a wake-up call today.

God has never taken lightly *any source* from outsiders or insiders
that threatens the spiritual health of His people. To review what angels
did against enemies of God's people should be a wake-up call today.
Among the seven things listed in Proverbs 6 that God hates is a person
"who stirs up dissension among brothers" (v. 19). The flip side of that is
for every member to "make every effort to keep the unity of the Spirit
through the bond of peace" (Eph. 4:3). Unity of the Spirit does not mean
just keeping people together; it also means to be one with the Spirit's
character in order to function as Christ's extended body on earth. When
negative "cells" within the body of Christ begin to spread like cancer, that
cell must either repent or be removed to protect God's people and to give
other potential cancerous cells a wake-up call. God will not allow His
people to be alienated (Josh. 5:14), even if it means wiping out an entire
army of 185,000 strong in one night (2 Kgs. 19:35; Isa. 37:36).

Regardless of the threats, God's people will be more than con-
querors, for if God is for us, who can be against us? He who did not
spare His Son for us will not spare what it takes to preserve His Church

Angels 5

on earth. Jesus promised it, "I will build my church, and the gates of Hades will not overcome it" (Matt. 16:18; See also Rom. 8:31-39).

From time to time, angels did do, are doing, and will do many other ministries including the following:

1. Affecting nature
2. Witnessing, which is really God's own self-disclosure through angels
3. Receiving Jesus' acknowledgements of us (Luke 12:8)
4. Traveling with people to whom they were so assigned to do (Gen. 32:1)
5. Joining in celebrations of joy over people who repent (Luke 15:10)
6. Providing provisions (Ps. 78:25)
7. Performing physical labor such as removing the stone from Jesus' tomb (Matt. 28:2)
8. Taking our prayers to God (Rev. 5:8; 8:3-4)
9. Having put the law into effect for Old Covenant people (Gal. 3:19; Heb. 12:2)
10. Guiding people toward what is right (Job 33:23)
11. Escorting dead saints to heaven (Luke 16:22)
12. Announcing the return of Jesus (Matt. 24:31)
13. Separating the righteous from the unrighteous at the end of the age (Matt. 13:40-41)
14. Accompanying Jesus' return (Matt. 25:31)
15. Fellowshipping with the saints in heaven (Book of Revelation).

These works do not exhaust the activities on earth. God is the God of the angels and can include them in any kind of service on earth for heaven's sake He desires. But angels are also working in heaven for earth's sake.

Their Work in Heaven for Earth's Sake

Their General Work

Generally angels in heaven are in God's immediate presence, gaze upon Him, and stand ready for any work He has for them to do (Rev. 7:11; Ps. 103:20). At one time they fought a terrible battle against those who were led by the Devil. The Satan-led angels lost and were expelled (Rev. 12:7-9). As God did not allow His created heavenly

angels to get away with bringing dishar- **Angels 5**
mony and destroying His heavenly com-
munity, He will not allow His earthly re-created
people to get away with bringing disharmony and destroying His earthly community. Church leaders must understand and accept this protective assignment from God. If not, they should work at understanding or
accepting it, or step aside. The expelled angels had power and still do,
as negative people in the church have power to influence many.

Now that the heavenly battle is over, the victorious angels are
doing many different things including the following, all of which are
revealed in the book of Revelation:

1. Leading in worshiping, praising the Triune God (4:8-11; 5:8-14;
   7:11, and singing the "hymns" scattered throughout the book).
2. Asking questions (5:2)
3. Waiting for power and assignments to protect or harm earthly
   realities (7:1)
4. Carrying prayers to God (8:2-4)
5. Waiting for power and assignments to affect nature on earth
   (8:12)
6. Declaring realities on earth and expressing disappointments
   (woes) for those negative happenings on earth (9:1-15; 14:8;
   18:1-24)
7. Affirming those who obey God (14:12)
8. Leaving heaven to warn people (14:9-12)
9. Instructing John to write (14:13; 19:9; 22:10)
10. Delivering the seven last plagues (chapters 15–16; 21:9)
11. Revealing God's plans (17:1-15)
12. Distributing God's wrath (14:14-20)
13. Will chain Satan (20:1-3)
14. Revealed Jesus and other realities to John (21:9ff), and may intro-
    duce us to Jesus when we get to heaven
15. Rejecting worship to self (22:8-9)

Some believe the 24 elders around the throne are angels.[22] However there is no hint of that in the book.

Eventually all God's people will join the angels to enjoy eternal
life in heaven as revealed in Hebrews 12:22-24, "But you have come
to Mount Zion, to the heavenly Jerusalem, the city of the living God.

---

[22] Robert H. Mounce, *Book of Revelation* (Grand Rapids: Eerdmans, 1977) 135-136;
Barth, *Dogmatics*, III.3, 464.

Angels 5

You have come to thousands upon thousands of angels in joyful assembly, to the church of the firstborn, whose names are written in heaven. You have come to God, the judge of all men, to the spirits of righteous men made perfect, to Jesus the mediator of a new covenant. . . ."

Those who do not believe in angels will no doubt be surprised to see them coming with Jesus at the end of the age (Matt. 25:31). They may also be embarrassed to live forever with those they refused to believe existed, while at the same time having believed in the Bible that continuously affirms the existence of angels. To believe the Bible, but not believe in angels is an interesting phenomenon.

Our belief in angels is not required to get to heaven; however, our belief in Jesus is, as He declared, "I am the way and the truth and the life. No one comes to the Father except through me" (John 14:6). Eternal life is not in God's angels, but is in God's Son, "And this is the testimony: God has given us eternal life, and this life is in his Son. He who has the Son has life" (1 John 5:11-12; 7:19; 8:14; and 11:25).

Eternal life is not in God's angels, but is in God's Son.

Any initial embarrassment for not believing in angels will be instantly eliminated when we connect up with Jesus and the angels, for we will experience the reality of the following: "Now the dwelling of God is with men, and he will live with them. They will be his people, and God himself will be with them and be their God. He will wipe every tear from their eyes. There will be no more death or mourning or crying or pain, for the old order of things has passed away." Then we will hear God's welcoming announcement, "I am making everything new! . . . It is done. I am the Alpha and Omega, the Beginning and the End. To him who is thirsty I will give to drink without cost from the spring of the water of life. He who overcomes will inherit all this, and I will be his God and he will be my son" (Rev. 21:3-7).

CHAPTER 6

ANGELS TODAY: YES OR NO?

Cessation of Believing

The reactions to the possibility of angels serving us today are diverse. Wink does not believe angels are actual beings, but instead are psychodynamic spiritual experiences which exist inside an individual, a church, and a work place.[1] Some believe the age of angels ended with Christ who is God's mediator; however, the only New Testament book that mentions Christ being our mediator also mentions the value of angels three times. Hebrews 1:14 does not say angels *were* (past tense) ministering spirits sent to serve those who will inherit eternal salvation, but *are* (present tense). And in that same book we are commanded to show hospitality to strangers, for by doing so may entertain angels without knowing it. That command is as significant as the one immediately before it, "Keep on loving each other as brothers" and the one immediately following it, "Remember those in prison as if you were their fellow prisoners, and those who are mistreated as if you yourselves were suffering" (Heb. 13:1-3). These were written *after* Christ ascended to heaven.

There is nothing in the New Testament that suggests the elimination of angelic services.

There is nothing in the teachings of Christ nor in any New Testament letter that suggests the elimination of angelic services. Lightner and Jones rightly observe that just because angels did certain ministries in the past doesn't mean they are prevented from doing those same kinds of services today.[2]

---

[1] Wink, *Naming*; *Unmasking*; Walter Wink, *Engaging the Powers: Discernment and Resistance in a World of Domination* (Minneapolis: Fortress Press, 1992).

[2] Lightner, *Angels, Satan, and Demons*, 163; Timothy Jones, "Rumors of Angels," *Christianity Today* 37 (April 5, 1993) 22.

Angels 6

However, Lightner rejects the idea that angels today give inspired messages.

He believes if that were the case it would mean the Scriptures are not complete.[3] I disagree with Lightner for the following reasons: (1) the basic function of angels is to be God's messengers; (2) anything they do or say comes from God's instructions which is then "God-breathed"; (3) that does not mean God would be adding or subtracting from the completed Scriptures; (4) if angels function today, we must view them as cooperating with God, Jesus, and the Holy Spirit; (5) we must not write a personal angelology that denies God freedom to use His angels. I agree with Westermann, "What a blessing it is that angels do not concern themselves with what people think about them or even whether people believe in them."[4]

Putting the Bible aside, there are two opposite poles from which people form their unbelief about angels. The first pole centers on personal experiences. Some line up with "doubting Thomas" and will not believe in what they have not experienced. Some are reluctant to believe anything they cannot see. But many things remained unseen for centuries before being affirmed as realities, such as germs, bacteria, DNA, cholesterol, radio waves, and frequencies. We cannot see the electricity we use, the actual wind that blows, sea life deep below the surface, a submerged iceberg, changes of white or red blood cells, blockages forming in the arteries, air pressure, cancer cells, and much more.

About angels, MacArthur wrote, "Natural human vision usually cannot perceive them except when their visual manifestation is necessary to their mission."[5] Spirits are not visible; therefore, as ministering spirits angels are invisible until assuming a material form. Not seeing is not the real cause for not believing, because those who refuse to believe in angels they cannot see believe in germs and atoms they also cannot see; and Christians believe in God and the Holy Spirit whom we have not seen. We may be shocked when God pulls back the curtain or rewinds the historical video of our lives to reveal all those times the "invisible" was in His service for our "visible" good.

Biblically what was invisible to some was very visible to others. Once God gave a donkey the ability to see an angel, which its master could not see until God opened his natural eyes to see the unnatural (Num. 22:21-31). Peterson notes that for the most part angels are invis-

---

[3] Lightner, *Angels, Satan, and Demons*, 50-51.
[4] Westermann, *God's Angels*, 11.
[5] MacArthur, *God, Satan, and Angels*, 125.

ible and inaudible like writers who are real and yet are not seen or audibly heard by the readers.[6]

The second pole that shapes unbelief centers on intellectualism. Angels do not fit into educational pursuits, and do not fit the tenets of a closed system (see discussion on closed system in chapter one).

Continuation of Believing

There is nothing in the Bible that puts angels today on the endangered species list. While some reject angels because they are not visible, and some because it is not intellectually keen to do so, others adopt a form of "biblicism" by restricting angelic activities to only the time frame covered within the Bible, their services to the kinds done or not done in the Bible, and their manifestations to those kinds revealed in the Bible.

While some scholars imprison angels to the past, many others affirm the continuation of angelic activity. Wayne Grudem believes the completion of the Bible does not mean God will not communicate to us through angels as He does through people, "If God can send another human being to warn us of danger or encourage us when we are downcast, there seems to be no inherent reason why he could not occasionally send an angel to do this as well."[7] Barth taught that angels continue to serve throughout history and stated, "The reality of the ministry of angels cannot be restricted to the history attested in the Bible."[8] Noll suggests lack of accepting the reality of angels today may be because we may not believe "there is a heavenly world that makes a claim on us."[9] Remarking about angels serving us today, Halberstam and Leventhal wrote, "The darkest moments of one's life may carry the seeds of the brightest tomorrow."[10] They view "coincidences" as "whispers that can awaken us from our stupor and remind us that the hand of God is always there guiding us through our days."[11]

Perhaps part of the problem for some is their lack of readiness to be served by the supernatural in unusual ways. Westermann triggers our thinking with, "What a difference it would make in our social min-

---

[6] Eugene Peterson, "Writers and Angels: Witnesses to Transcendence," *Theology Today* 51, no. 3 (October 1994) 395.
[7] Grudem, *Systematic Theology*, 408.
[8] Barth, *Dogmatics*, III.3, 516.
[9] Noll, *Angels of Light*, 95.
[10] Yitta Halberstam and Judith Leventhal, *Small Miracles: Extraordinary Coincidences from Everyday Life* (Avon, MA: Adams Media Corporation, 1997) 131.
[11] Ibid., 47.

Angels 6

istry if we really expected to encounter the messenger of the One who is beyond us in the persons of the helpless whom we encounter."[12] His point is that when we encounter people with needs, we may be encountering angels. No wonder we are admonished to entertain strangers, for they may be angels in disguise (Heb. 13:2). If the Devil can disguise himself as an angel of light (2 Cor. 11:14), then God can disguise His presence as an angel in need. Jesus affirmed that what we do or do not do for the needy, the outcasts, the oppressed, the neglected, and stereotyped, we do and do not do for Him (Matt. 25:31-46). Jesus is the model for caring for the needy, and there is no reason to assume angels may not motivate us to do the same.

Van der Hart wrote, "It is important for the Christian Church to make sure that her members always have a clear consciousness of the position of the angelic forces."[13] But it is possible that only a few members have a clue about their position on the reality and ministry of angels today. Is that because church members keep the reality of angels at a distance, in a "Star Wars" kind of fantasy, or like a childish concept that belongs to the prescientific primitive third world cultures? Why think it is more nonsense to believe in the reality of angels than to believe Jesus will return in a way that every eye will see Him, the moon will turn to blood, the sun will not shine, the stars will fall, the whole world will be gathered together and then separated as shepherds separate sheep from goats; and Christians will live in heaven where there is no death, cancer, heart attacks, colds, crying, aging; nor need for cosmetics, medicine, vitamins, hair spray, shots, insurance, banks, investments, wheelchairs, crutches, walkers, food stamps, shelter houses, and bridges for the homeless?

Surely out of respect for God (to whom angels belong and from whom they are sent) and out of compassion for those to whom God sends angels, we should immediately stop disregarding the reality of angels today and stop denying that God uses them for ministries on earth. After all, God could stop sending angels to the culture that refuses to believe in His ministry through angels. Shedd asks a pertinent question, "What if we believed in God's power and in his unusual ways the way the early Christians did?"[14] I wonder what we would miss by neglecting what God wants to share with us? For instance, we might

---

[12] Westermann, *God's Angels*, 84.
[13] Van der Hart, *Theology*, 89.
[14] Charlie W. Shedd, *Brush of an Angel's Wing* (Carmel, NY: Guideposts, 1994) 29.

miss being protected and helped in various ways. Would we want to deny God's varied benefits in heaven when we get there, because they don't fit our understandings, experiences, or beliefs? If not, why continue to do that on earth?

On the one hand, some attempt to restrict the power, plans, priorities, and practices of the Creator by teaching what God can and cannot or will and will not do for people on earth. On the other hand, others disregard the teachings in the Bible about angels and create their own understandings, some of whom profit from writing and speaking to the emotions of people who really want to be open to God's gracious ministries. Since God is God regardless of what we may choose to believe or are able to understand, perhaps we should be more open to giving Him freedom in our thinking and living to function the way He wishes including how He chooses to use angels.

Missionaries and Christians in all cultures have experienced angelic visitations along with many Jews who believed in angels and sensed their presence and ministries during Hitler's demonic holocaust. Grudem summarily writes, "There seems no compelling reason to rule out the possibility of angelic appearances today."[15]

Since the Bible did not describe, determine, or declare the termination date of angelic ministries, we should be extremely careful not to declare that God no longer utilizes His angels. There is no biblical teaching that directly restricts any kind of angelic manifestation and ministry to only past centuries. To pretend there are is to build our theological house on the foundation of quicksand. But if angels exist and God continues to use them, then what on earth are they doing for heaven's sake?

Consistency in Serving

MacArthur shares a list of general but diverse angelic ministries today which includes watching, protecting, delivering, taking prayers to heaven, rejoicing over repentance, and being our companions.[16] Since we are often aware of God's presence among us in ordinary situations and ways, it is easy to miss the presence of angels in those same kinds of situations, and thus think we need extraordinary angelic experiences. Perhaps God sends angels in such ordinary situations to refresh and

---

[15] Grudem, *Systematic Theology*, 408.
[16] MacArthur, *God, Satan, and Angels*, 179.

Angels 6

energize us when we feel like giving up. Billy Graham remembered times he felt he received energizing services from invisible angels when he was physically and mentally wiped out.

Perhaps some Christians shy away in order to avoid being linked to the New Age movement.

Perhaps some Christians shy away from affirming angelic activity today in order to avoid being linked to the New Age movement. However, by accepting the reality of God, of God's angels, and of God using them as He desires, Christians can build the following bridges that might help others draw closer to God:

1. A bridge to New Agers that might help some affirm God's incarnated Spirit in Jesus and in Christians as the primary means by which God serves various needs of people on earth.
2. A bridge to the Rationalists and Deists who think we live in a closed system with no involvements and influences from outside the universe. Perhaps this bridge will help some be open to the transcendend God who cares for this universe in ways beyond explanation.
3. A bridge to Atheists to help them know that at times mysterious experiences have no other explanation than the reality of a Being that exists beyond the limitations of people. After all, that is precisely what confirmed the life and ministry of Jesus. The Church began with a message from Peter who reviewed some things those people could not disregard because they were acquainted with the historical events, "Men of Israel, listen to this: Jesus of Nazareth was a man accredited by God to you by miracles, wonders and signs, which God did among you through him, as you yourselves know" (Acts 2:22). That Church began in the cocoon of miracles, "Suddenly a sound like the blowing of a violent wind came from heaven and filled the whole house where they were sitting. They saw what seemed to be tongues of fire that separated and came to rest on each of them. . . . 'Are not all these men who are speaking Galileans? Then how is it that each of us hears them in his own native language?' . . . Amazed and perplexed, they asked one another, 'What does this mean?'" (Acts 2:2-12). Christianity spread across the known world as people like Paul demonstrated the reality of God not just by preaching powerful sermons, but also by demonstrating miraculous

services to people. For the modern Church to use Scripture to teach that such a God is no longer active is antibiblical.

And by doing that, the Church is helping to raise a generation of people who place more power on the media than on the Master; more commitment to gadgets than to God; more attention to lust than to the Lord; more time with the Internet than with God's inspired "Internet"—the Bible. If God has put His power inside a closet and locked the door to keep it from touching this planet, what practical use is God for our very complex, confusing, and powerfully influential world? If the Church thinks only the "god of *this* world," who is Satan, has power (2 Cor. 4:4), then that Church refuses its role of being God's soldiers in the cosmic spiritual battle. It does little good to talk about the "good old days"— the days of the Bible—when God demonstrated power, if He has none today. Not many unchurched people are influenced by or want that kind of "has been" God. This world needs *the* God who is alive and active in this world, and His Church being willing to invite His power to penetrate our world of predicaments via any means He chooses.

4. A bridge to the "Pan-angelists" who insert angels into every kind of experience, and who believe every good event comes from activities of angels. On the one hand, we do not need to "see" angels even once; but on the other hand, we do not need to "see" them in every minor or major event in order to affirm that God continues to use angels according to *His* concerns, not according to *our* creations. As it is not helpful to take angels *out of* events when they have revealed themselves, it is also not helpful to insert them *into* events when they are not clearly revealed. After all, we know only about the ministry of angels in the Bible when their involvement was reported. We have no idea how many other times they were involved, but God's people did not dream them up in order to affirm angelic presence, power, practices, and possibilities.

While some, particularly New Agers, affirm angels for angels' sake, Shedd counterbalances that by writing that angels do not function to affirm their own reality, but the reality of God. Shedd's remarks are helpful, "I believe that the God who created us did not go off and leave us. In his love, he is constantly trying to reach us, lead us, and guide us. Or maybe he wants to warn us, detour us, and perhaps bring us to an abrupt stop for our own good. I believe that all around us, all the time his angels are there wanting to direct us and for what reason? Because he loves us."[17]

In his book, Shedd shares nearly fifty experiences in his own life and ministry he considers to have included angels. Those include such things as an internal voice and/or a strong popped-in impression or awareness of something to do or not to do, answered prayers, and protection. Many of his experiences sound like coincidences, but how do we know whether or not they were random coincidences or real "God-cidences" that included God's Holy Spirit or His angels? For instance on one occasion Shedd heard a voice in his head, "The Haroldsens. They need you. Go! Go now at once." Upon arriving at the house, Shedd heard Mrs. Haroldsen screaming with a baby in her arms and two small children at her side. She was on the phone listening to the news that her husband had just been electrocuted in an accident. She needed the presence of a calm person. I have also had times when a person's name popped into my mind. When I went to see that person at the house or the hospital, there was always an immediate need to address. How do we explain that? Perhaps Kinnaman is correct that sometimes a coincidence is "God performing a miracle anonymously."[18] That sounds much like the fabulously unassuming, humble, and helpful heavenly Father.

However, we must be cautious about listening to every strong inner impression.

However, we must be cautious about listening to every strong inner impression. While I was preaching a revival in Wisconsin, a young mother who was a member of the church heard a voice in her head ordering her to decapitate her infant baby, and she did. If angels can give us impressions of something good to do, the devil can give us strong impressions of something bad to do, because he can disguise himself as an angel of light (2 Cor. 11:14). Here's the rest of that story. That mother was placed in a mental institution for several years. The church reached out to her family and to her. Her husband took the other children to visit her as often as permitted. They took every vacation near her in order to visit her and to love her. Around ten years later, a couple of women picked me up at O'Hare Airport to take me to the

---

[17] Shedd, *Brush*, 101.
[18] Gary Kinnaman, *Angels Dark and Light* (Ann Arbor, MI: Servant Publications, 1994), 111.

Wisconsin Christian Convention that was meeting in the same church where I had spoken ten years earlier. On the way to the church, I asked about the young mother who decapitated her infant. There was strange silence, then the words, "things turned out well." During the convention, one of the women who picked me up told me that the other woman in the van was that young mother about whom I asked. That's when I discovered what the church and her family did for her. So I met with her and her family, hugged them, and affirmed how wonderfully God had worked in all their lives, and how much they ministered to me by knowing them and their love for God and each other.

Commitment to Openness

What can we do to communicate to God that we are open to His ways, including using His angels for us when He so desires, whether or not we recognize the angels who serve us? Here are some suggestions:

1. Prioritize pleasing God in all we think and do (John 8:29; Col. 1:10; Gal. 1:10; 1 Thess. 4:1).
2. Keep in constant contact with God through prayer. Our prayers may trigger God's protection or deliverance for us and others. Paul wrote to a church that God had delivered him from peril and would continue to do so "through your prayers" (2 Cor. 1:9-11). Remember an angel warned Paul of danger (Acts 27:23) and delivered him from prison *during the same time* people were praying for him. (Acts 12:1-17). On what biblical "hook" do we hang the teaching that God did that for some of His leaders/people a couple thousand years ago, but not today when we are living in a world that is increasingly hostile toward God?
3. Practice the presence of God throughout the day and let Him know we sense His presence.
4. Invite God to be personally involved in every minor and major situation.
5. Bury pride. God is more likely to let His angels be known to those who will receive the visit in humility with little interest in exploiting it for personal attention or profit. Not one biblical person to whom angels visited bragged about it.
6. Communicate gratefulness to God for those events, relationships, situations, people who see us as precious and encourage, include, value, lift up, and make a positive difference in how we view and live with self, events, others, and God.

Angels 6

7. Verbally and nonverbally communicate love to God. Visualize hugging and kissing God whom we dearly love. Say those precious words to Him, "I love you."
8. Express compassion for all kinds of people in all kinds of situations as Jesus did (Matt. 9:35-38).
9. Be open to continuously change into the likeness of Christ (Rom. 8:29; 2 Cor. 3:17-18; Rom. 12:1-2).
10. Do not neglect worshiping with others, while being aware that angels surround genuine worship services.
11. Use our aptitudes, personality traits, and charisma to serve others.
12. Express our faith through love feelings and love functions (Gal. 5:6).
13. Practice living in the Spirit with the fruit of the Spirit growing and glowing through our intentions, actions, and reactions (Eph. 5:18; Gal. 5:16-26).

Either angels *are* God's ministering spirits sent out to render service, or they *were* His ministering spirits. No theologian or church member has the right to change God's "are" to our "were."

No theologian or church member has the right to change God's "are" to our "were."

We do not have the capacity to exhaust God's reasons, ways, and means. The world is too complex with too many comprehensive problems to think we have a corner on what God needs to do, can do, and will do for a world He loves so much that He did not stop the crucifixion of Jesus.

After all, God and His angels live through all time zones, and are not uninterested and are not not involved. Here is a short list of God's probable use of angels today, because they are ways God used them in the past:

1. Answering prayers (Acts 12:7 in light of 12:12)
2. Encouraging (Acts 27:23-24)
3. Nudging us to witness to another who may be crossculturally different from us (Acts 8:26-40); however, we are never to wait for such nudging, for we have the command to do so and doing so is part of what it means to be a new creation in Christ (2 Cor. 5:15-19).
4. Warning us (Heb. 12:25; Acts 16:6-8)
5. Enhancing our awareness of the presence of the unseen God
6. Slowing us down. We live in a rushaholic, goaholoic, active-

aholic, workaholic, busyaholic, and belongaholic world with noise and stress all around us and in us. As Jesus got away

from demands of his time and urged his disciples to do likewise, so should we (Mark 6:31-32). If the devil cannot make us too bad to sense and enjoy the presence of God, he can make us too busy. Many of us are too busy to rest and relax for the re-creation of our holistic needs.

7. Being our companions in what can be a lonely, disconnected world

8. Rejoicing with us in positive times

9. Grieving with us in disappointing times

10. Watching our holistic behavior

11. Strengthening us when we are weakening

12. Lifting us when we are down

13. Delivering us from immediate danger. Grudem applies Psalm 91:11-12 with the following possible examples: when "a car suddenly swerves from hitting us, when we suddenly find footing to keep us from being swept in a raging water, when we walk unscathed in a dangerous neighborhood, should we not suspect that God has sent his angels to protect us? . . . Should we not therefore thank God for sending angels to protect us at such times? It seems right that we should do so."[19] Even if an angel had not been sent, would it not be appropriate to thank God for our safety regardless of the reason?

14. Enriching our worship. The natural function of angels is worshiping as viewed in the book of Revelation.

15. Helping to move us from fear to faith (Gen. 22:24-30)

16. Impressing upon us some ministry to do (Moses with the burning bush and Paul with the Macedonian call). I loved being a senior air traffic controller at O'Hare airport in Chicago and advanced rapidly. Nothing I have done since was as stress-free, easy-to-learn, and easy-to-do as that. With that fulfilled joy, I cannot explain the intense call to enter a different kind of ministry—the teaching, preaching, and writing ministry. That call did not come from a psychological internal unfulfilled wish. Oh, no, for being selected as a controller at the world's busiest airport was my internal wish, after being a control tower supervisor in the Air

---

[19] Grudem, *Systematic Theology*, 406.

Angels 6

Force. God may have sent His angel to nudge me to make the break, and again years later to keep me from returning to the control tower when I was very tempted to do so.

17. Giving courage and motivation to speak judgments to situations
18. Influencing us to leave certain situations (Num. 20:16; Isa. 63:9)
19. Changing addictions from self-centeredness to God-centeredness
20. Escorting us to heaven when we die
21. Appearing to us as we are dying. Recently a grandfather told me about his nine-month-old grandson who was dying of cancer. As he breathed his last, he looked straight up, raised one arm straight up with his hand open as if to take someone's hand, smiled widely, and died. Billy Graham reported that just before his grandmother died, she sat up, and then said she saw Jesus with His outstretched arms, her deceased husband, and angels; then she slumped and died.[20] Our 20-year-old daughter, Rachel, was literally cremated in her car that was stuck in the desert sand and exploded. A woman in our church received a vision that fire engulfed the car. She described the terrain where the car was stuck, and saw Jesus walking away from the car with Rachel. She then saw Rachel look back at the burning car, and heard Jesus ask, "What's the matter, Rachel?" And her reply was, "I'm concerned about my family." Jesus said, "I'll take care of them, Rachel." And she turned away and walked off with Jesus. What is interesting about that vision is that the terrain she described—a little hill on the left with a small tree or shrub is the precise description of the area, which we did not see until about six weeks after the explosion. That accident happened as she was on the way to walk the trails at the Valley of the Fires State Park north of Las Vegas. Upon receiving the bad news, we immediately went to Las Vegas to meet with the investigators. On the way home in the car, all of a sudden my wife, Julia, said "I just clearly heard Rachel say, 'Mom. Don't worry. I am OK, and very happy.'" Julia is not one who is prone to that kind of experience.
22. Being companions with our loved ones in heaven
23. Returning with Jesus for those saints who are still living when God pulls down the curtain to end the drama of earth's history (1 Thess. 4:14)

---

[20] Graham, *Angels*, 152.

89   The Bible does not suggest all
Christians or any Christian should know
they are experiencing angels or have experi- **Angels 6**
enced angels. But the Bible reveals that we may encounter angels
without knowing it (Heb. 13:2). Perhaps not knowing is one way God
keeps us from getting big heads in thinking we are more privileged or
superior to others. And it may be one way to keep us from getting so
hooked on angels that we focus more on them than on God, the Father,
Son, and the Holy Spirit, even if the focus is on our own personal
guardian angel, which we may or may not have.

To that topic we turn next.

CHAPTER 7

GUARDIAN ANGELS: GOD'S IDEA OR OUR'S?

Looking at Various Positions

The idea of Guardian angels is a hot button topic among both Christians and New Agers. Westermann suggests the idea that everyone having a guardian angel may be closer "to the enigmatic unfathomabiliy of a misfortune."[1] Most Christians probably relish the knowledge that God is with us as we go through one of life's valleys. Just as appealing and comforting is the idea of having a personally assigned guardian angel especially in a world of so much disconnectedness from others.

The concept of a guardian angel assigned to everyone is not biblically well developed.

However, the angelology that includes a guardian angel assigned to everyone is not biblically well developed. Some feel the following passages introduce the reality and presence of guardian angels:

1. ". . . the Angel who has delivered me from all harm" (Gen. 48:16).
2. "If you make the Most High your dwelling—even the LORD, who is my refuge—then no harm will befall you, no disaster will come near your tent. For he will command his angels concerning you to guard you in all your ways" (Ps. 91:9-11).
3. "The angel of the LORD encamps around those who fear him, and he delivers them" (Ps. 34:7).
4. "Yet if there is an angel on his side as a mediator, one out of a thousand, to tell a man what is right for him, to be gracious to him and say, 'Spare him from going down to the pit; I have found a ransom for him'—then his flesh is renewed like a child's; it is restored as in the days of his youth" (Job 33:23-25).

---

[1] Westermann, *God's Angels*, 32-33.

5. "Jacob also went on his way, and the
   angels of God met him" (Gen. 32:1).
6. "See that you do not look down on one of
   these little ones. For I tell you that their angels in heaven always
   see the face of my Father in heaven" (Matt. 18:10).
7. "Suddenly an angel of the Lord appeared and a light shone in the
   cell. He struck Peter on the side and woke him up. 'Quick, get
   up!'" (Acts 12:7).
8. "Peter is at the door! You're out of your mind. . . . It must be his
   angel" (Acts 12:14-15).
9. "Last night an angel of the God whose I am and whom I serve
   stood beside me and said, 'Do not be afraid, Paul. You must
   stand trial before Caesar; and God has graciously given you the
   lives of all who sail with you'" (Acts 27:23-25).

However, it is easier to read a guardian angel into those texts
(eisegesis) than to read them out of the texts (exegesis). In many of the
above instances God sent His angels on special rescue missions like
the movie *Saving Private Ryan*. There is no objective reason to conclude that such deliverance by angels in a given situation points to a
guardian angel permanently assigned to that person, as those who rescued Private Ryan were not his protective guards prior to the start of the
mission or after the completion of the mission.

To conclude that the "angel of the Lord" or "of God" is a
guardian angel in selected passages (such as Ps. 34:7 and Acts 12:15
above), but not in the many other passages, is to conclude what is not
in those selected passages. There is no hint that the angel of the Lord
in the other passages are permanently assigned *guardian* angels, but
rather are *simply* angels sent by God for specific ministries to specific
people facing specific situations.

Early Church Fathers (biblical scholars who greatly influenced
Christian thinking and Church Doctrine) developed the concept of
guardian angels. For instance, Origen believed every human is under
the direction of an angel who is like the Father, and Basil believed God
sends an angel to guard every believer like an army would. Church
Fathers viewed guardian angels as guards, overseers, assistants, shepherds, protectors, and superintendents.[2]

However Church Fathers differed on when a person acquired a
guardian angel—at birth, at baptism, or when facing a specific situa-

---

[2] Danielou, *Angels and Mission*, 69-70.

Angels 7

tion. They also differed on the specific functions these angels did, such as the following:

(1) Guarding new Christians
(2) Assisting ministers to preach
(3) Protecting people from trouble
(4) Reprimanding and punishing people who turn from the right way
(5) Helping people participate in spiritual warfare
(6) Guarding a person's moral weaknesses from yielding to temptations
(7) Bringing interior peace to a troubled soul
(8) Giving happiness
(9) Removing sorrows
(10) Putting the devil to flight
(11) Inducing people to repent
(12) Presenting prayers of saints to God
(13) Giving good thoughts to a person

Parente has a similar list combined from the specific beliefs of several different Church Fathers including the following:[3]

1. Surrounds us with love and care
2. Leads us safely through life
3. Defends and protects the soul from Satan, especially little children
4. Gives us pious thoughts and desires
5. Mediates between God and us by taking our needs and prayers to God
6. Serves as our Spiritual Director
7. Reduces temptations and can break their force
8. Prays with and for us
9. Joins us in preaching
10. Receives our soul at death and escorts us to heaven and to God
11. Goes on errands for us
12. Leads us into purgatory for additional cleansing, if we are not ready for heaven
13. Inspires our friends to pray for us, and to offer masses for our release from purgatory
14. Introduces us to God in heaven after we have been released from purgatory
15. Shares with us in never-ending worship of God in heaven

---

[3] Parente, *Angels*, 23-24.

The Roman Catholic Church affirms the doctrine of guardian angels by teaching that "Beside each believer stands an angel as protector and shepherd leading him to life."[4] The New Ager Janice Connell agrees, but believes every good and bad person (not just believers) has a guardian angel that is equipped to provide power, courage, strength, wisdom, consolation, understanding, and knowledge.[5] My students at the university would like to link up with such an equipping angel.

Some believe a different guardian angel is not only assigned to individual people, but also to individual nations, and to individual congregations. These national and congregational angels are assigned to be advocates, protectors, fighters, teachers, guides, and preservers. But one wonders why a guardian angel is needed for a nation and a congregation if each person in that nation and congregation already has a competent guardian angel.

After reading the above functions, it seems as if life on earth should be trouble free as a taste of heavenly living. In fact with such protection we might not notice much difference between earthly and heavenly living beyond the fact that there will be no death and marriage in heaven. Anyone reading the developed angelology of guardian angels might ask, "What ever happened to mine? Has mine taken a long siesta, sabbatical break, or a century-long vacation?"

Looking at Two Passages

It is essential to consider the two texts that on the surface appear to be more guardian angel–related than others.

Matthew 18:10

Jesus declared, "See that you do not look down on one of these little ones. For I tell you that their angels in heaven always see the face of my Father in heaven." Hagner sees this as an example of Hebrews 1:14, "Are not all angels ministering spirits sent to serve those who will inherit salvation?"[6] However, this text does not imply a private and permanent guardian angel for each child or person.[7] These are certainly

---

[4] *Catechism*, 87:336.

[5] Connell, *Angel Power*, xiii.

[6] Donald A. Hagner, *Matthew 14–28, Word Biblical Commentary*, vol. 33b (Dallas: Word, 1995) 14-18.

[7] Barth, *Dogmatics*, III.3, 518.

not angels who had the mission of guard- **94**
ing and protecting the related children
from harm, because they were being mistreated,
which is hardly a supporting text for those children having guardian
angels. Morris does not believe these angels guard the little ones, but
bring their situations to God.[8] This text also shows that Jesus believes
angels connected life on earth with heaven.

Barth's position is that permanent guardian angels are not needed since all the hosts of heaven are called God's ministers to watch
over us.[9] Grudem does not believe angels in this passage support the
idea that there is *one angel per child*, but rather a plurality of angels for
children as a whole.[10] The angels in this text seem to be *watching and
reporting from heaven*, and *are not guarding on earth*. They are not in
the presence of children on earth, but are in the immediate presence of
God in heaven, for they "always see the face of my Father in heaven."

Matthew 18:1-14 is a devastating condemnation on those who
abuse children, and should be preached and taught more often around
the world where children are endangered while still in their mother's
womb, and then while growing up in a messed up world. In this section of Scripture Jesus said more about the abusers than about the
abused. He made it clear that it is better to go to heaven helping children than to go to hell harming them. When Jesus spoke about cutting
off the hand or foot and gouging out the eye, he was giving a vivid picture of stopping the hurtful actions at their source—nip it in the bud.
God is the good shepherd who is not willing for one of His little lambs
to be hurt or lost (vv. 7-14).

Acts 12:15

A servant girl had just announced, "Peter is at the door!"

"You're out of your mind," they told her. When she kept insist-
ing that it was so, they said, "It must be his angel."

In the broader context, King Herod had executed the apostle,
James. Seeing it pleased the Jews, he had Peter arrested with the intention of bringing him to trial and execution after the Passover celebration; "but the church was earnestly praying to God for him" (12:1-5).
After an angel led the activities of Peter's prison break, Peter went to

---

[8] Leon Morris, *The Gospel according to Matthew* (Grand Rapids: Eerdmans, 1992)
465.
[9] Barth, *Dogmatics*, III.3, 518.
[10] Grudem, *Systematic Theology*, 400.

the location of the praying church and a girl answered his knocking. But in her excitement, she left him standing there while she ran to tell others (something like little children would do when they see their grandparents at the door).

Does the statement, "It must be his angel," prove the existence of a guardian angel for Peter and thus for all people? Could his "angel" be literally his "messenger" as it is in Matthew 11:10; Mark 1:2; Luke 7:24; 2 Corinthians 12:7; James 2:25; plus 98 other times in the Old Testament? Perhaps the people thought Peter had sent a messenger from prison with some information, gratitude, or request. Perhaps they had been praying for some kind of intervention which they thought might have happened; if so, they might have thought Peter would not stick around, but send a messenger. Perhaps they thought a messenger had arrived to share the bad news that Peter had been executed, in spite of Herod's intention to wait until after the Passover, for Herod was quite unpredictable.

We do not know what they thought, but whatever it was, their statement communicated nothing about the reality of guardian angels. At that time, Jewish people believed in guardian angels, and this statement may do nothing more than reveal their theory about God's use of angels. That is how Barth,[11] Marshall,[12] and Grudem[13] understand the passage. Barth suggests the whole idea of guardian angels comes not from biblical passages, but from paganism, and was first introduced into Christianity by Origen. He adds, "Where in the Bible are the ideas of guardian and national angels so substantial and important as to compel or even to allow us to understand the function of angels according to this norm?"[14]

Noninclusive Evidence

The belief in guardian angels is not part of most Christian angelology, except within the doctrines of the Roman Catholic Church. Calvin did not see the benefits of guardian angels as long as we have a host of angels around us.[15] Westermann sees no need of a guardian

---

[11] Barth, *Dogmatics*, III.3, 518.

[12] I Howard Marshall, *The Acts of the Apostles* (repr., Grand Rapids: Eerdmans, 1989) 210.

[13] Grudem, *Systematic Theology*, 400.

[14] Barth, *Dogmatics*, III.3, 383-384.

[15] Calvin, *Institutes*, 1.14.7, 16.

angel based upon Jesus' promise, "I will **96** be with you," and upon God's promise, "If God is for us, who can be against us?" Westermann also states, "It is the intention of the Bible not to provide a special figure apart from God and in addition to God, but rather to emphasize God's care for what is endangered and unprotected in particular proximity to a person." Thus for Westermann whatever can be said about a guardian angel can be said about God.[16]

The belief in guardian angels is not part of most Christian angelology.

It does not appear that Jesus had a guardian angel for the following reasons:

1. Angels in the plural (not one guardian angel) ministered to Him *after, but not during* His wilderness temptations.
2. Jesus did not refer to the possibility of asking His guardian angel to stop the crucifixion. Instead He spoke about calling 72,000 angels. But one effective guardian angel would have been enough in light of the fact that only one angel killed 185,000 soldiers during one night in the Old Testament.
3. No guardian angel reduced His sorrow in the Garden of Gethsemane when He was "overwhelmed with sorrow" (Matt. 26:38).

Complex Questions

There are many complex questions that need to be resolved somehow if each person, nation, and congregation has a permanently assigned guardian angel:

1. If each person has a different protective guardian angel, are those angels in conflict with each other when two people are in conflict with each other to the point of trying to kill each other?
2. Where are the guardian angels when two soldiers are warring against each other and both are Christians from different countries, or from the same country engaged in a civil war? Does that mean guardian angels take a break during conflict, or does God withdraw a guardian angel from one side when two are in conflict? Where is the biblical evidence for such selectivity?
3. How do guardian angels relate to a person's freedom of choice?

---

[16] Westermann, *God's Angels*, 104-105.

4. What is a guardian angel doing when a little girl is snatched from her bed, raped, and killed?
5. Why didn't James's guardian angel protect him from Herod's sword?
6. Why didn't guardian angels keep the other apostles from being executed?
7. Why didn't our daughter Rachel's guardian angel whisper to her to turn off her car, or it would explode?
8. Why does a congregation's guardian angel not intervene when members are dividing over various issues?
9. Do guardian angels of conflicting nations call in other angels to take sides in warfare?
10. Where were all the guardian angels in this country on 9/11/2001, and during other tragedies?
11. What are guardian angels of little children doing in other countries where they are starving to death by the hundreds of thousands?
12. What are guardian angels of individual women doing in those countries where they are being terribly mistreated?

Those kinds of questions are endless.

A Human Idea or God's

It seems highly likely the idea of individual guardian angels being permanently assigned to individuals, nations, and congregations is the creation of the wishes of humans, not the creation of the will of God. Sidney Callahan brings reality to the concept of guardian angels with, "If they cannot be expected to protect against fire, and each robber . . . then how can guardian angels be intervening in the things going on in the world?"[17] Leon Morris makes a compelling point that if a guardian is meant in Matthew 18:10, then "it would point to something so significant that we would expect references to guardian angels elsewhere and we do not find them."[18]

It should be support and comfort enough for us to know that we have a person with us—a stick-to-it companion who is the triune God—the Father, Son, and Holy Spirit. With freedom of choice, it is our responsibility to imitate the Father, to be conformed to the Son, and to

---

[17] Callahan, "Trouble," 7.
[18] Morris, *Matthew*, 464.

Angels 7

be filled with the Spirit. Nowhere does the Bible suggest that a guardian angel will help us mature, for that is our responsibility with the help of other members in Christ's Body, the Church (Rom. 12:4-6; Eph. 4:11-16; and all the "one anothers" in the New Testament).

We may face dangers, disappointments, devastations, misunderstandings, mistreatments, and mishandling; but when we do, there is no reason to wonder where our guardian angel is. Instead we can be full of *wonder* in God who promises that we will eventually cross over from death into life (John 5:24), for to be absent from the body is to be present with the Lord (2 Cor. 5:6) because He is *the* resurrection and *the* life (John 11:24). Thus our focus is to please Him while on earth (2 Cor. 5:9).

There is practical benefit for not depending upon weak and non-biblically supported ideas about having a guardian angel; but there is pertinent benefit for depending upon the strong and biblically supported reality that God is so much on our side that nothing shall separate us from His love (Rom. 8:31-39).

What more could a guardian angel add?

But there are unexplainables that we can experience. And to that we turn next.

CHAPTER 8

EXPERIENCING
THE UNEXPLAINABLE

Living with Incomplete Knowledge

Since the Bible did not develop a systematic theology about angels, there is much about them that remains unknown and unexplainable. But that should not surprise us, because there is much about God that is unexplainable. Part of the magnetic majesty of God is His mystery. He is above us. We cannot "own" Him by mastering all there is about Him, including angels and His use of them. Instead, we are to be mastered by God partly through what we do know about Him.

Part of the magnetic majesty of God is His mystery.

If we think we know all there is about God, our knowledge of Him is more like picking up one grain of sand from a massive beach that has no end to its width and length, and claiming we hold the entire beach in our hand. Or it is like filling a cup with water from the Pacific Ocean and claiming we have the entire ocean in that cup. As Paul put it, "We know in part, . . . Now we see but a poor reflection as in a mirror. . . . Now I know in part; then I shall know fully, even as I am fully known" (1 Cor. 13:9-12).

Living with Faith, Hope, and Love

While it is important to glean our knowledge of God from biblical studies, teachings, and personal experiences (including biblical culture and languages), we also rely on faith, hope, and love. "These three . . . but the greatest of these is love" (1 Cor. 13:13). Eventually hope will be absorbed by reality, and faith by clear sight. However, love will never be absorbed or replaced by anything. We will take love with us to heaven, and God will touch it and transform our incomplete and immature love with His. We will be full of His mature love without reservations or limitations.

Angels 8

Until then hope and faith are part of human living. We live by anticipating what we have not yet experienced. In Christ we have been born to a "living" hope (1 Pet. 1:3). That kind of hope is not passive; it is alive with motivations, energies, and stimulating openness to the unexpected. A live hope is ready to embrace and rejoice in God's serendipitous surprises. Otherwise we would not actively anticipate heaven. But we do anticipate it regardless of our very limited knowledge about it.

As we live with hope in the realities that are not yet exposed, we also live with faith in what we do not see, "We live by faith, not by sight" (2 Cor. 5:7). While hope is the anticipation of realities not yet known or experienced, faith is the confidence of things hoped for, but not yet seen or experienced (Heb. 11:1). So hope and faith are closely related.

Hope and faith are motivators for living. We cannot live long without the combination of both. For instance, without the active exercise of hope and faith, we cannot drink water, eat food, or inhale the next breath of air; for we do not know with certainty that something is not in the water, food, or air that will poison us. We cannot drive a car around a blind corner not knowing whether or not another car is in our lane coming toward us. We cannot enter an intersection with a green light not knowing for certain whether or not the cross traffic has a red light. We cannot cross a bridge not knowing for certain it will hold us; we cannot get on an airplane about to be piloted by people we do not know. We cannot live an hour without hope and faith, which linked together function as our "sixth sense" for making decisions, and is just as essential as sight, touch, taste, smell, and hearing. The issue is not whether or not someone has hope and faith, for all of us have some degree of hope and faith. The issue is the object of a person's hope and faith.

While we live daily with the unknown, unseen, un-understood, and unexplainable realities of the physical aspects of life, so it is with the spiritual aspects. We are constantly experiencing the unexplainable in both aspects. We have not and will not be able to comprehend and explain all there is about either the physical or the spiritual worlds.

The Finite Living with the Infinite

We are not able to capture all there is about God and His ways. The creature cannot fully explain the Creator. Our limited minds cannot contain all there is about His limitless mind. Our finiteness cannot fully fathom the infinite. We who began in time and space cannot fully comprehend God who is timeless and spaceless. Even Jesus cannot be fully explained. For instance how can He be both fully human and fully God? How can anyone fully explain the Trinity? No wonder the apostle Paul referred to Jesus as the "indescribable gift" (2 Cor. 9:15). He is indescribable because He is unexplainable, but not unexperienceable even by those who have never seen Him as He promised His apostles, "Because you have seen me, you have believed; blessed are those who have not seen and yet have believed" (John 20:29).

The Infinite Reaching the Finite

And so it is with the unseen, indescribable, unexplained, and un-understood realities of the incomprehensible God and His ways. This awesome God has always come to humans through mediators, and "angels are a part of the complex structure of the divine mediation."[1] We are still in need of God coming to us, thus the continual necessity of mediation.

In His humanity Jesus needed the service of His Father through the mediation of angels. He who was full of the inner Holy Spirit welcomed the service of angels. Why then shouldn't we? Is it possible that the more gadgets we have the less we think we need God; the more services we enjoy the less we need God's ministering spirits; and the more affluence we acquire the less we need or want angels?

He who was full of the inner Holy Spirit welcomed the service of angels. Why then shouldn't we?

Living with the Realities beyond Us

In the past God chose angels as one way to bridge the distance between Himself and humans—between the Creator and the creatures—between the Commander-in-chief and the front-line troops in the spiritual battles that continue on earth. Perhaps one reason God uses angels is to remind us there *is* a reality beyond us—beyond the material—beyond the natural phenomenon—beyond what we see—beyond what we touch—beyond what we hear—beyond what we smell—beyond what we taste—beyond all the senses—and beyond what we have or may experience.

[1] Ramm, "Angels," 67.

Angels 8

Perhaps our addiction to earthly things creates an inner emptiness that opens us for experiences of eternity touching us. The reality of angels affirms the openness of heaven to this world. Heaven and earth are two sides of God's creative love, and we should not deny either one.

Living with Angels among Us

Why do some Christians believe our unseen God materialized Himself in Jesus, but refuse to believe God can or would materialize angels? That unbelief is anchored to human perceptions rather than to God's productions. Unbelief may restrict what God is waiting and wanting to do for and through us. However, He can do with His angels whatever He wants to do, whenever He wants to do it, for whomever He wants to do it, and for whatever reason He wants to do it whether or not we understand the unexplainable.

Doesn't it make sense to believe in the ongoing reality and presence of angels when we read they have existed since before the creation of the earth; visited earth from the first book in the Bible through the last book; will return with Jesus, and live in heaven with God's people forever? What kind of logic concludes that angels are in some kind of holding pattern between the end of the New Testament and the end of our life on earth? Their interim passivity is in our perception only, but not in God's past, and probably not in His present or future plans and practices.

Why did our spiritual forefathers and foremothers believe in angels while we do not? What would have been lost to those before us had they adopted the denial stance of some of us? For instance, they might have lost the help of that angel who killed 185,000 enemy soldiers; they might have missed the food sent by angels; the shepherds might have missed the announcement on the night Jesus was born; the women might not have been addressed by angels at the tomb of Jesus. And what is being lost by that denial stance today? We may never know this side of heaven.

With all the negative things happening in our world today, Burns suggests that our belief in angels is a "refuge from the tide of secularism."[2] If 2 Timothy 3:16-17 is correct that all Scripture is advantageous for us to be "thoroughly equipped for every good work," then the God-

---

[2] Robert E. Burns, "On a Wing and a Prayer," *U.S. Catholic* 63, no. 9 (October 10, 1998) 2.

inspired record of angels is also profitable for us to be and to do what God wants us **Angels 8**
to be and to do. Our doing comes from our being. And our being comes partly from our beliefs. And our beliefs come or should come out of God's enlightenment, not just out of our experiences.

Living with God for Us

If we continue to disbelieve God is involved with life on earth as He was in the past, we may come close to being functional deists, who believe God is not engaged in our time and is not engaging in affairs on earth. Deists believe God started life on earth and then restricted Himself to watching it wind down on its own. For deists, God could die—the "Death of God" theology—and life would go on without Him and without His "Godufactured" Operations Manual, the Bible. Of course Christians do not believe that factually, but do we behave as if we believe it functionally?

We must be careful that we do not hold off God by disbelief in the unseen and the unexperienced. By doing so we may put ourselves outside the boundaries of some of God's services for us through His ministering spirits, the angels. Davis observes that if God is immortal and angels are immortal, then on what ground do we stand in denying their ministry today? The various reported claims about their appearances and ministries today "raise the possibility of such intervention being available at any time[3]"

People may be revealing more about themselves than about their understanding of God's world.

Could Paul's criticism of Sadducees for saying "there is no resurrection, and that there are neither angels nor spirits . . ." (Acts 23:8) also be directed to some of us? Barth noted that when people do not think angels are needed, they may be revealing more about themselves than about their precarious understanding of God's world.[4] He also believed that it is not so much what we think of angels as it is what that thinking reveals about our Christian faith and churchmanship by neglecting what the Bible does not ignore.[5] Jesus taught us to accept (bind) and to

---

[3] P.G. Davis, "Divine Agents, Mediators, and New Testament Christology," *Journal of Theological Studies* 45, no. 2 (October 1994) 482.

[4] Barth, *Dogmatics*, III.3, 412.

[5] Ibid.

reject (loose) on earth what has already **104** been accepted and rejected in heaven (Matthew 16:19; 18:18).

It behooves us to align ourselves with the realities revealed from heaven and not expect heaven to align itself with our rationalities. To accept God without the Spirit world or without the world of the spirits is to re-create God's world, ways, and relationships to our designs, likings, and limited understandings of reality. Fackre notes that the many biblical accounts of angels conform to the real order of things, and we cannot reduce the biblical characters to our conventions.[6] If God's people in the past entertained angels unaware, Christians should be the first to not only welcome their visits, but also to help those visits to be delightful and productive.

Practicing the Presence of God

Philosophically, scientifically, and scripturally there is nothing impossible about spirits having no bodies and then becoming materialized into bodies. While some claim Christianity borrowed the concept of angels from false religions or erroneous cosmology, the philosopher Adler believes it is a serious mistake to think the three Great religions of the West got their understanding of angels from pagan concepts.[7] Grudem believes God wants us to be aware of the existence of His angels.[8] Angels are not necessary for God as if He could not do without them, but may be necessary for us—to comfort our weakness, to encourage our hope, to affirm God's presence and care.

Angels are not necessary for God as if He could not do without them, but may be necessary for us.

Since we have God's life in us through His Spirit, we have the capacity to sense the presence of God in ordinary meetings, experiences, and events. But in our noisy and "rushaholic" world, we can easily crowd out noticing and practicing God's presence. Knowingly or unknowingly to us, angels may help wake us up to the presence of God. I suspect some of us will be pleasantly shocked someday to know how active angels may have been in our lives.

[6] Fackre, "Angels Heard," 356-357.
[7] Adler, *Angels and Us*, 107.
[8] Grudem, *Systematic Theology*, 405.

A contemporary and essential question remains: Are all reported appearances of angels God's involvements or humanity's imaginations? Wiederkehr correctly notes that it is possible angels "are in danger of being trendy."[9] It seems as if the concept of angels has become a fad in some circles. Angelic items in stores and published stories are financially marketable and profitable. Many reported angelic involvements seem to be humanity's inventions rather than God's interventions. Some stories border on being unbelievable; however, Clark reminds us, "We may disbelieve these stories, but it makes no sense to do so on the ground that they report things too unusual, too poorly attested to be believed."[10] Shedd also reminds us that angels operate in God's ways not ours.[11]

It is possible angels "are in danger of being trendy."

After all, many, if not most, angelic visitations recorded in the Bible are quite surprising and unbelievable. It is even surprising to some Christians who know biblical stories to see angels in some of the most familiar biblical events, such as being in a burning bush (Exod. 3:2), closing hungry lions' mouths (Dan. 6:21-22), keeping human bodies from being burned when engulfed with fire (Dan. 3:28), one angel killing 185,000 troops on one night (2 Kgs. 19:35), disconnecting Peter's chains and going through locked doors without being seen or encountered by guards (Acts 12:6-10), rolling back the stone at the tomb when soldiers were guarding it (Matt. 28:2), and so on.

At times God borders on being unusual and unbelievable. The resurrection of Jesus after a horrible execution is the mother of all unbelievables from our human objective reasoning. In fact much in the Bible fits that category such as creating the world out of nothing, the flood, the ten plagues, crossing the Red Sea, people wandering around for forty years without wearing out their clothing or shoes (wonder how women handled *that*), appearances of manna, stopping death from poisonous snakes by looking at a bronze one, bones scattered across a valley taking on flesh and blood and coming to full life, the virgin conception, dead people coming out of their graves at the crucifixion of

[9] Macrina Wiederkehr, *A Tree Full of Angels: Seeing the Holy in the Ordinary* (San Francisco: HarperSanFrancisco, 1995) i.

[10] Stephen R.L. Clark, "Where Have All the Angels Gone?" *Religious Studies* 28 (June 1992) 223.

[11] Shedd, *Brush*, 15.

Jesus, the ascension of Jesus, and the way
He will return. Those kinds of events are
endless in the Bible. But people experienced the
unexplainable and were blessed by doing so. And they are part of the
great cloud of witnesses who are watching us to see if we will pick up
the torch and run with the unbelievable as they did, in spite of not
understanding the unexplainable.

Living with Openness and Caution

Christians today need to balance openness to believe with caution to accept because the devil would like to detour us from affirming
the unexplainable God and His ways. After all, to disguise himself as a
snake and talk with a woman was quite sneaky, but successful. He
even disguised himself as a prophet of God claiming to have a message
from God (1 Kgs.13:18). So we need the balance of listening to the
reports of angelic visitations today with looking into the biblical revelation concerning the nature and function of authentic angelic visits
and messages. We need the balance of accepting authentic angelic visits with caution, so we do not shift our allegiance from God to them;
from the Master to the messengers; from the Sender to the ones sent;
from the One being represented to the representatives; from the Abba
to the angels; from acting on what we know God wants us to do, to
doing nothing about it until we get a confirmation from an angel.

Christians today need to balance openness to believe with caution to accept.

Living with Scripture and Experiences

We need the balance of Scripture with experiences. Rhodes
emphasized that balance, "By understanding what Scripture says about
the doctrine of angels, believers become aware of one of the most
exciting ways God takes care of us during our earthly sojourns."[12]
Scripture shifts the focus from angels to people as God intended by
allowing Christ to suffer and die on the cross, "For surely it is not angels
he [God] helps, but Abraham's descendants" (Heb. 2:16). Abraham is
not only the historical father of the Jews, but also of Gentile Christians
as Paul wrote, "So then, he [Abraham] is the father of all who believe
but have not been circumcised, in order that righteousness might be

---

[12] Rhodes, *Angels among Us*, 163.

credited to them" (Rom. 4:11). There is no biblical reason to believe that angels will not continue to minister to the biological descendants of Abraham today as they did in the past. And there is no biblical reason to believe that angels will not also minister to the spiritual descendents of Abraham—Christians, for anyone who belongs to Christ is "Abraham's seed, and heirs according to the promise" (Gal. 3:29). All God's people are potential recipients of various ministries from God's authentic angels. It is possible to keep God at such a distance that we are not aware of His angelic ministries.

All God's people are potential recipients of various ministries from God's authentic angels.

Experiencing Authentic Angels

If we balance openness to angelic visitations with caution and openness to Scripture with commitment, how then will we know the difference between authentic angelic visits from God's intervention and inauthentic visits from humanity's inventions? Here are some guidelines gleaned from Scripture:

1. Angels never draw attention to themselves.
2. Angels always shift a person's focus to God.
3. Angels refuse to be worshiped.
4. Angels will never contradict anything in Scripture.
5. Angels will never contradict anything Jesus said or did.
6. Angels will never introduce a person to another Savior than Jesus.
7. Angels will never introduce a person to another God, than the God of the Bible.
8. Angels will never introduce a person to another Spirit than the Holy Spirit.
9. Angels will never lure people away from the Christian Church.
10. Angels will never honor a person being a "lone ranger" kind of Christian.
11. Angels will never suggest doing something that is immoral.
12. Angels will never affirm a different religion than Christianity.
13. Angels will always encourage a person to grow toward the likeness of Christ.
14. Angels will never divide Christians from other Christians over matters of opinion about Scripture or theology.
15. Angels will never belittle another Christian.

Angels 8

16. Angels will never challenge the inspiration of the Bible.
17. Angels will never direct a person to any inspired source other than the Bible.
18. Angels will help Christians know they are united with all other Christians everywhere.
19. Angels will never suggest or entertain the idea there is another way to be saved except through Jesus.
20. Angels will never weaken a person's belief in the unseen realities of heaven and hell.
21. Angels will never remain in the center of a person's interest and focus.
22. Angels will never detour a person from doing any of the "one anothers" in the New Testament.
23. Angels will never contradict the character and fruit of the Holy Spirit or encourage anyone to do that.
24. Angels will never encourage us to do or say anything that would hurt others.
25. Angels will never give us a rationale for doing wrong.
26. Angels will always encourage us to do as Jesus would do and say what Jesus would say were He here in person.
27. Angels will always direct us to be subordinate to God's Word and Ways.
28. Angels will never feed our selfishness.
29. Angels will never feed our ego at the expense of others.
30. Angels will always bring honor and praise to the Father, Son, and Holy Spirit.
31. Angels will never encourage disunity among members of a congregation.
32. Angels will never try to control people by taking away their freedom of choice.
33. Angels will never function as substitutes for doing what others can and should do for one another.
34. Angels will do nothing to encourage us to shift our interdependence from one another to angels, thus weakening God's desire for community.
35. Because of 33 and 34 above, angels will probably not do minute things like making a bed, planting a flower, finding a parking place, fixing a flat tire, and so on that others can and should do, but they may as evidence of God's love.

Angels 8

It was never, and still is not, God's intention to replace angels with people or to replace people with angels. Angels are not surrogate members of the Church to do what God gifts people to do for both fellow Christians and outsiders.

Intimate Living with God

God desires an intimate companionship with us, but will not manipulate nor force us into it. His love is enough to draw out love as John reminded us, "We love because he first loved us" (1 John 4:19). However, it is possible for us to keep God at such a distance that we may not be aware of His presence among us nor the ministries of His angels for us. Sometimes we get so busy with our agenda that we become oblivious to His. Wiederkehr raised a pertinent question for all of us to ponder, "Are you able to be still enough to become intimate with the One who lives within?"[13] and "Have we learned to be present with quality to God, to self, to others, to experiences and events, to all created things? *We are in the midst of nourishment and we starve*"[14] (italics added). It may be that to live in the presence and ministries of angels is to exist in the midst of nourishment at the banquet table of God's service for us, but we starve.

Sometimes we get so busy with our agenda that we become oblivious to His.

Shea referred to angels as "companions of human adventure."[15] I would add "for the purpose of directing us to God and each other in those adventures." Surely angels may serve us in the diverse and meaningful ways they served people in biblical days because those angels belong to the same God and for the same purpose, and God loves and cares for His people in the modern world as much as He did in the ancient world.

But what kind of ministries might angels do with and for us? As God's sent servants, they would surely extend His love and desires for us. Consequently, with or without our awareness, they may engage in similar kinds of services that fellow Christians in the Body of Christ do

[13] Wiederkehr, *Tree*, xvi.
[14] Ibid., 26.
[15] Shea, "Angels We Have Heard," 37-38.

Angels 8

for one another, which at times may function to help us to make progress in some of the following needs:

1. Being closer to God
2. Being closer to one another
3. Being more evaluative of our own life style
4. Being more committed to keep unity within God's community
5. Having a lessened sense of loneliness in the midst of dysfunctional relationships
6. Feeling buoyed up during sinking times
7. Functioning with our own charisma without envying others
8. Being more content with what we have and more grateful for what we do have
9. Seeing light not only at the end of the tunnel, but also in the tunnel
10. Desiring to grow into whom we can become in Christ
11. Practicing the presence of God more
12. Praising God more throughout the activities of the day
13. Authentically worshiping God without pretense. Calvin believed that "in every sacred assembly we stand before the sight of God and the angels."[16] We sing about "standing on holy ground with angels all around."

God sends His love in various packages— the ordinary and extraordinary.

Of course the live-in Holy Spirit is doing some of the functions angels did in the past, but that does not automatically eliminate the ministry of angels who function in tandem with the Spirit. God sends His love in various packages—the ordinary and extraordinary. When all looks bleak and impossible, we need to be open to the possibility of miracles and the unexpected through the intervention of God's presence and power regardless of the avenue He chooses to utilize.

Living with God Who Is Bigger Than We Thought

Our view of God is too small if we have him locked up inside our theological, experiential, nonexperiential, intellectual, traditional, rational, and comfortable lock boxes. Ancient Judaism thought they had God trapped inside the Holy of Holies in the temple where they

---

[16] Calvin, *Institutes*, 3.4.11, 635.

wanted Him. Only one person (The High Priest) could enter inside and on only one

day a year (the Day of Atonement—Yom Kippur). But with Jesus' crucifixion the curtain that kept people away from the immediate presence of God was split from top to bottom symbolizing that God was not in that "prison," and anyone can immediately be with God.

That should not have been surprising because God declared that He was too big for any one place to contain Him, "Heaven is my throne, and the earth is my footstool. Where is the house will you build for me?" (Isa. 66:1; Acts 7:49-50). That was God's way of saying that He does not live in houses built by people, for there is not enough lumber in the world to build a house big enough to contain even His little toe. When Stephen reminded the Jews of that, they stoned him to death (Acts 7:54-60). There is no denomination or tradition big enough to keep God in "our" place that we believe is also "His" place. The Psalmist declared it well, "Our God is in the heavens; He does whatever he pleases" (Ps. 115:3, NASB). He does not need our vote to do whatever He pleases. He does not need to pass the test of what pleases us. He will not honor our veto. He does what pleases Him. And what pleases Him is always for our good whether or not we recognize it, appreciate it, or honor it.

Living with the Unexplainable

What God does that pleases Him is quite mysterious at times. Barth wrote, "Where the Kingdom of God is . . . the mystery of God is at work, and therefore . . . the angels."[17] It is certainly an unexplainable mystery why some people are healed or helped in various ways while others are not; some are physically protected, while others are not.

I wish I knew why an angel did not whisper to our daughter to turn off the car immediately, but evidently one did not. Instead of criticizing God for not sending an angel to do that, I will stick with trusting God who declared, "For my thoughts are not your thoughts, neither are your ways my ways" (Isa. 55:8). I also believe the Psalmist who declared, "The LORD is compassionate and gracious, Slow to anger and abounding in lovingkindness. . . . He has not dealt with us according to our sins, Nor rewarded us according to our inequities. For as high as the heavens are above the earth, So great is His lovingkindness toward

---

[17] Barth, *Dogmatics*, III.3, 516.

Angels 8

I trust God who has that much love for
me and for others. I believe God who speaks to us through what He spoke to His people of old when He said, "When you pass through the waters, I will be with you; And through the rivers, they will not overflow you. When you walk through the fire, you will not be scorched, Nor will the flame burn you. For I am the LORD your God. . . . Since you are precious in My sight . . . and I love you . . ." (Isa. 43:2-4, NASB). That means as Rachel was sitting in that car with her skin burning off, her two arms, two legs, and her head falling off, her ribs scattered, and with only one knee cap and one ankle bone found, *she herself* was not being scorched—her body, yes, but not her. She was untouched by the flames. I believe angels escorted her to heaven. And that Rachel crossed over from death into life (John 5:24), for to be absent from the body is to be present with the Lord (2 Cor. 5:8). I believe those words, because I believe God. God's love is bigger than what we see or the bad news we receive, because God is bigger than all of that. He is always God-for-us.

It is time for Bible-believing people to stop being reluctant in accepting what God reveals because it may not fit into our scheme of things. Angels are God's idea, not man's imagination; God's servants, not man's superstitions; God's purpose, not man's perceptions.

Perhaps we would all do well to utter the prayer Charlie Shedd uttered to God for him and his wife on their first pastoral call, "Lord, may we both be ever more alert for even the smallest brush of an angel's wing."[18]

Yes, I believe in angels. I believe they are God's ministering spirits sent to serve those who will inherit salvation (Heb. 1:14). And I believe what David wrote, "This I know, that God is for me" (Ps. 56:9). And this I know, that God is for all of you who are reading this right now.

So, come Heavenly Father, the Divine Son, and the Holy Spirit. And if you wish to come with and through your angels, then *come and meet us experiencing the unexplainable.*

---

[18] Shedd, *Brush*, 39.

WORKS CITED

Adler, Mortimer F. *The Angels and Us.* New York: Macmillan, 1982.

Anderson, Joan Webster. *Where Angels Walk: True Stories of Heavenly Visitors.* New York: Ballantine Books, 1992

_____. *Where Miracles Happen: True Stories of Heavenly Encounters.* New York: Ballantine Books, 1994.

Angels among Us. Compiled by the editors of *Guideposts.* Carmel, NY: Guideposts, 1993.

"Angels: Good or Evil." History Channel. Two-hour special, April 7, 2003.

Banks, Edgar J. "Angel." *The International Bible Encyclopedia.* Edited by Geoffrey W. Bromiley et al. Rev. ed., 1:124-127. Grand Rapids: Eerdmans, 1979.

Barth, Karl. *Church Dogmatics.* Edited by G.W. Bromiley and T.F. Torrance. Vol. III, Part three. Edinburgh, Scotland: T&T Clark, 1960.

Bietenhard, Hans. "Angel, Messenger, Gabriel, Michael." In *The New International Dictionary of New Testament Theology.* Edited by Colin Brown, 101-103. Grand Rapids: Zondervan, 1975.

Bloesch, Dondald G. *God the Almighty.* Downers Grove, IL: InterVarsity, 1995.

Bultmann, Rudolf. "New Testament and My Theology." *Kerygma and Myth.* Edited by Bartcsh. Vol. 1. London: SPCK, 1964.

_____. *Theology of the New Testament.* Translated by Kendrick Grobel. Vols. 1 & 2. New York: Charles Scribner's Sons, 1955.

Burnham, Sophy. *A Book of Angels: Reflections on Angels Past and Present and True Stories of How They Touch Our Lives.* New York: Ballantine Books, 1995.

Burns, Robert E. "On a Wing and a Prayer." *U.S. Catholic* 63, no. 9 (October 10, 1998) 2.

Bush, Trudy. "On the Tide of the Angels." *Christian Century* 112, no. 8 (March 1, 1995) 236-238.

Callahan, Sidney. "The Trouble with Angels: My Conversion Ex-   **114** perience." *Commonweal* 122, no. 21 (December 1, 1995) 7.

Calvin, John. *Institutes of the Christian Religion*. Book I. Chapter 14. Sections 3-19.

Catechism of the Catholic Church. Second edition. Revised and Promulgated by Pope John Paul II. Rome: Liberia Editrice Vaticana, 1997.

Charles, J. Daryl. "The Angels, Sonship and Birthright in the Letter to the Hebrews." *Journal of the Evangelical Theological Society* 33, no. 2 (June 1990) 171-178.

Church, Forrester. *Entertaining Angels: A Guide to Heaven for Atheists and True Believers*. San Francisco: Harper & Row, 1987.

Clark, Stephen R.L. "Where Have All the Angels Gone?" *Religious Studies* 28 (June 1992) 221-234.

Cohen, A. *The Psalms*. London: The Soncino Press, 1974.

Connell, Janice. *Angel Power*. New York: Ballantine Books, 1995.

Conrad, Edgar W. "The End of Prophecy and the Appearance of Angels/Messengers in the Book of the Twelve." *Journal for the Study of the Old Testament* 73, no. 1 (1997) 65-79.

Cunningham, John. "Christology and the Angel of the Lord." *Journal from the Radical Reformation: A Testimony of Biblical Unitarianism* 6, no. 2 (Winter 1997) 3-15.

Daniel, Alma, Timothy Wyllie, and Andrew Ramer. *Ask Your Angels*. New York: Ballantine Books, 1992.

Danielou, Jean. *The Angels and Their Mission: According to the Fathers of the Church*. Translated by David Heimann. Westminster, MD: Christian Classics, 1976.

Davidson, Maxwell J. "Angels." *Dictionary of Jesus and the Gospels*. Edited by Joel B. Green & Scot McKnight, 8-11. Downers Grove, IL: InterVarsity, 1992.

Davis, P.G. "Divine Agents, Mediators, and New Testament Christology." *Journal of Theological Studies* 45, no. 2 (October 1994) 479-495.

Dickason, Fred C. *Angels: Elect and Evil*. Chicago: Moody Press, 1975.

Fabian, Allison. "Readers Swear: Angels Are Out There." *Cosmopolitan* 223, no. 5 (November 1997) 174-176.

Fackre, Gabriel. "Angels Heard and Demons Seen." *Theology Today* 51, no. 3 (October 1994) 345-358.

Fass, David E. "How the Angels Do Serve." *Judaism* 40, no. 3 (Summer 1991) 281-289.

Fox, Rory. "Can There Be a Reason to Believe in Angels and Demons?" *The Downside Review* 115, no. 399 (April 1997) 112-138.

DEMONS

LEONARD THOMPSON

COLLEGE PRESS PUBLISHING COMPANY· JOPLIN, MISSOURI

CONTENTS

Author's Preface   6

Part One — The Reality of Evil and the Evil One

1 **The Concept of Evil:** From the Beginning   10
2 **Satan—His Origin and His Nature:** The Devil Made Me Do It **13**
   Origin of Satan   13
   The Biblical Teaching   14
   Nature of Satan   19
   Satan's Objectives   21
3 **Satanic Strategy and Agenda:** Deeds Done in the Dark   **24**
   Satan's Tactics   24
       Temptation   24
       Deception   26
       Imitation   27
       Accusation   28
       Destruction   30
   The Destiny of Satan   32

Part Two — The Realm of Demons

4 **Demons—Their Being and Existence:** Where Satan Leads,
      Demons Follow   **36**
   Demons—Terminology Used   38
   Demons—The Reality of Who They Are   40
       Disembodied Spirits   40
       Disembodied Spirits of a Pre-Adamic Race   41
       Offspring of Angels and Earthly Women   42
       Fallen Angels   43
5 **Demonic Confrontations in the New Testament:**
      Kingdoms in Conflict   **46**

6 Demons and Their Characteristics: What Dark Angels
    Do for a Living   **50**
Demons Are Real   50
Demons Have Personality   51
Demons Have the Ability to Occupy Bodies
    of All Kinds, Animate and Inanimate   52
Demons Have Supernatural Powers   52
Demons Are Perverted and Depraved   54
Demons Have Specific Duties to Perform
    and Jobs to Carry Out   54
Demons Are Organized   55
7 Demonic Tactics and Activities: Strategies from
    the Underworld   **56**
Demonic Oppression of the Mind   57
    Temptation   57
    Deception   59
    False Teaching   60
    Cults   61
    False Religions   62
    Mental Invasion   62
Demonic Assaults on the Body   63
    Bodily Illness   64
    Addictions and Obsessions   65
Demonic Control of Our Spirits   65
8 Demonic Possession: Intruders and Squatters
    in Unwanted Places   **67**
Demonic Influence   73
Demonic Domination   73
Demon Possession   73
    Specially Possessed Objects   75
    Symptoms   77

Part Three — Dealing with Demons

9 Who Let Them In? Doors to Demonism   **82**
Sinfulness   82
    Sexual Sin   83
    Lack of Forgiveness   85
    Depression   86
    Desire and Craving for Power   86
Pagan Religions   87

5

Occult Practices 88
    Occult Institutions 89
    Occult Apparitions 91
    Spiritism 91
    Occultic Entertainment 91
    Other Possible Doors 92
Ancestral Sin 93
Transference 94
Pronouncement of Curses 95
Child Abuse 96
10 Barricade the Gates: Protection from Demonic Influence **97**
Begin a Relationship with the Christ 98
Protect Yourselves with Godly Armor 99
Cover Yourself with Prayer and Petition 100
Shelter Yourself in the Fellowship of the Kingdom 101
11 Evacuating the Premises: Deliverance and Exorcism **103**
Need for Deliverance 105
Authority for Deliverance 105
Preparation 106
Exorcism 108

Addenda

Addendum One: Pagan Religions and Demons **114**
Addendum Two: Christians and Demons **121**
Demons Can Influence Christians 123
    False Miracles 125
    False Tongues 126
    False Deliverance 126
Demons Can Oppress Christians 126
Demons Can Control Christians 128
What Can Be Done? 130
Addendum Three: An Inquiry into the Subject of Territorial
  Spirits and Strategic-Level Spiritual Warfare **131**
Terminology 132
Territorial Spirits in Scripture 134
Spiritual Warfare 137
Strategic-Level Spiritual Warfare 138
Conclusions 140
Demonology Bibliography **142**

PREFACE

I do not fancy myself as a great or accomplished writer, and even though I did, in college and graduate school, take several classes in journalism, I think of myself more of an investigative reporter, presenting hard and often unlovely facts. Thus, when Prof. Mark Moore of Ozark Christian College asked if I would undertake the writing of a book on demons, to be co-authored with the very popular and prolific writer, Knofel Staton, my hesitation on being linked with such a great person was soon overcome by the challenge of investigating the whole subject of demons and demonism. But the challenge grew first into frustration, and then into a task that seemed beset by problems—some understandably strange.

Several years ago my theology professor at Cincinnati Bible Seminary, Dr. Jack Cottrell, warned us never to undertake any project, be it just study or deep research or any investigation concerning Satan and his demons, and the entire occult world, without being fully and completely covered by prayer. I now understand what he meant and why. I did make sure of this though, and a team put together by my second daughter Karen, then a graduate student at Purdue University, provided primary prayer coverage. She got members of her active prayer group to cover me with daily and constant prayer. I am deeply grateful to the Purdue Grad. School prayer group for this.

Undertaking this project reinforced what I already knew, that the demonic world is real and active. When researching and writing, I experienced an uncanny desire—extremely strong and real at times—to quit the whole project. Sitting at the computer with a whole lot of research to be sorted out and put together I would experience total mental blocks for vast periods of time. I did most of my writing in the late hours of the night and early morning. I would return home at times without a single word having been written. It was not just writer's block, for I am in the habit of "dashing" off the editorial and other arti-

7   cles in the periodical we publish called **Preface**
Christindian. Rather, the mental blocks
were accompanied by bizarre mental activi-
ties—eerie thoughts, evil suggestions, unwanted flashbacks, and the
like. And, yes, they did make me often turn around and look for who
was behind me!! Of such I have no desire to experience again. I was
acutely aware at the same time of the prayer coverage I had. At home,
my wife expressed how, during those times, she herself went through
feelings and awareness that something strange was occurring. No,
there were no apparitions seen or voices heard or other such things.
We were just made aware that evil was about and real, and that evil
did not want me to finish the project.

Quite a lot of material has been written and published on this
subject. Some are in the area of providing speculative scenarios bor-
dering on fantasy. These cannot be overlooked, for the ways of the
demonic world are certainly in the realm of the weird. Other writings
are intended to inform and warn and go to great lengths to show how,
the world over, Satan is at work endeavoring to destroy and delete the
things of God. Yet others have been written to document biblical evidence concerning demonic origins and workings, and to thereby inform
as well as alert us to the "wiles" of the devil. I have written so that we
could know what the Word of God teaches concerning demons and
their leader Satan, and to relate these teachings with what is happening in the world today. In doing this I have labored hard to stay away
from the fantastic and from fantasy; to separate "fact" from "fiction";
and to avoid supplying whimsical data that would seek to create fear
and panic. I believe that any work written about the demonic world
must make it clear that the Cross of our Lord Jesus Christ rang the
death knell for Satan and his followers and His Resurrection gave us
humans power over them. Victory over evil was made possible through
Christ's redemptive act on Calvary!!! I hope that this is made clear
through my writing.

I am grateful to my wife Pamela for all the support she gave me
in this project, standing by me in difficult times. My daughters, Kristina
(the eldest) and Karen moved me along, expressing their confidence
that I could meaningfully undertake this writing, and I am thankful to
them for their encouragement and support in many ways. The office
staff of Strategic World Evangelism, our mission based in Chennai, India,
helped me tremendously, especially one "little" (about 4 ½ ft. tall) girl,
Louisa Menezes, whose computer and DTP expertise was of tremen-

Preface

dous help to me. The mechanics of this book are mostly due to her hard work and the immense and intense interest she took in it. And I thank Mark Moore for even thinking I could do it.

I dedicate this book to those who will one day stand victorious around the throne, having overcome evil and the evil ones.

Leonard W. Thompson

A malignant being . . . subtle and full of hate

— Donald Grey Barnhouse

PART ONE

THE REALITY OF EVIL
AND THE EVIL ONE

CHAPTER 1

THE CONCEPT OF EVIL
FROM THE BEGINNING

To begin a book on demonism without looking at the concept of evil is in some ways putting the cart before the horse. We need to know from whence came evil and the Evil One, for in the most basic of understandings demons are creatures of an evil disposition. There are modern philosophies and related theories that decry any belief in demons, dismissing their existence and activity as nothing more than either delusion or mental inadequacy. Some religions also deny their existence, exemplified by some Hindu schools of thought that state that demons are the product of ignorance in a man (ignorance again being equated with sin). The ignorance of course is not one of value or intellect but is described rather as the spiritual ignorance that prevents a man from knowing his oneness with the Brahman, that monistic concept of a Supreme Being. Other religions dichotomize the belief of demons into good demons and evil demons. Yet, why call a demonic being a good demon when the whole concept of demons is consistent with the idea of evil? Demons are by logic and association with the Evil One, creatures of evil.

Demons are by logic and association with the Evil One, creatures of evil.

But what is evil? Simple philosophic definitions begin with evil being the negative of good. There is the almost childish concept that evil must be if there is good, just as light implies that there is darkness. A rather comprehensive statement with regard to the existence of evil is given by William Wallace in a book entitled *The Elements of Philosophy*.

> *Evil* is opposed to good, which is the integrity or perfection of being in all orders: material, moral, and spiritual. . . . Taken in itself evil is a negation of the perfection due to a nature or to a being. As such, however, it is not a simple negation; rather evil consists in a

10

privation, i.e., in the fact that a certain being lacks a good it requires to enjoy the integrity of its natures. While this implies that evil is non-being, it does not imply that evil is non-existent. . . .

Since evil is a privation it can exist only in a *subject* or in a being that, as such, is good. Evil presupposes good, both as the subject that it affects and as the perfection that it negates.[1]

The above philosophical look at evil does not in any way deny or contradict any biblical concepts of evil. Wallace himself later says, "God is not and cannot be in any way the *cause* of evil, for he is infinite goodness and desires only to communicate good."[2]

Among the various and varied religions of the world we cannot find any without some understanding, right or wrong and good or bad, with relationship to evil. Even Hinduism with its strong monistic and pantheistic base, which in turn seems to necessitate the existence of evil as being merely illusory, yet has its sacred literature filled with the activities of numerous evil beings and creatures who need to be both placated and defeated.

Animism also has a concept of evil, seeing it as that which is opposed to what is good, and this is clearly seen in their array of good and evil spirits. True, they are vague in their ideas regarding what is good and bad, and this again is related to nature all around so that what is good for one animistic group could possibly be evil to another. Yet there is that almost instinctive perception that evil exists.

The biblical teaching of the origin of evil is centered around the Creation account and presents evil in a personified way, with an evil being or person opposing Him who is not just Creator but also the Righteous and Holy One. So great is the contrast between Goodness and Evil in the Bible that as one person said, it takes your breath away.

The biblical teaching of the origin of evil presents evil in a personified way, with an evil being or person opposing the Righteous and Holy One.

What the Bible tells us of the origin of evil is so astounding, so utterly contrary to the conjectures and philosophies of men, that, but for a divine revelation, such a thing would never have crossed the mind of man. It simply takes your breath. It leaves you trembling with awe.

[1] William A. Wallace, *The Elements of Philosophy: A Compendium for Philosophers and Theologians* (New York: Alba House, 1977) 143.
[2] Ibid., 148.

Demons 1

Your first reaction is to deny the possibility of such a thing. But when it is taken in connection with the facts of life as a whole and with the redemptive work of Christ, it becomes the necessary link in the chain of events without which nothing is intelligible.[3]

We can look into evil in an abstract manner and argue for or against its existence for all of time itself, but not only is that defeating the purpose of this book but also it goes against an empirical fact. There is an evil being, both in the singular and in the plural. The concept of evil is "personified" in Satan and his own angels and their very existence is what causes man to be plagued with the promptings of evil in all spheres of his very being. From whence then comes Satan?

---

[3] F.J. Huegel, *The Mystery of Iniquity* (Minneapolis: Bethany Fellowship, 1968) 19.

CHAPTER 2

SATAN—HIS ORIGIN AND HIS NATURE
THE DEVIL MADE ME DO IT

Origin of Satan

Unger in his book, *Demons in the World Today,* says, "The history of various religions from the earliest times shows belief in Satan and demons to be universal."[1] And indeed a study of world religions makes this evident. Hinduism, as already stated, in spite of its monism and in spite of its explanations of lack of knowledge being the reason why concepts of evil are prevalent, still has references to evil and evil spirits and demonic creatures and so on. Islam has its El Shaitan and its Jinn.

> *I shall tell you now of the Two Spirits at the beginning of Creation.*
>
> *The Holier of the two thus speaks to the Evil One:*
> *"Neither our thoughts nor our teachings,*
> *Neither intentions nor choices,*
> *Neither our words nor our deeds,*
> *Neither our consciences nor our souls ever agree."*
>
> Taken from the Zoroastrian Scriptures, *The Avestas*

In the ancient religion of Zoroastrianism there is the belief in an Evil Being or Spirit who coexisted and is co-eternal with the Good Being or Spirit. Zoroaster (also known as Zarathustra) the founder of Zoroastrianism in around 660 B.C. specifies in the Avestas,[2] the Zoroastrian scriptures, that the two were the exact opposites of each other. The Supreme Being, endowed with all virtuous and noble attributes is referred to as *Ahura Mazda,* but the opposite of this being is an evil

---

[1] Merrill F. Unger, *Demons in the World Today* (Wheaton, IL: Tyndale House, 1971) 10.
[2] Numerous translations of the Avestas exist. A good book that teaches and explains concerning Zoroastrianism is *The World's Religions,* a Lion Handbook, published by Lion Publishing of Icknield Way, Tring, Herts., England in 1982.

Demons 2

hostile spirit called *Ahura Mainyu*. Even though the term *Ahura Mainyu* is mentioned only once in Zoroastrian scriptures there are other names and references to this spirit in many sections of their scriptures. But of interest is the constant admonition of Zoroaster himself, and those who followed him, regarding the avoidance of evil in the world. So ancient Zoroastrians had a well-defined concept of evil and the Evil One. Whether Zoroaster got his beliefs from the Judaism which was around in ancient Persia (Iran) or not is debatable but the Zoroastrians have an easy concept regarding evil. Interestingly, the religion also has a distinct eschatology.

Islam teaches of the existence of *jinn,* angelic-like created beings, created out of fire. Jinn are both good and bad, and the rebellious jinn are the devils and demons of Islam. They are also called *shaitans* and their leader is called *Iblis* or *The Shaitan.* Thus there is a definite doctrine of demons in the Koran, and the Islamic demons particularly are involved in leading men astray and opposing the prophets.

The origin of the Iblis is interesting. When Adam was created, all angelic beings were ordered to prostrate before the newly created being, man, and all obeyed except the Iblis. As a result the leader and the other rebellious jinn are cast down to earth where they devote themselves to causing men to draw away from God. In the Koran, Sura 72 deals at length with the jinn.

Concerning the relationship between Satanic influences and non-Christian religions, Robert Morey has a meaningful perspective:

> People have a natural religious desire. Satan has created pagan religions to provide counterfeit satisfaction of these natural desires. He then binds these religions to the surrounding culture, making it very difficult for someone to receive Christ in the midst of a culture that is spiritually antagonistic to Christianity.[3]

The Biblical Teaching

The Bible gives us a rather symbolic insight into the origin of Satan and consequently the origin of sin in the human race. We are not told specifically who the serpent was or whom the serpent represented. But it is clear from the book of Genesis that the serpent was the manifestation of evil. In Revelation 12:9 Satan is referred to as the serpent of old.[4] Yet,

---

[3] Robert Morey, *Satan's Devices* (Eugene, OR: Harvest House, 1993) 181.
[4] Reference to Satan's appearance to Eve and Adam in Genesis.

15 though he makes his first recorded appearance in the Garden of Eden and on that occasion does his first job of deceiving man, we have to go elsewhere in the Bible to learn more of his origin or of his beginnings.

Demons 2

It is clear from the book of Genesis that the serpent was the manifestation of evil.

In that same passage of Revelation 12:9 we read of Satan being "thrown down to earth, and his angels were thrown down with him." So we find glimpses of both his beginnings and his followers and of their involvement with the rest of creation. Satan is pictured here as having a new domain and that being the earth. In the Gospels Jesus Himself refers to him as the "prince of this world," and we find this repeated three times in John's Gospel, 12:31; 14:30, and 16:11.

Elsewhere in Scripture we find him mentioned as an angel of light who went bad (extinguished his "light" and went into darkness?—grand symbolism here) and lost his place and position in Heaven where there is room for only one Sovereign.

To understand his "beginnings" or origin let us look at some of the names and titles, that often overlap each other, given to the Evil One, beginning with the word "Satan." His titles describe his being, his origin, his agenda, and his *modus operandi*. References to him in the Bible occur over two hundred times.

The most common name is *Satan* which in the Old Testament is from a Hebrew word, *satan*, used 52 times. Its common meaning is an opponent or an adversary, and it is used for the Devil in 1 Chronicles 21:1; Job 1:6ff. and Job 2:1ff.; and Zechariah 3:1-2. In the latter two instances Satan is seen as "The Accuser" and in the first passage he is "the instigator of evil."

In the New Testament the Greek word *Satanas* is used 33 times. One reference is Matthew 12:26. Here again the connotation is that of an accuser. The Greek word, *diabolos*, is used 35 times with the general meaning and connotation of a slanderer, one who deliberately puts down somebody else. These are the two most common words for the Evil One in the New Testament, though other names are also mentioned. Josh McDowell provides us with an ancient perspective on Satan's names from a work called *Malleus Maleficarum*.[5]

---

[5] Josh McDowell and Don. Stewart, *Understanding the Occult* (San Bernardino, CA: Here's Life, 1982) 128

Demons 2

> Malleus Maleficarum, a fifteenth-century treatise by Heinrich Kramer and Jakob Sprenger, indicates that Satan may be invoked under several names, each with a special etymological significance:
>
> As Asmodeus, he is the Creature of Judgment. As Satan, he becomes the Adversary. As Behemoth, he is the Beast. Diabolus, the Devil, signifies two morsels: the body and the soul, both of which he kills. Demon connotes Cunning over Blood. Belial, Without a Master. Beelzebub, Lord of Flies.

Here is a list of names and titles given to Satan found in both the Old and New Testaments:

Abaddon	Rev. 9:11	Power of darkness	Col. 1:13
Accuser of our brothers	Rev. 12:10	Prince of this world	John 12:31
Adversary	1 Peter 5:8	Prince of devils	Matt. 12:24
Angel of the Abyss	Rev. 9:11	Ruler of the king-dom of the air	Eph. 2:2
Apollyon	Rev. 9:11	Power of this dark world	Eph. 6:12
Beelzebub	Matt. 12:24; Mark 3:22; Luke 11:15	Serpent	Gen. 3:4,14; 2 Cor. 1:3
Belial	2 Cor. 6:15	Spirit at work in those who are disobedient	Eph. 2:2
The devil	Matt. 4:1; Luke 4:2; Rev. 20:2		
Enemy	Matt. 13:39	Tempter	Matt. 4:3; 1 Thess. 3:5
Evil spirit	1 Sam. 16:14		
Father of lies	John 8:44	The god of this world	2 Cor. 4:4
Great red dragon	Rev. 12:3		
Liar	John 8:44	Unclean spirit	Matt. 12:43
Lying spirit	1 Kings 22:22	Evil one	Matt. 13:19,38[6]
Murderer	John 8:44		
Ancient serpent	Rev. 12:9; 20:2		

Yet the Scriptures are not comprehensive on the subject of Satan's origin. The nature of the revelation of God's Word is to show man the

---

[6] H. Wayne House, *Charts of Christian Theology and Doctrine* (Grand Rapids: Zondervan, 1992) 78.

17   grandeur and majesty of His Sovereign
Lord God, seen in His relationship to man # Demons 2
as Creator, Redeemer, and Sustainer. It is, there-
fore, reasonable not to expect a complete and time-related (physical or
otherwise) thesis on the origin of Satan.

Because of the nature of God's revelation, we should not expect a complete thesis on the origin of Satan.

> The Scripture gives but veiled glimpses of his origin and home. Their
> purpose is more expressly to reveal God and His Christ as the
> Redeemer of men, the history of the redeemed from the fall of Adam
> in Eden, their way of salvation through the Cross, and their eternal
> destiny when the Christ shall have "abolished all rule and all author-
> ity and power" contrary to the reign of God, and God Himself shall
> be All in All.[7]

It is generally accepted that Satan was once an angel of high
standing in heaven, a created being of splendor and beauty who
rebelled against God together with his own followers and associates
and consequently was thrown out of the realm of the presence of God.
Two passages in the New Testament make this clear, namely, 2 Peter
2:4 and Jude 6. Both references imply rebellion against God and a
desire for usurping God's position and authority. Second Peter 2:4
specifies ". . . angels who sinned . . ." (NIV) and Jude 6 mentions ". . .
angels who did not keep their positions of authority but abandoned
their own home . . ." (NIV).

Two Old Testament passages are often used to describe what
happened in heaven when Satan and these angels "sinned." One is
from Isaiah 14:12-17, and the other is Ezekiel 28:12-19. The Isaiah
account has a direct reference to the King of Babylon and his downfall.
The language used however is of such a literary nature that it does
seem to refer also to a nonearthly being: morning star, raise my throne
above the stars of God, enthroned on the mount of assembly, etc. But
this is not necessarily conclusive that the fall of Satan is also being
referred to, for just a few verses further down the language becomes
definitely Babylon related: "Is this the man who shook the earth and
made kingdoms tremble . . ." etc.

Again, it is not conclusive that Ezekiel 28:12-19 refers to Satan's
going against His Creator and God and subsequently being thrown out

---

[7] Jesse Penn-Lewis, *The Warfare with Satan* (Madras, India: Evangelical Literature Service, 1975) 15.

Demons 2 of Heaven. A cursory reading of the passage makes it rather evident that the person being referred to is the Prince of Tyre and is descriptive of Tyre's eventual overthrow. But again, the imagery used seems to refer to the time of creation. But the context does not warrant an interpretation that the passage is an account of Satan's rebellion against God.

New Testament passages often used to prove Satan's fall are Luke 10:18 and Revelation 12:7ff. Here again the context does not imply that the origin and fall of Satan are being referred to. The passage is one of excitement as the seventy return and joyously report their power over evil spirits; in response Jesus mentions what He knew was happening, which is that Satan was being defeated. With reference to the statement, "I saw Satan fall," Lewis Foster in his commentary to the Gospel of Luke in the NIV Study Bible says, "Even the demons were driven out by the disciples which meant that Satan was being defeated."[8]

Once again we must acknowledge a lack of both total revelation on the matter of Satan's fall or rebellion and as Huegel, whom we already quoted above, says, it is a mystery.

> We are told that it is a mystery—"a mystery of iniquity"—and are given to understand that it will remain such even after the reception of all the light Scripture casts upon the dark and awful facts of life. Nothing of this nature (the loftiest of the angelic hosts and with him a third part of the celestial beings rebelling against God and setting up a government of their own in defiance of the divine order) would ever have been conceived by man. Much less would we understand this bearing upon life here upon earth. It is too vast, too strange, too awful, too mysterious. Angels of God taking up arms against the Most High. A cataclysm of infinite dimension. Angelic beings "starting a row" that upsets the moral order of the universe and which ends in hell! . . .[9]

We are limited to Scripture to know of Satan's beginnings and his going against God.

We are limited to the revelation of Scripture to know of Satan's beginnings and his going against God. I confess that I, like Huegel, am in almost fearful awe when I try to understand rebellion against the Most High, when His Presence, His Holy and Majestic and Magnificent

---

[8] Lewis Foster, "Study Notes on Luke 10:18," *NIV Study Bible* (Grand Rapids: Zondervan, 1985).
[9] Huegel, *Mystery,* 20.

Presence, was in full manifestation, in all His Glory, to those then created beings! It was in the context of such a heavenly environment that we find the rebellion of Satan and his angels. Who can comprehend adequately such an event? Who can explain it with clarity? Who can fathom the depths of evil that brought forth such a conception and such an action?

But though we leave it in its mysterious context, yet the lesson we learn is just as impactful. How can we, endowed with a salvation so grand and glorious, join such a rebellion? How can we today, sharing in and enjoying the bounteous endowments God has given to us in all of His creation and above all in the Gift of His Son as our Savior, who died to effect that salvation, how could we align ourselves with the Evil One and his demonic retinue? The sad and almost incomprehensible fact is that mankind since the dawn of creation and the appearance of the created Adam, has chosen the path of evil promoted by Satan and his followers. And mankind has joined the rebellion!!

Nature of Satan

It is important to know what kind of a being Satan was, for his nature and his personality will certainly be reflected in those of his followers who joined him in rebellion against the Sovereignty of God. The nature of demonic beings will be similar to that of their leader. If he personified evil, those personifications would of necessity be in those angels who are his followers.

What was Satan originally like? Was he equal with Michael and Gabriel? Like an angel of light? A morning star? An angel of exceptional powers? From the teachings concerning his fall, and his natural being as evidenced by the names and titles given to him, he was probably an archangel-type creature but filled with pride and desire, both of which led him to seek beyond the privileges and glory given to him by his Creator.

Satan's pride and desire led him to seek beyond the privileges and glory given to him by his Creator.

After his "fall" and his "downfall" he was relegated to earth and is designated in Scripture as Prince of this World. (John 12:31). This is where the sphere of his activity is accentuated, and this is where man faces him and his onslaughts. Here is where Satan is in his element. And here is where man can withstand him. To do this requires an

Demons 2

Without resorting to speculation we can see what he is like through these revelations of Scripture.

1. *Satan is a created being.* An important point here is with regard to overcoming Satan. Being created, he is like man, who is also created. Satan, being a spirit, an angel, he has certain powers, but man must remember that Satan is not like God who is without beginning or ending, Alpha and Omega.

2. *Satan is powerful.* Titles and descriptions of Satan specify this:
   a. God of this world—2 Cor. 4:4 (god of this age, NIV)
   b. Prince of this world—John 12:31
   c. Prince of the power of the air—Eph. 2:2
   d. Ruler of demons—Matt. 12:24, NASB
   e. Has angels under him—"the devil and his angels"—Matt. 26:26
   f. Ruler of darkness—"For our struggle is not against flesh and blood, but against the rulers, against the powers, against the world forces of this darkness, against the spiritual forces of wickedness in the heavenly places"—Eph. 6:12, NASB
   g. Can manifest signs and false wonders—2 Thess. 2:9.

Despite having these powers Satan also has weaknesses (mentioned next) and hence man need not live in fear of him even though aware of his powers.

3. *Satan is also extremely cunning.* We read about the "wiles" of the devil in Ephesians 2:11 ("schemes" in NASB). His causing of Adam and Eve to sin is evidence of his cunning.

4. *Satan is by very nature an imitator.* "The devil is God's ape" is the way some have described Satan. He imitates God's work (signs and wonders) and can even masquerade as an "angel of light" (2 Cor. 11:14). Herein, perhaps, is his most dangerous mode. In his pretense roles he can even convince the very elite. We need to remain constantly close to the Word of God to distinguish truth from falsity.

In spite of his powers and in spite of his deceptive methods Satan has limitations.

Yet we should never fear him. Mark Bubeck, in a book called, *The Adversary*, says, "Satan is an enemy to be respected and understood for his God-created and granted position and power, but we must

not fear him."[10] And we need not fear him, for in spite of his powers and in spite of his deceptive methods he has limitations. Satan is not an "unlimited" being.

1. *Satan is a created being* **while God alone is Creator and therefore the only Sovereign ruler over ALL of creation.**

2. *Satan is* **not** *omnipresent.* He is limited as to both time and location. (See Job 1:6-7.) An important implication of this is that, since he is not omnipresent, *his work in different areas is carried out by his angels.*

3. *Satan is* **not** *omniscient.* God alone is truly omniscient. Hence, neither Satan nor his demons are endowed with unlimited knowledge.

4. *Again, Satan is* **not** *omnipotent.* God is unlimited in power, and whatever power Satan wields is under the permission of God. Satan's power therefore is definitely limited. (See Job 1:6-12.)

5. *Satan is not eternal.* As mentioned above, only the Lord God is without beginning and ending. Satan is limited as to his existence, which began when he was created. Therefore his rule and his dominion are limited.

6. *Satan's manifestations are limited to other physical bodies and entities.* We find that he utilized the body of a reptile to tempt and deceive Adam and Eve. He must take on some physical form to appear on earth. He does not have the power of the Son of God who in pre-incarnate form appeared as the Angel of the Lord.

7. *Satan can be resisted and overcome.* James says that when we resist the devil he will flee from us (Jas. 4:7). Likewise, John in his first epistle states that young men had overcome the evil one (1 John 2:13, NASB). Take heart, both young and old; you can overcome the evil one. Stand firm and you will resist him.

Seeing how Satan is limited and allowed by the Lord God to operate within certain boundaries, we should take heart and be fully confident that we can overcome his subtleties. Yet awareness of his being and his methods is of paramount importance.

Satan's Objectives

Opposition to God's will is Satan's main objective. The word "Satan" itself, connoting "adversary," is descriptive of this. In this the

---

[10] Mark I. Bubeck, *The Adversary* (Chicago, IL: Moody Press, 1975) 79.

Demons 2

main adversary of Satan is God Himself, and because of this man becomes his next main target. The Bible indicates that Satan desires God's position and power and place, forgetting a cardinal implication of Divine truth: There is only *one God*. There can be no others beside Him. Satan's desire was therefore to usurp God's authority. His main objective is to stand in opposition to God. Hence he endeavors to thwart all of God's purposes and to do this mostly through that creation which was first in the image of God.

Satan's desire was to usurp God's authority.

We can see how his agenda to oppose God progressed and developed. Thrown or banned from the presence of God, he actively pursued mankind right from creation itself. He deceived mankind's first forefathers, but the Lord God rescued them from total surrender to the Evil One by promising and planning a way out of their sin, a way through the Redeemer Himself, God's own Son.

Satan moved towards the rest of the world, endeavoring to get the nations of the world to turn towards him. We can see this quite clearly in the religions of the world that demonstrate evil foundations. And the followers of these religions unwittingly submit to Satan's intentions, validating practices and customs that are deeply steeped in evil, in the name of worshiping the divine, appeasing the supernatural, and placating the spirit and spiritual world. Ritual prostitution, human sacrifices, child molestations, and demonic rituals have all been made acceptable because they are religious. But their Satanic origins, though clouded by both ceremony and time, can be clearly seen, for they are not part of what God intended for man. Thus they are nothing else than the tactics of Satan to achieve his primary goal—oppose the Living God. But here again the Lord frustrates him, for Scripture states that the message of salvation which came through His Son can turn such people from "darkness to light and from the dominion of Satan to God . . ." (Acts 2:18, NASB).

The message of salvation through God's Son can turn people from the dominion of Satan to God.

The ministry on earth of the Son of God was under the constant onslaught of Satan. Seeing how the Cross was looming near and large, he opposed God's Son relentlessly. The Herodic attempts to get rid of the baby Jesus, the wilderness temptations, and the direct demonic

23 confrontations are all indicative of Satan's almost desperate attempts to sideline the purposes of God and usurp them with his own.

Demons 2

His usage of Judas to betray Jesus (John 13:2) shows how Satan felt that perhaps His death would end the ministry of Jesus, but he failed. His assaults on the Savior in His dying moments on Calvary are indicative of Satan's attempts to prevent or perhaps misdirect the planned redemption of man. He failed. He failed to prevent the Cross, and he failed to retain the tomb with its buried body of Jesus. The Resurrection destroyed his aim of subverting the work of redemption.

But he still pursues with obsessive energy his objective of usurping God's place and authority. Thus he focuses on man, the main object of the redemptive event. He strives to keep man from accepting that redemption and puts obstacles and hurdles in the path of those who desire to change their lives. The apostle Peter gives us his classic warning about this, stating in 1 Peter 5:8, "Be of sober spirit, be on the alert. Your adversary, the devil, prowls about like a roaring lion, seeking someone to devour" (NASB). And his demons carry out his bidding in this. His bidding is to make himself to be God in the place of He who is truly God of All, the King of kings and the Lord of lords.

CHAPTER 3

SATANIC STRATEGY AND AGENDA
DEEDS DONE IN THE DARK

Satan's Tactics

How does Satan operate in attempting to accomplish his futile goal? What methods does he use? What are his tactics? His activities? His realm and sphere for those activities? Here again we can look at some of his titles and some of the descriptive names given to Satan to determine his modus operandi. We can accordingly categorize his main works under the labels of:

1. Temptation
2. Deception
3. Imitation
4. Accusation
5. Destruction

The above classifications are not exhaustive and similarly they are not exclusive. There is overlapping in about all of them. For example temptation and deception go together. But we can, through these labels, understand Satan's workings better.

Temptation

Satan is referred to as the tempter in Matthew 4:3. In that chapter and its complements in the other Gospels we find him trying to lead the Son of God to deviate from the Divine plan of Redemption through varied forms of temptation, and three are specifically mentioned. These three detailed temptations of Jesus in the wilderness give us special insight into the temptation. Likewise, at the time of creation when all of the world was fresh and new, in the Garden of Eden Satan appears in reptile form with a deceptive message for Adam and Eve. In Genesis chapter 3 we read how he approached them with guile and subtlety. His smooth operation there corresponds with John's warnings regarding the "lust of the flesh, and the lust of the eyes, and the boastful pride

of life" (1 John 2:16, NASB). But looking at Adam and Eve's succumbing to Satan's

Demons 3

temptation we find him being at least consistent with his basic goal of going against God's plans and purposes. Thus Kreeft says, "The fundamental temptation is to disobey the First and greatest Commandment: to love God with our whole heart."[1]

Satan's smooth operation in Genesis 3 corresponds with the warnings in 1 John 2:16.

Lust of the Flesh

The show-and-tell type of tactic that Satan used with Adam and Eve involved food and a food element. A fruit was used that was in Eve's estimate good for eating. Satan was using a legitimate desire. Thus whether it is the need for food, or comfort, or companionship, or sex, Satan takes that natural human desire and turns it around for his evil purposes. In the wilderness, while the Son of God was in a state of fasting, Satan approached him with a natural human desire to make bread and satisfy physical hunger. The subtlety of his tempting is thus seen: Fulfill legitimate needs outside of the boundaries set by the Lord who is Creator of our human bodies.

Lust of the Eyes

Eve saw that the fruit was not only good for eating but also a delight to the eyes. How could it be wrong to eat of such a gourmet item? And why should the Lord God prohibit such a glorious activity? After all, the Lord God Himself had created both the desire for food and the attractive food element. Could something seemingly so right be so wrong? Thus Satan set the stage for Adam and Eve to doubt the Word of God. Common tactic of Satan. Doubt the Lord God's injunctions. Did God really mean what He said? In the wilderness He tempted Jesus to prove He was the Son of God by throwing Himself down, testing the validity of what was promised by God, that angels would prevent His fall. And so then what follows is oh so natural—justify the disobedience. It is right because of its beauty and its charm and its satisfaction. But it is contrary to the Will and Word of God. Yet Adam and Eve submitted to the tempter.

---

[1] Peter Kreeft, *Angels (and Demons): What Do You Really Know about Them?* (San Francisco: Ignatius Press, 1995) 121.

"You will be like God," said Satan
to Eve. It's a privilege due to you is what Satan
was saying, and implying that the Lord God was preventing them from
that privilege. You can fulfill yourself. You can find yourself, as the present generation says. You can be a purposeful being. Control your own destiny. Take charge. And in essence, you will be your own God. And similarly He approached God's Son in the wilderness. Fall down and worship me, and you will have all things. You will have it minus the destined way of the Cross. Take charge to attain all things and in doing so deviate from the plan of God set for you His Son. Thus Satan tempted both the first and second Adam.

Today we see man's yearning to be his own god and create his own destiny. The Pride of Life fills us, and Satan uses it to bring about our rebellion against God. Self-worship becomes really worship of Satan who uses our obsession with ourselves to supersede our need to be under the Lord's control.

Satan, the tempter, uses the three channels of temptation to get man to go his own way in opposition to the role and boundaries set for him by his Creator. Kreeft sums up Satan's method of tempting man thus:

> The two main parts of this satanic strategy—arousing selfish passions
> (biological or psychological) and dimming the light of reason—reinforce each other. Passion clouds reason, and clouded reason fails to
> enlighten passion.[2]

Deception

Satan is a deceiver. He is a liar (John 8:44). He lied to Adam and Eve, and he continues to lie to God's creation. He tempts man to believe his deceptions and accept his lies as truth. And in this he draws fine lines, so that man's mind, as Kreeft said, is clouded. The target here is the mind of man. James 3:15 talks about demonic wisdom. The wisdom of Satan pervades just about all of man's living, and man can only withstand by knowing God's truth, a truth that will set him free (John 8:32).

Satan tempts man to believe his deceptions and accept his lies as truth.

The deception of Satan is seen in the rise of both old and new false religions, cults, humanistic teachings, and secularism. It is given

---

[2] Ibid.

the garb of biblical acceptance and man-
ifested in miracles and signs and wonders **Demons 3**
that are false and fake. It is cloaked and cloud-
ed in scriptural language while being all the time nothing but hermeneutical heresy. It is made manifest in everyday life even under the
guise of national pride and patriotism.

The basic intent of Satan is to make man believe his lies and go against God's revelation in Scripture.

The basic intent of Satan as a deceiver is to make man believe
his lies and thereby go against God's revelation in Scripture. The main
thrust of Satan's opposition here is against the Word of God. And he
validates his lies with his false miracles. We must never forget that, as
believers in the truth and veracity of God's Word, Satan can empower
people to perform his Satanic wonders thereby even deceiving the very
elect (Matt. 24:24).

How do we overcome Satan's lies and other deceptions? Apart
from an awareness of his tactics as a deceiver we must know the truth.
Our antidote to being led to believe his lies and fall to his fake demonstrations is to be ourselves deeply rooted in His Word. In John 17:15-17
Jesus prays that we be sanctified in the truth so that we could resist the evil
one. And in that definitive armor we use to stand against the devil, we are
asked to grasp firmly the "sword of the Spirit, which is the word of God"
(Eph. 6:17). But the truth must be used and not just displayed. "We must
take it into our hearts, and delight in it, and guard it, and wield it boldly
and proudly in our personal lives and in our church activities."[3]

Imitation

We live in a world of imitation. Cheap fakes of valuable mer-
chandise fill our stores. Beauty parlors make you up to be what you
really are not! You can be dressed to imitate the high and mighty.
Imitation is part of modern-day living. In 2 Corinthians 11:13-15 we
read of Satan's use of imitation. This again is in keeping with his nature,
his modes of operation, and above all his primary goal which is to be
in God's place and position. In the Scripture referred to, we see that
Satan can be transformed into an angel of light. His servants can be disguised from what they really are to resemble ministers of righteousness.
His workers put on the imagery of apostles of Christ—all imitations and

[3] Jack Cottrell, *Demonology* (Cincinnati: Cincinnati Bible Seminary, Unpublished
Class Notes) 16.

far from reality. But the imitations are being accepted as the real thing, and reality is being rejected. Again, we see Satan's cunning strategy at work: make people believe they are seeing the real truth when what is presented is a fake.

Satan's cunning strategy: make people believe they are seeing the real truth when presented with a fake.

The Word of God has incidents and injunctions that illustrate Satan's strategy of imitation. Moses before Pharaoh saw the Egyptian magicians bring forth serpents from rods, just as Moses did through his being empowered by God to perform that miracle. In the Corinthian passage referred to earlier, we are warned about imitation preachers proclaiming an imitation gospel presenting an imitation Jesus (2 Cor. 11:4).

Mistaken concepts of satanic strategies often lead many well-meaning people to believe his lies and accept his imitations. Forgetting that Satan masquerades as an angel of light, some feel that if something is not grossly evil, or decidedly wicked, or glaringly un-Christian then it is all right and can be accepted as the real thing. But Satan, in his nature, is a usurper. In his desire to usurp God's authority, *he strives to imitate Him*. As the Son of God is declared the Light of the World (John 8:12), Satan too endeavors to portray himself as an angel of light. Imitation to deceive!

And what should be our means of determining what is imitation and what is real? John puts it in graphic terms when he says to "test the spirits" (1 John 4:1). We need to examine everything that is akin to truth by aligning it with the Word of God. No other examination would reveal the true identity of whether something is from God or not. Emotion, experience, miracles, signs, wonders, and even gospel, *must* be found in complete reconciliation with the divinely inspired Word of God. Everything else must be rejected and exposed as imitation. It must be seen as a work of the great imitator, Satan.

Accusation

Here we find a strategy of Satan which is paradoxical. Satan is the accuser of the people of God to God Himself. He is actually called the "accuser of the brethren" in Revelation 12:10. The same Scripture says that he accuses the brethren "before our God day and night."

Satan as accuser builds upon his tactics of temptation. Temptation by Satan and accusation by Satan complement each other. Satan

tempts man to sin. Man falls into the temptation and sins against God. Then Satan turns around and accuses us before God. And in man, guilt takes over, and that guilt leads to various other mental situations making man become unsure of himself, as well as inadequate and insufficient.

Satan tempts man to sin.
Man falls into the temptation and sins against God.
Satan turns around and accuses us before God.

Why does Satan do this when he has already had a "victory" when man succumbs to his temptations? Perhaps Satan, being by nature an adversary of God and of man too, develops a perverse pleasure (satanic pleasure) in being an accuser of the believer. But there is more. Herein Satan develops a domination of a person's conscience itself.

Two biblical incidents give us insight regarding Satan's role as an accuser before God. In the book of Job, when the Lord God praises the faith of His servant Job, Satan launches his accusations against him. "Does Job fear God for nothing? Hast Thou not made a hedge about him and his house and all that he has, on every side? Thou hast blessed the work of his hands, and his possessions have increased in the land. But put forth Thy hand now and touch all that he has; he will surely curse Thee to Thy face." (Job 1:9,10, NASB). Accusation! Job has vested interests in pleasing God. Job is a fair-weather servant of God. Job's true colors will show when adversity strikes.

Satan here is falsely accusing Job, and Job never curses God as Satan said he would. But the lessons we learn about the Accuser are important. Satan has access to the throne of God. At times, the Lord God allows us to be tested by and through the Accuser. But the Lord God knows His own. He knew Job and his consistent faith. When the scene was repeated as shown in Job chapter 2, again there is the accusation and the defense of Job by God Himself.

Take heart, for the Sovereign Lord knows who we are. And we have more than an accuser before the throne. We also have an advocate and intercessor, He being the Son of God Himself, Jesus our Savior. Romans 8:34; Hebrews 7:25; and 1 John 2:1-2 make this very clear to us, providing us therefore encouragement and confidence.

In the Old Testament we find another scene. In Ezekiel 3:1, Satan accuses the High Priest before God. But he cannot pass judgment on Joshua the High Priest for the Lord God alone is the judge! In Zechariah

Demons 3

garments in replacement of that which was filthy. And therefore, though Satan should stand before the Lord as our accuser, we can rejoice that his accusations are not received. The Omniscient Lord and our Advocate Jesus Christ the Righteous One knows us as we really are. There is righteous judgment pleaded for us through Jesus, and praise God for that!

Christian, do not let guilt of past sins override you. Distinguish between Satan's accusations to enhance your feelings of guilt and the convictions that come from the Holy Spirit to create in us both remorse and repentant response. Satan wants you to feel guilty. Our Heavenly Father wants us to have the assurance of His forgiveness.

Destruction

Satan does attack man through afflictions to his body. Again we see the scheming of the evil one, schemes that display his extreme cunning, his "wisdom," if you may. On the cross of Calvary Jesus died for the whole man, so that man is redeemed as a person. The Holy Spirit indwells the redeemed man, and man's body becomes the temple of the Living God, the earthly housing of His Holy Spirit (1 Cor. 6:19-20). Therefore our bodies become targets of Satan, targets for his bodily afflictions.

Satan seeks to control our bodies and possess them. Hence we encounter demonic possession! We have already seen how Satan is a powerful being and has the power to bring pain and suffering to our physical bodies. Again, we have seen how he had permission to trouble Job through his body, and Job endured agonizing bodily ailments, particularly pertaining to his skin. And in the Gospels we find again and again Jesus relieving those whose bodies were distressed by Satan. Some were mute and dumb due to his attacks (Matt. 9:32ff.; Mark 9:17-27; etc.). Even mental illnesses can be caused by satanic control as we allow sin to dominate our brains and thought processes.

However we should be acutely aware that not all diseases have satanic origins. Often a physical disease might be due to definite physical causes alone—neglect of good health habits and hygiene, epidemics, carelessness of our bodies, etc. Yet and again however, we should also be cognizant of the effects Satan can have on a physical body that is under his control.

And the prevention and cure for this? The apostle Paul, in 2 Corinthians 12:7-10 details how he dealt with his bodily ailment

31 which he refers to as "a messenger of

Demons 3

Satan." He falls back on the grace of God which for him was all-sufficient to combat the problem. (Some scholars would deny that in the stated account Paul's problem was a physical one, but was limited to a spiritual malady. I see it as both physical and spiritual—physical suffering brought about through spiritual attack).

We can also deal with Satan's attacks on our bodies by donning the full armor of God (Eph. 6:12ff.). With His protection over us we can thwart Satan's attempts to control and distress our bodies.

With God's protection over us we can thwart Satan's attempts to control and distress our bodies.

As we are made aware of the strategies and agenda of the evil one, we can see how he seeks to dominate man in totality.

1. Satan is the tempter, seeking to control the *will* of man.
2. As deceiver he endeavors to take charge of our *minds*.
3. As the accuser he influences our *consciences*.
4. And Satan as the destroyer uses his wiles against the human *body*.

And how does he accomplish all of this? That is, in this his goal of dominating God's prime creation man, how does he bring it about? Satan uses his *demons* to control and dominate man. We can perhaps say that Satan has to use his demons, for he himself is not omnipresent, and of course neither is he omniscient. So Satan's *demons* are designated to carry out Satanic planning. Demonic activity in our world today is nothing more than the work of Satan being carried out by his angels, the *demons*.

But we should also be aware of another reality, and that is that Satan uses demons to do his bidding, and demons act to control and dominate people so that they, in turn, become instruments of Satan. In a little booklet entitled *The Strategy of Satan*, Warren Wiersbe makes a simple statement that has profound implications. "Demons work through people. That is why Paul instructs us not to fight against 'flesh and blood.'"[4] The hosts of Satan are active in our world and they follow their master's leading and goals. Demons indulge in temptation and deception, in imitation and destruction. They can wield immense power and influence as they are empowered by Satan himself. But

[4] Warren W. Wiersbe, *The Strategy of Satan: How to Detect and Defeat Him* (Wheaton, IL: Tyndale House, 1979) 145.

Demons 3

Scripture encourages and urges us on to combat their attacks saying, ". . . Greater is He who is in you than he who is in the world" (1 John 4:4, NASB).

The Destiny of Satan

Since Satan had a beginning, being a creature created by God, then he must have an ending too. What would that ending be like? What is his destiny?

In Matthew 8:28ff., Jesus encountered demons in the province of the Gadarenes (Gergesenes, KJV). They recognized who Jesus was and acknowledged Him verbally as the Son of God. Then they referred to their judgment to come, asking if Jesus was going to bring about their destined eternal damnation "before the time." Hence they were aware of their final judging and destruction. Satan is a doomed creature, and his demons likewise are doomed creatures.

Satan will be conquered. His great and final weapon is death. Paul cries out with a great joy, "Death is swallowed up in victory" (1 Cor. 15:54). The resurrection of Jesus conquered death and the grave, and so Satan was defeated through the Cross event and the Resurrection event that followed. He is now bound and gagged but continues his guerrilla warfare against the Lord's anointed. But his eternal destiny is sealed, and he is condemned to eternal destruction.

Satan's eternal destiny is sealed, and he is condemned to eternal destruction.

The Lord Jesus, the Creator and Sovereign, will judge all creatures, including evil angels (John 5:22). He defeated Satan and his demons during His career by invading Satan's territory and casting out demons from those possessed (Matthew 12:28-29). He anticipated the final defeat of Satan when His disciples returned with reports of demons being subject to them through Christ's power (Matthew 10:1,17-20).

Through His death and resurrection, Christ sealed the final judgment of Satan and demons. The cross reveals God's hatred and judgment of all sins. The just One had to die if the unjust ones were to be forgiven (1 Peter 3:18).[5]

Satan is man's greatest enemy, wielding both spiritual and physical force against him. Yet we can overcome all his attacks and with-

---

[5] C. Fred Dickason, *Angels: Elect and Evil* (Chicago: Moody Press, 1975) 210, 212.

stand all his temptations. This quote from Josh McDowell can be an apt conclusion
to this section:

> We need to realize that Satan is not all-powerful, he has been defeated by Christ's death on the cross. The power of sin over us is broken. Therefore, we need to respect his power but not fear it to the point of thinking he can in-dwell believers and make them do things they do not wish to do. The power of God is greater but the great deceiver would have you doubting that. Therefore, be aware of the limitations of Satan and the unlimited power of God.[6]

---

[6] McDowell and Stewart, *Understanding*, 135.

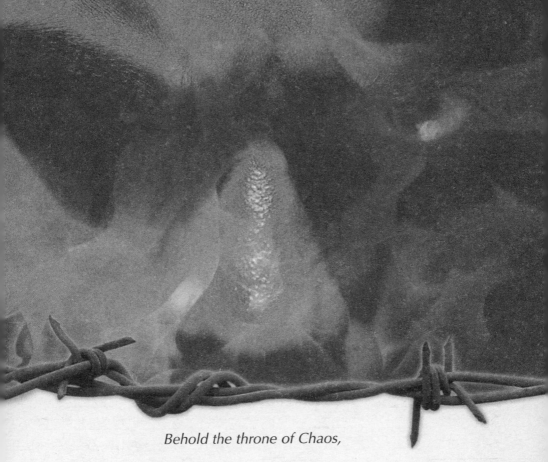

Behold the throne of Chaos,

and his dark pavilion spread wide on the wasteful deep.

— John Milton

PART TWO

THE REALM OF DEMONS

CHAPTER 4

DEMONS—THEIR BEING AND EXISTENCE

WHERE SATAN LEADS, DEMONS FOLLOW

Who and what are demons? What is their origin or source? What kind of an existence is theirs? How much power do they have? Can they influence man and, if so, then how?

These are all valid questions which need to be answered. And the need for answers are varied and many. First, an awareness of them will allow us to avoid being influenced or controlled by any demonic powers. Second, we could help those who are afflicted by them. Third, we can rejoice that regardless of how strong they might appear, we have the assurance that He who indwells us is greater than any and all of them. So says 1 John 4:4. We should also know as much as we can about demons since there is a host of references to them in the Gospels.

We should know about demons since there is a host of references to them in the Gospels.

What is a demon? A spirit? A person? A force or some energy? An imaginary creation of man? Or just a metaphor for either physical illness or some other form of bodily distress, and therefore making some of the assumptions mentioned in the previous paragraph irrelevant?

There are many modern ideas and philosophic concepts that would deny the existence of demons. Most of these are part of the ideologies that deny any kind of supernatural existence or occurrence. Reports and accounts of demonic activity are therefore relegated to either the area of medical illnesses or the realm of imagination and fantasy. Surprisingly, many Christians who have a strong foundational belief in God, deny any existence of demons. And there are those who say that, yes, at one time demons did exist but not any longer, since science and technology has allowed man to advance in his thinking, his religion, and his faith!

But there is a logical explanation as to the existence of demons. This ties in with the concept of evil. We know evil exists and that it is

37 the opposite of good. We know, and have **Demons 4**
had it revealed to us, and have experi-
enced it, that the source of Goodness is the
Alpha and Omega, the Everlasting Sovereign Lord and Creator of all
things. We know, and it has been revealed in Scripture, and we from
time to time even experience the fact, there is an Evil One, that fallen
angel called Satan. We know of the existence of supernatural beings
called angels and know that they have the privilege of choice. Well, if
some chose good, then it is only logical to assume that some chose
evil. And that is exactly what did take place in the realms of the supernatural. Peter Kreeft says,

> Here is a logical argument for the existence of demons:
> If angels are persons (selves) they have intellects and wills. If they
> have wills, they can choose between good and evil. If they can choose
> between good and evil, they can choose evil. If they choose evil, they
> become evil. So, if there are good spirits, there can be evil spirits.[1]

Kreeft goes on to rightly say that philosophic reasoning is not
enough to prove the existence of demons. Revelation proves they exist.
But in what form? And can they be identified by man?

Belief in demons and/or evil spirits goes way back into antiqui-
ty. Ancient Hinduism has its demons and so do many other religions.
In the Hindu pantheon of gods and goddesses there are demonic
beings mentioned by name. But of course, in keeping with the concept
of *Brahman*[2] they are explained away as being results of man being
ignorant of his being part of Brahman.

> Who creates the demonic forces in the world? We ourselves, indi-
> vidually and collectively by our selfish and destructive thoughts,
> words and actions, give birth to a multitude of demons. Hinduism
> calls these demons Kritiyas. These demonic forces attack the weak
> and young among us.[3]

Similarly, archaeological records provide evidence for a strong
belief in demons among ancient Babylonians, Assyrians, Iranians (Zoroastrians), and others. Regarding the Assyrians, the online Catholic Encyclopedia reports:

---

[1] Kreeft, *Angels,* 111.
[2] *Brahman* is the Hindu Monistic concept of deity/ultimate reality, from which all else emanates and of which all else are a part.
[3] Viswanathan, ed., *Am I a Hindu? The Hinduism Primer* (New Delhi, India: Rupa and Co., 1944) 298.

Demons 4

From certain cuneiform texts which are more especially described as "religious" it appears that besides the public and official cult of the "twelve great gods" and their subordinate divinities, the Assyrians had a more sacred and secret religion, a religion of mystery and magic and sorcery. These "religious" texts, moreover, together with a mass of talismanic inscriptions on cylinders and amulets, prove the presence of an exceedingly rich demonology."[4]

We find, therefore, that among the ancients belief in demons was very common. The Old Testament gives us the Jewish concepts of demons but more in terms of prohibitions and laws concerning worshiping them rather than protracted descriptions of their being. The New Testament, as mentioned earlier, has numerous accounts of not only the existence of demons, but more particularly, accounts about our Lord's encounters with them. The biblical teachings regarding demons are where we place our emphasis.

Among the ancients belief in demons was very common.

Demons—Terminology Used

Demons did not always exist, for the Lord God alone is without beginning or ending. We have seen that Satan himself is a created being and so are his angels. But how did their existence come about? An answer to this question would of course explain what they are. Let's take a brief look at the biblical records where the word "demon" or its synonyms are used.

The Old Testament has some references to demons, and three distinct words are used. Deuteronomy 32:17 refers to "demons who were not Gods" (NASB), and Psalm 106:37 talks about the abominable custom of sacrificing children to "demons." The Hebrew word used here is *shedim*. The two other words are *se'irim* and *Lilith*.

1. *shedim*—meaning shades. Some scholars believe that the word is derived from the Assyrian *sedu,* which was a spirit sometimes worshiped for protection.
2. *se'irim* is more demon oriented in background, referring to demon satyrs and to goat demons. More literally it signifies "hairy ones." These were all "gods" and deities to whom sacri-

4 Web site: **http//www.newadvent.org/cathen/04713.a.htm**.

fices were made by the nations round about Israel (Lev. 17:7; 2 Chr. 11:15).

3. *Lilith*—used in Isaiah 34:14 (translated as "night monster" in the NASB and as "night creature" in the NIV) is a mysterious creature often associated with a Semitic word which means "night demon," and with Babylonian literature where it refers to, "a mysterious female night spirit who apparently lived in desolate places. . . ."[5]

In that Isaiah passage we read also about wild goats, words often connected with demons. (See *NIV Study Bible* comments on the passage.) And in modern day Satanism, Satan is often part goat and part man, termed *Baphomet*.

There are three common words used to refer to demonic spirits in the New Testament. They are:

1. Demon from *daimon* and *daimonion*
2. Evil spirits from *poneros* meaning "evil" and *pneuma* ("spirit")—used about 6 times in Luke and Acts
3. Unclean spirits from *akathartos* meaning "unclean or impure"—used about 20 times in Luke, Acts, and Revelation

Interestingly, in Luke 4:33 we read about a man possessed by "the spirit of an unclean demon . . ." (NASB).

The Greek word most translated as demon in various versions of the New Testament is *daimonion*. However, due to translation some problems arise. For example, in the King James Version, *daimonion* has also been translated as "devil." The other word often translated as devil is *diabolos*. Yet the most common NT word that is translated as demon is *daimonion* which is neuter and singular. The adjective form is *daimonios*. It is interesting that *daimonion* is adjectival in form but regularly used as a noun.

Daimon is used just once in the New Testament while *daimonion* is used over 60 times. Unclean and evil spirits occur about 43 times in the NT.

There are just a few more derivatives from *daimon and daimonion* but the basic meanings are the same. And it is from the verb form of *daimonion*, which is *daimonizo*, we get the English word "demonize." However, the usage of these words, and their etymology, still does not answer the question, Who or what are demons?

---

[5] Ibid.

Christians hold more than one view regarding who or what demons are, and as to their origin. As we have seen earlier, some non-Christian religions have different views regarding demons and their origin, but here we limit ourselves to what, in general, Christians believe. Accordingly, we will look at four main concepts regarding who and what demons really are.

1. Disembodied spirits
2. Disembodied spirits of a pre-Adamic race
3. Offspring of angels (spirit beings) and women (humans) who cohabited.
4. Fallen angels.

Prominent scholars align themselves with each of these viewpoints. However, our endeavor here is to ourselves be aligned as closely as possible to what is revealed in Scripture.

Our endeavor here is to be aligned as closely as possible to what is revealed in Scripture.

Disembodied Spirits

A description by Derek Prince explains this perspective. "I describe demons as disembodied spirit beings that have an intense craving to occupy physical bodies. Apparently their first choice is a human body; but rather than remain in a disembodied condition, they are willing to enter even the body of an animal (see Luke 8:32-33)."[6]

An important clarification will be made later, in another section, to explain the phrase "occupy physical bodies." We can remember at this point that demons are spirits and are not spatial. Yet, we can agree with Derek Prince that they do desire to occupy or control or take over human bodies and use them for their own evil purposes.

There are variations to this main concept of demons being disembodied spirits.

a. Spirits of wicked dead only
b. Spirits of those who met violent and untimely deaths
c. Spirits of those who committed suicide, taking their own lives

Alexander Campbell, one of the fathers of the Restoration Movement, held this view. In an address delivered to the Popular

---

[6] Derek Prince, *They Shall Expel Demons* (Christchurch, New Zealand: Derek Prince Ministries—South Pacific, 1998) 97.

Lecture Club, Nashville, Tennessee, on March 10, 1841, and later published in **Demons 4**
the *Millennial Harbinger* of October 1841,
Campbell said, "We have, from a careful survey of the history of the term *demon*, concluded that *the demons of Paganism, Judaism, and Christianity were the ghosts of dead men."*[7]

Campbell argues throughout the lengthy lecture that his viewpoint is a valid one. He elaborates on his definition by later adding that disembodied spirits *"have taken possession of men's living bodies, and have moved, influenced, and impelled them to certain courses of action."*[8] In support of his beliefs he cites both Josephus and Philo and says that the Christian Fathers, Justin Martyr, Irenaeus, Origen, and others all accepted the belief that demons were the souls of dead men. And he quotes Plutarch as saying, "The spirits of mortals become demons when separated from their bodies."[9]

Victor Knowles, in his book, *Angels and Demons*, not only accepts the view of Campbell, but defends it extensively.[10] But there seems little or no real scriptural validation of this theory.

Disembodied Spirits of a Pre-Adamic Race

Some scholars view the creation account of Genesis 1 as being a re-creation. In the context of this book it is not possible to get into detailed theories of creation and the variations thereof, but in the pre-Adamic theory it is believed that prior to the earth being ". . . formless and void . . ." (Gen. 1:2, NASB) there was a former creation which came to some kind of a cataclysmic end, and in which Satan was involved. Following this, the theory says, God re-created the world as we know it now. This is often referred to as the "Gap Theory" of creation, signifying two creations, with a gap of unknown limits between Genesis 1:1 and Genesis 2:2.

While the argument itself might seem plausible as a theory of creation, yet there is no absolute biblical proof to determine the origin of demons as a result of this. Acts 23:9 is cited as showing that the Jews believed in a distinction between "angels" and "spirits,"*and they conclude that the spirits are demons who seek a body. But this is conjecture, so consider the following:

---

[7] Alexander Campbell, *Millennial Harbinger* (October 1841). Downloaded from the web site: **http://www.mun.ca/rels/restmov/texts/acampbell/mh1841/DEMON1.HTM**, 5.

[8] Ibid., 9.

[9] Ibid., 3.

[10] Victor Knowles, *Angels and Demons* (Joplin, MO: College Press, 1994).

Demons 4

a. Even if there were some kind of pre-creation catastrophe, there is not any shred of evidence to prove the existence of any kind of human race being existent at that time.

b. Again, even if there were a cataclysm of some sort, the fall of Satan at this time would remain hypothetical, for the classic passages that are cited to deal with Satan's fall (Isa. 12:14ff. and Ezek. 28:1-9) also have hermeneutical plausibility for other interpretations.

c. Even if the Isaiah and Ezekiel passages are seen as referring to the fall of Satan, there is no evidence linking it up with the "Gap Theory."

d. And again, even if there were such a race of "humans," there is no connection or evidence that they became demons.

e. That there is a distinction between spirits and angels and the spirits are demons is an unfounded presupposition.

Therefore, the belief that demons are the disembodied spirits of a pre-Adamic race is highly speculative, and does not have much scriptural or logical support.

The belief in a pre-Adamic race is highly speculative.

Offspring of Angels and Earthly Women

In Genesis 6:2 we read, " that the sons of God saw that the daughters of men were beautiful; and they took wives for themselves, whomever they chose" (NASB). This theory says that the "sons of God" (*bene elohim*) were angels and they cohabited with women of the earth before the flood. As a result of this strange and unnatural union, the offspring were monstrous creatures.

The Scriptures in Genesis 6:4 indicate that these offspring were "Nephilim" meaning "fallen ones" though translated as "giants" in the KJV. They seem to have become heroes and mighty men of renown but by all indications perished in the flood that followed. Their disembodied spirits are now demons. The theory has little support though in the second century A.D. Justin wrote,

> God committed the care of men and all things under heaven to angels whom he appointed over them. But the angels transgressed this appointment, and were captivated by the love of the women, and begot children who are those that are called demons.[11]

---

[11] Quoted from Clement by Gary Kinnaman, *Angels Dark and Light* (Secunderabad, India: Ben Publishing, 1994) 143.

Merrill F. Unger cites the Book of Enoch concerning this theory:

Wicked spirits came out of the body of them (i.e., of the women), for they were generated out of human beings, and from the holy watchers (angels) flows the beginning of their creation and their primal foundations. The spirits of heaven—in the heaven shall be their dwelling. And the spirits of the giants will devour, oppress, destroy, assault, do battle, and cast upon the earth and cause convulsions.[12]

However, this theory does not have too many modern advocates. The concept of sexual involvement between angels and humans seems preposterous. And also, there is no reason to believe that, even if such unions did occur that the offspring became demons in any form.

Fallen Angels

The majority of Bible teachers and scholars accept the theory that demons are fallen angels, "angels who sinned." Second Peter 2:4 says, ". . . God did not spare angels when they sinned, but cast them into hell and committed them to pits of darkness, reserved for judgment" (NASB). And in Jude 6: "And angels who did not keep their own domain, but abandoned their proper abode, He has kept in eternal bonds under darkness for the judgment of the great day . . ." (NASB).

The fall of these angels coincides with the fall of Satan. There are many passages that refer to Satan and his angels: Matt. 25:41; Matt. 12:24 (Beelzebul and demons); Revelation 12:7 (dragon and his angels); etc. Satan is termed as Beelzebul, the Great Dragon, etc., and so his angels and followers are the same as demons.

Many passages refer to Satan and his angels.

Many believe that the two passages most descriptive of Satan's fall are Isaiah 14:12-17 and Ezekiel 28:12-19. Earlier it was said that this may or may not be the case, but even if so, then it enhances the description of Satan's fall. But the certainty of Satan's rebellion and fall cannot be denied, nor can the fact that many of the angelic realm chose to rebel with Satan and hence fell with him.

When did this happen? Apparently before the world, as we know it, was created. It appears that Revelation 12:4ff. is a picture of the fall and how it happened. If so, then Satan probably took about a third of the angelic realm with him to become his angels or his demons.

---

[12] Merrill F. Unger, *Biblical Demonology* (Wheaton, IL: Scripture Press, 1957) 46.

Demons 4

And what were the consequences for those rebellious angels? What resulted from their fall? The result of the fall was eternal condemnation. Their eternal doom was already sealed. Matthew 25:41 refers to the "eternal fire prepared for the devil and his angels. See also 2 Peter 2:4, Jude 6.

Some scholars believe that the fallen angels were divided into two groups, one allowed to be free, and therefore active in opposing God's people (Rev. 9:14; 16:14), while the other is already confined to their designated prison (2 Peter 2:4; Jude 6). Again, there is a divided opinion, some believing that part of the confined angels are in hell (Tartarus) awaiting final judgment. Yet again, opinions as to who these demons are and why they are in this place now vary. Opinions:

- These are there not because of their original rebellion but because possibly of some great evil after the fall of Satan.
- These demons are the offspring of the "sons of God" who cohabited with the "daughters of men" (Gen. 6:2,4).

Those demons who are not confined in Tartarus are believed to be confined in the "abyss" (Luke 8:31) or "bottomless pit" (Rev. 9:1-3) and have been sent there by Christ when He rebuked and expelled demons during His ministry on earth.

We cannot conclude with finality on this. Scripture is silent regarding any detailed clarification as to why and if some angels are confined to await their doom while others are allowed to roam the world as workers of Satan.

In a book by Fred Dickason entitled *Angels Elect and Evil* the author gives four reasons why the theory of demons being fallen angels is biblically sound and therefore the most acceptable.

1. *Similar Relationship to Satan*, meaning that demons are intrinsically related to Satan as disciples to a master, for example, Matthew 25:41—devil and his angels; Revelation 12:7—the dragon and his angels; Matthew 12:24—Beelzebul the ruler of the demons, etc.
2. *Similar Essence of Being.* Scripture identifies angels as spirits and demons as evil spirits. Satan is the Evil One
3. *Similar Activities.* Demons, like Satan their ruler, share in opposing the things of God and the people of God.
4. *Sufficient Identification.* No other real origin of demons is revealed in Scripture. Demons and Satan are both related to the Fall of Satan.

In summation of this theory Dickason says,

Demons, like angels, are not the product of an overactive imagination nor the superstitious designation for certain natural diseases. Neither are they the disembodied spirits of a supposed race of men before Adam. Nor are they the monstrous offsprings of angelic cohabitation with women before the flood. There is little, if any, evidence for these views that can stand critical evaluation. However, there is solid and substantial evidence to believe that they are fallen angels. They were part of Satan's original rebellion and share in his work today.[13]

---

[13] Dickason, *Angels*, 172.

DEMONIC CONFRONTATIONS IN THE NEW TESTAMENT
KINGDOMS IN CONFLICT

The Old Testament does not have as many direct demonic confrontations as are found in the New Testament, particularly in the Gospels. References to demons, as we have seen earlier, are limited to practices involving demonic worship among the ungodly nations and warnings to the Israelites to stay away from such pagan ceremonies and rituals. One Old Testament passage, however, does need mention, and that is the reference to the "prince of Persia" and the "prince of Greece" (Dan. 10:13,20,21). It is generally believed, and probably correctly, that this refers to demonic beings who were "guardians" over the two territories. (Note that the geographical boundaries and national allegiances changed rapidly during this period of time.) Since Michael the archangel is referred to here as one of the chief princes, and Michael is an angelic being, it is logical to assume that the prince of Persia and the prince of Greece were angelic beings too, albeit evil beings. So we have mention of a direct confrontation between Michael, God's prince, and demonic beings who were Satan's princes with influential power over Persia and Greece.

In the Gospels there are numerous confrontations between demons and Jesus, and in the book of Acts between the servants of God and demonic forces. It appears that there was a spate of these confrontations, and we can see the logical causes for this increased and focused activity of the demonic realm.

There was a spate of these confrontations.

Jesus, the Incarnate Son of God, came to earth for the precise purpose of bringing people back to God. That meant getting man to turn from his own way of living, which is what Satan motivated them to do, towards God's way of life which brought to man eternity with God on the basis of sins forgiven. Satan's domain was therefore under attack by God Himself through His Son. The King had arrived on

Satan's territory to establish the Kingdom of God. The coming of the King heralded **Demons 5** the inauguration of His Kingdom, and that translated into doom for Satan and his kingdom. The prince of the power of the air was now facing expulsion from his realm. The prince of this world was staring into defeat at the hands of the King of kings who was on earth as the Savior of mankind. Satan's kingdom was now under siege and attack, and he launched, as it were, a no-holds-barred assault on the King. This is clearly demonstrated by the three offensives with which he approached Jesus in the wilderness.

Satan's domain was under attack by God Himself through His Son.

Jesus' ministry on earth specially included the driving out of demons. On several occasions He was directly confronted by the demons themselves as in the first direct contact He had after His ministry had begun (Mark 1:1-28; Luke 4:31-37). Further, He commissioned His disciples to cast out demons (Matt. 10:8). Throughout His time on earth He was again and again involved with rebuking demons, casting them out, and providing relief to those who were possessed by them.

Some would label every illness and every physical disability as being demon oppression. However, we must distinguish, particularly in the ministry of Jesus on earth, as to what were real demonic confrontations and what were not. Perhaps some of the diseases were caused by demonic influence or intervention, but we will deal here only with the very obvious and direct confrontations Jesus had with demons during His earthly sojourn.

The first of such contacts is found recorded in both Mark 1:23-26 and Luke 4:33-35. Here, a man in the synagogue in Capernaum screamed out to Jesus, saying, "What have we to do with You, Jesus of Nazareth? Have you come to destroy us? I know who You are—the Holy One of God" (Mark 1:24, NASB). Jesus spoke to the demon and commanded that he be quiet and come out of the man. Immediately the demon left the man, leaving with a loud voice, probably screaming horribly.

We can glean from this first parallel account of Jesus' dealing with demons (Mark and Luke) a few extremely important perspectives, perspectives to help us as we deal with demonic powers:

1. The demons recognized who Jesus was, were conscious of His position and power, and were vocal about it.
2. Similarly, the demons were aware of their ultimate end.

Demons 5

3. Jesus, while on earth, did not include in His ministry a witch hunt against demons. His main thrust was to proclaim the gospel of the Kingdom, which He ushered in through His death and Resurrection. This was opposed by Satan and his minions, and Jesus dealt with them as they confronted Him.
4. There was absolutely no fear by Jesus in any of the confrontations.
5. Jesus was always victorious on these occasions.
6. He constantly forbade the demons from publicizing who He really was. We could say that He shunned the fanfare that casting out demons could have produced.

Jesus did not carry on a witch hunt against demons. His thrust was to proclaim the gospel of the Kingdom.

Other passages in the Gospels indicating direct confrontation between Jesus and demons:

Matt. 8:28-34; Mark 5:2-20; Luke 8:27-34	Two men in Gadara— demons cast into swine
Matt. 9:32-33	Dumb man, possessed
Matt. 12:22; Luke 11:14	Demon-possessed, blind and dumb
Matt. 15:22-29; Mark 7:25-30; Luke 9:37-42	Syro-Phoenician woman's daughter, unclean spirit
Matt. 17:14-18; Mark 9:17-27	Lunatic child
Matt. 4:24; 8:16; Luke 4:41	Demons cast out (varied)
Mark 16:9; Luke 8:2-3	Mary Magdalene—demons cast out.

Together with the above passages there could have been more confrontations, missed in the list because of the variations in translation. (The above list is as per the NASB translation.) And further, there were probably numerous instances in the ministry of Jesus where Satan and his demons were at work opposing the Son of God, but indirectly. Was Satan or his demons behind the taunts and insults hurled at Jesus while He was on the Cross? Probably he was. Were demons involved when at Nazareth they tried to throw Him over a cliff? Again, perhaps yes. But we have enough of recorded direct conflicts for us to realize that demons were disturbed and furious at the coming of the Son of God to earth, while Jesus demonstrated, again and again, His power over them.

Whenever Jesus was faced with sick people he ministered to them according to the root cause of their condition and not just according

49 to the presenting symptom. Where the root cause was a sickness or disease he healed the person. Where the root cause was a demon he cast it out. Where there was both demonization and sickness he delivered and healed.[1]

Demons 5

In the book of Acts we find the Church of Jesus Christ coming into its corporate existence with power and glory on the Day of Pentecost. The ministry of the Body of Christ had begun. The gospel was going forth with power and with a dedication among its adherents that perhaps has never been reproduced. And the demonic world was not happy. The demonic world was in disarray. Peter J. Horrobin, the British writer quoted above, says of those times, "The reaction to all of this in the demonic realms must have been one of sheer horror. Jesus had gone, but replacing him was an army of men and women, behaving just like Jesus."[2]

The apostles continued to drive out demons just as Jesus did. Peter and the other apostles healed people "afflicted with unclean sprits" (Acts. 5:16, NASB). We find similar healing situations in Acts 8:7; 16:16-18; 19:12. In the account recorded in Acts 8:7, it was not an apostle involved but rather Philip, the evangelist.

In a situation reminiscent of Jesus' own dealings with demons, we find evil spirits recognizing who the Lord's servant was, in this case the apostle Paul. In Acts 19:12ff. an evil spirit literally attacked the seven sons of Sceva, declaring, "I recognize Jesus, and I know about Paul, but who are you?" (Acts 19:15, NASB). Here again the demons know who Jesus is. They know who the servants of Jesus are. We then need to be aggressive in our approach when dealing with demonic confrontation. Satan and his demons know who we are and how we are covered with the righteous blood of Jesus, and know that we are under His protection.

Demons know who Jesus is and who the servants of Jesus are, so we need to be aggressive when dealing with demonic confrontation.

In yet another incident in Acts, Paul rebukes a magician (sorcerer) by the name of Elymas and tells him, "You are a child of the devil" (Acts 13:10, NASB). The sorcerer is immediately struck blind, again showing the Lord's power over the world of evil spirits.

---

[1] Peter Horrobin, *Healing through Deliverance 1: The Biblical Basis* (Tonbridge, Kent, England: Sovereign World Ltd., 1994) 197.
[2] Ibid., 200.

CHAPTER 6

DEMONS AND THEIR CHARACTERISTICS
WHAT DARK ANGELS DO FOR A LIVING

The accounts in the Gospels and the book of Acts help us to be cognizant of the nature and characteristics of demons. We must never forget that Satan is the ruler of demons. Hence, their basic nature would be similar to their ruler, Satan himself. But what about their characteristics which enable them to do what Satan wants, characteristics which empower them to fulfill his desires? What distinguishes a demonic angel from an angel who does the Lord's ministry?

Demons Are Real

Though this seems an irrelevant statement, yet we must consider it for we are looking at angelic beings—not just a force or an influence or a mental idea or effect. Demons are living entities. In their encounters with Jesus they spoke to Him and He spoke to them. They are spiritual beings, no doubt, but spiritual beings with wills, emotions, and personalities.

Right here we dispel all those concepts that deny the reality or the "aliveness" of demons. There are varied concepts about their "reality" even though there might be facile agreement that they somehow exist in some manner and some form. Scripture, however, provides us with the chilling fact that demons are alive and active in our world of today. Paul says in Ephesians 6:12, "For our struggle is not against flesh and blood, but against the rulers, against the powers, against the world forces of this darkness, against the spiritual forces of wickedness in the heavenly places" (NASB). But even though this is in some ways a terrifying admission, yet Paul follows it with that glorious, reassuring assertion that we can withstand these forces, we can overcome, and we do have resources *par excellence* with the whole armor of God (Eph. 6:13-17).

Scripture provides us with the chilling fact that demons are alive and active in our world of today.

51   But be aware—demons are *real.* **Demons 6**
They might be spirit beings, but by the
same token they do not have bodies that die.
They can occupy and take residence in bodies of all kinds and transfer
from one to another too. They are real.

Demons Have Personality

Demonic personality might seem hard to both accept and understand, but when we look at the encounters Jesus had with demons during His ministry, we find them, the demons, reacting to Jesus, as they knew Him, which was as the Son of God. So in those direct confrontations there was conversation, requests, "arguments," and forms of resistance—all indicative of demons having the attribute of personality. Also, personal pronouns are used by the demons and to refer to them. And in this personal aspect they even have names (e.g., Legion).

We need to be cautious in this for the personality of demonic beings should not be understood as being similar to that of humans when they are involved with other humans. They are spirit beings, and they are evil spirit beings, so their personality is founded in evil. Therefore, regardless of how they might appear to be in their personality manifestations, we must never forget that their very essence is evil. Some personal characteristics:

a. *Demons can speak.* We need go no further than the first confrontation Jesus had with demons, in Capernaum. There the demon cried out to Jesus ". . . I know who you are. . . ." This ability can actually lead to conversations (beware of deeper implications here) with demonic beings. (Often demonic speech is alien to the person controlled by the demon, such as a male speaking in a female voice, or a language unknown to the controlled person, etc.)

b. *They have knowledge.* This knowledge however is limited, for demons, like Satan, are *not* omniscient. They *do not* have unlimited knowledge. Yet, their knowledge should never be misunderstood.
   • Intelligence. They showed knowledge of Paul—Paul *and* his ministry (Acts 16:16-17).
   • They are knowledgeable about themselves—of who they are. "My name is Legion . . ." (Mark 1:24).
   • Awareness of their destiny—"Have you come to torment us before our time? . . ." (Matthew 8:29).

c. *They have wills.* They have the ability to determine things. The well-known account of the demons pleading with Jesus to send

them into the swine at Gadara is evidence of this (Mark 5:11-13). And demons can certainly exercise their wills.

d. *They have, and do display, their emotions.* Demons also believe and tremble, James tells us in his epistle (2:19).

Regardless of how demons might appear to be, we must never forget that their very essence is evil.

Demons Have the Ability to Occupy Bodies of All Kinds, Animate and Inanimate

We must realize two facts concerning control or occupation of any bodies by demons.

a. As spirit beings demons, like angels, are firstly invisible.

b. Secondly, however, since demons are spirit beings parallel to angels in terms of existence but completely unlike them in character and purpose, they too can manifest themselves in different forms. Again, logically, Satan can manifest himself in various ways (as in the Garden of Eden, as a serpent), and therefore so can his demons. Very often they appear as hideous beings, but can also manifest themselves in seemingly beautiful appearances.

Demons Have Supernatural Powers

Satan has supernatural powers, and therefore so do demons. Likewise angelic spirits beings have supernatural powers and so do demonic spirits have supernatural powers.

a. *Supernatural strength.* In Acts 19 we read of a demon overpowering the sons of Sceva. The evil spirit, "leaped on them and subdued both of them and overpowered them, so that they fled out of that house naked and wounded" (Acts 19:16, NASB). The demon-possessed man in Gadara was uncontrollable and could not be bound (Mark 5:4). And other scriptural passages give evidence of extraordinary strength being demonstrated by those under demonic control. In addition, numerous accounts of supernatural physical strength come to us from those who have encountered demons in today's world.

Many times the supernatural strength of demons is turned inwards towards those controlled by them. It appears that when this kind of extraordinary strength is found among demonically controlled persons, it becomes self-destructive and ends up

greatly hurting and injuring the person concerned.

Also, demonic strength is used to perform amazing feats and "miracles." Satan, their ruler is able to deceive people with "all power and signs and false wonders." (2 Thess. 2:9, NASB). Naturally then his demonic followers could also demonstrate those kinds of astonishing abilities. This is most vividly seen in the context of those non-Christian religions that grossly indulge in appeasing the Evil One through their worship and allegiance.

Demonic strength is used to perform amazing feats and "miracles."

The superhuman strength of demons is also seen in the way they wreak physical ailments and physical defects in humans they control. Demons afflict the human body with all kinds of disease and suffering.

It is of vital importance that we realize that the extraordinary power of demons does *not* make them omnipotent. They are limited and their supernatural powers **cannot** equal that of God our Creator. He alone is Almighty, and He alone can be truly omnipotent. Demonic power is both a limited power and only a permitted power.

b. *Supernatural movements.* Demons are not hampered by any kind of normal, human obstacles or barriers. Being supernatural beings, and angels at that, they can traverse through space very rapidly. This is enhanced by not having physical bodies. Thus it appears that they are in more than one place at the same time, but that cannot be for demons are limited in time and space. They are neither omnipresent nor ubiquitous.

Demonic intelligence is the accumulation of vast knowledge resources, for they have lived for eons.

c. *Superphysical knowledge and intelligence.* We have seen that demons possess knowledge. But that knowledge is in the supernatural dimension, unhampered by what hampers man's intelligence from increasing in intelligence. Demonic intelligence is the accumulation of vast knowledge resources, for they have lived for eons. Yet, this knowledge is focused almost unreservedly on their goal of opposing God and His children. And

again, this knowledge and intelligence is **54** definitely limited and not comparable to the wisdom of God. Demonic intelligence is not the same as omniscience.

Demons Are Perverted and Depraved

Demons are extremely wicked, but by very nature they are morally depraved. We can see how this came about, for they had their own angelic nature totally corrupted when they rebelled against God. Matthew 12:45 shows us how some demons are more wicked than others. Hence, when there is absolutely no restriction on their evil nature, they indulge in the most gross and sometimes indescribable immoral activities. That is why a demon-possessed person indulges in all kinds of perverted moral acts. That is why nudity is common amongst them. That is why sex has been lifted from its sanctified spiritual purpose and made into just a physical activity providing an ever-increasing desire for more and more sensuousness, giving rise to abnormal, depraved, and perverted acts.

A quote from Merrill F. Unger describes their depravity:

> The moral turpitude of demons is everywhere evidenced in Scripture by the harmful way they produce in their victims, deranging them mentally, morally, physically and spiritually, and by the frequent epithet of "unclean," which often describes them (Matt. 10:1; Mark 1:27; Luke 4:36; Acts 8:7; Rev. 16:13). Fleshly uncleanness and base sensual gratification are the result of demon control of the human personality (Luke 8:27).[1]

Demons Have Specific Duties to Perform and Jobs to Carry Out

All these duties are under the direction of, and because of devotion to, their father, Satan himself. Hence all these duties are concentrated on opposing the Lord God and therefore going against His righteousness.

Satan is a limited creature, even though he is endowed with supernatural powers. He is a spirit being, but he is also a created being making him *not* unlimited. Hence his presence and power are not limitless. But he extends himself and his power and his presence through the myriads of his angels who are devoted to him and his purposes. He

---

[1] Merrill F. Unger, taken from *Zondervan Pictorial Bible Dictionary*, ed. by Merrill G. Tenney (Grand Rapids: Zondervan, 1963) 212.

is their god and ruler (Mark 12:24), and **Demons 6**
they obey and serve him.

We can say then that the primary function
of demons, their reason for existence in a way, is to serve Satan in continuing his rebellion against God and to control God's highest creation,
man. Demons use various tactics, strategies, and deceptions to carry
out their primary function. Christians need to be aware of this single-
minded attitude and *raison d'etre* of demons to better understand the
hatred, wickedness, violence, and viciousness that demons demonstrate when they endeavor to control man. (More of this in the chapter
on Demonic Activities).

Demons Are Organized

Ephesians 6:12 seems to imply some kind of organization among
the hordes of demons, and Mark 9:29 likewise seems to indicate "types"
of demons. Similarly, the references to the Prince of Persia and the
Prince of Greece in Daniel 10 could imply demonic ranking. However,
we are not certain as to how they are organized or what rankings exist
among them, etc.

Are demons, if they are ranked according to power and responsibilities, given charge over specific geographic territories? Are the references to the Prince of Persia and Prince of Greece indicative of high-
ranking demons given Satanic authority over these nations? And if there
are demons with responsibility over nations, then is there a graded
breakdown, so there are demons over states, over counties, over cities,
over towns, etc.?

The concept of territorial spirits is a current widely debated controversy with vehement advocates on both sides. One of the foremost
proponents of demons having territorial jurisdiction is Peter Wagner,
who is one of the leading proponents of Strategic-Level Spiritual
Warfare (SLSW). Yet there are others who deny the idea of there being
territorial spirits and who question some of the concepts associated
with SLSW. This will be dealt with in another section in greater detail.

**The concept of territorial spirits has
vehement advocates on both sides.**

CHAPTER 7

DEMONIC TACTICS AND ACTIVITIES
STRATEGIES FROM THE UNDERWORLD

Satan and his forces are not endowed with the wisdom of God the Creator. But to take too lightly their ability to plot and scheme is tantamount to giving permission to be influenced by them. Again, awareness of their tactics and strategies are crucial to combating them.

The work of demons—their tactics and activities—is limited to a single aspiration and singular goal. Their desire is to please Satan their ruler and their god. Satan needs them to carry out his objectives since he, in spite of all his powers, is limited, he not being equal with God who is unlimited and sovereign. So Satan uses demons to fulfill his wishes, and demons, in turn, are designed to carry them out. And the goal of demons is the same obsessive goal of the Evil One, Satan, which is to thwart and oppose the will of God. Everything demons do is toward that end. And their father, the Devil, empowers them to work toward that goal. Gary Kinnaman has said it in a unique way, ". . . Where Satan leads, demons follow. . . . Together they cooperate in a celestial conspiracy against God, God's purposes, and God's people."[1]

Since man is Satan's prime target on earth, his demons, likewise, seek to dominate, control, possess, and defeat him. And how do they do this? Perhaps we should ask, how do they try to do this, for not all men succumb to their tactics.

Demons concentrate on man's weaknesses. They know where a person is most vulnerable. Hence the importance of surrendering our whole beings to the Lord Jesus Christ, becoming His captive rather than being captured by Satan and his demons.

> ## Demons concentrate on man's weaknesses. They know where a person is most vulnerable.

There is a mistaken notion that demons only attack a person

---

[1] Kinnaman, *Angels*, 147.

through his spirit and his mind. Man (and demons know this) is a combination of

Demons 7

body and spirit, an integral whole. Therefore we can expect demons to assail a person through his body, as well as his mind and his spirit. So though temptations come through the mind, the body (of which the mind is really a part when we consider the brain) is also a target of the demonic world. And demons focus on the body, assaulting it through sensuousness, illness, physical disasters, and other means. Demons leave no stone unturned when trying to develop control over a person.

We can see how demons work toward dominating men by understanding their characteristics and being aware that their tactics are toward man and his body and his mind and his spirit. We must realize however that we cannot exhaust demonic methodology. Also, though we categorize some of the strategies of Satan and his demons, there can be tremendous overlapping, for, after all, we are dealing with spiritual forces and not laboratory experiments.

Demonic Oppression of the Mind

In the Bible we are asked to turn every thought captive to the obedience of Christ (2 Cor. 10:5). The mind is the center of man's being and it must come under the Lordship of Christ. If not, it is open to the possibility of various kinds of demonic influence.

Temptation

First and foremost demons *tempt* man to sin, and in this they have both a master teacher and a classic example. We refer to Satan's tempting of Adam and Eve in Eden and the tempting of Jesus in the wilderness. The lust of the eyes, the lust of the flesh, and the pride of life are synonyms for the areas of demonic activity and focus. We have dealt with this when we looked at demonic activity in the Gospels and analyzed it. Be aware though that the tempting work of Satan and his demons is *not* limited to Gospel times.

> *Jesse was a friend of mine, and I had known him for several years. He was at one time president of his youth group and a good president at that. He had even preached the Word of God in various situations. But then came a career and the need to establish himself as a migrant in a foreign land. He pursued further education and secured a great job and kept moving ahead. At this time he chose a hobby—that of collecting knives.*

Demons 7

> *Different kinds of knives, small ones and big ones, daggers and swords, ordinary knives and weapons of assassination. He would work hard and come home late in the evening, and when everybody else was asleep, he would pull out his knives and look at them and admire them. He would run his fingers around their sharp edges and marvel at what the knives could be used for. And then one day it happened. He took out his beloved knives on which he had spent a great deal of money, and longingly and caressingly handled them. Glancing across the room he saw his beautiful wife fast asleep. I personally knew her and she was beautiful. Then the desire came into him like a sharp and hard heart attack! It did strike him in the heart really, the desire to take one of his knives and slit his wife's throat. The urge became stronger, and the feelings of delight that began to accompany it became more and more real to him. What would it be like to slit the throat of a human being? What would it be like to see the warm blood pumping out of a slit artery? But this was his wife of many years, the mother of his children. From where was this desire to kill, and to kill a beloved? Gathering the knives together quickly into a bundle and throwing them into his cupboard, he dropped to his knees seeking God's help.*
>
> *He spoke to his preacher the next day. The preacher concluded saying, "Jesse, you were being possessed by a demon that was wanting you to come under its control. The evil thought of murder, especially the murder of someone you love, is not characteristic of your own nature. However your obsession with weapons of destruction gave room for demonic activities. But thank God you found out at the right time. It was not you wanting to kill your wife. It was somebody else. This was," the preacher said, "the beginnings of demon activity in you."*

Temptation starts as impulses in the brain, evil impulses. Satan capitalizes on our weaknesses and our desires, mostly our hidden desires. Perhaps he works on our subconscious as what is residing in our mental storage is put to work, all those conscious evil thoughts and imaginations. Perhaps Satan uses other methods to get the temptations moving. The longer we fail to recognize these temptations as evil and demonic, the longer we take to do battle against them. Then, as James tells us, we are enticed, we are cajoled about the good sensations of the temptation. We go on to conceive in our minds the actions to come, and then, even as the tempter so desires, we sin. But James makes it absolutely clear that these are not from God, for God *does not* tempt a person to sin. This is the work of the tempter and his demonic agents. See James 1:13-15.

We therefore *must* be conscious of **Demons 7**
two important facts, and the first is that
demonic activity usually starts with mental
activity, temptations in the mind. "Evil spirits also have access to our
brains. They can tempt us by introducing thoughts into our minds.
Satan even did that with Jesus. Demons went much further than that
with the Gadarene demoniac."[2] The second fact is that we *must* put
our thought processes and contents under the control of the Holy Spirit.

Demonic activity usually starts with mental activity, temptations in the mind.

Deception

We have already seen how temptation works in having our minds
being captured by demonic influence. In our spirits, in our wills, in our
desires, temptation is a beginning step. We are tempted to look at things
differently, to believe differently, to act differently. We are tempted, *even
when we are not fully aware of it*, to decide in favor of evil.

Deception is synonymous with the demonic world, for Satan is a
liar from the beginning. If Satan can appear as an angel of light, then so
can his demonic angels deceive people, making evil look good and sin
look like an act of worship or something spiritual. Sin develops when
we believe a lie, and then it is turned around and the lie causes us to
sin. Romans chapter 1 talks about "exchanging the truth of God for a
lie . . ." (Rom. 1:18, NASB). Paul also says in 1 Timothy 4:1, "But the
Spirit explicitly says that in later times some will fall away from the faith,
paying attention to deceitful spirits and doctrines of demons." (NASB).

If Satan can appear as an angel of light, then so can his demonic angels deceive people, making evil look good and sin look like an act of worship or something spiritual.

And the areas of demonic activity where falsehood and lies are
rampant are numerous. This helps us to see why and how blatant
deception is acceptable to vast numbers of people in areas such as false
religion, modern day cults and cultic practices even in churches, occult
practices and magic, and direct Satanic worship through witchcraft and
related activities.

---

[2] Timothy M. Warner, *Spiritual Warfare* (Wheaton, IL: Crossway Books, 1991) 85.

Undermining the authority of God's Word is where Satan has gained a major foothold, starting of course with this in the Garden of Eden. Remember the classic questioning of the authority and veracity and interpretation of God's prohibition to Adam and Eve? "*Indeed,* has God said, 'You shall not eat from any tree of the garden'?" (Gen. 3:1, NASB). The subtle deception had begun, encouraging Eve to use her own intellect to determine what God meant. Then comes the direct denial of the Word of the Lord: "You shall not surely die!" (Gen. 3:1, NASB). And then the *coup de grace,* the enticing possibilities of going away from the Lord's command: ". . . You will be like God . . ." (Gen. 3:5, NASB). And ever since, Satan has in a lot of mankind a ready audience for his deceptions regarding God's Word.

Undermining God's Word is where Satan has gained a major foothold, starting in the Garden of Eden.

In 1 Timothy 4:1, we are expressly warned about demonic deception through false teachings. "But the Spirit explicitly says that in later times some will fall away from the faith, paying attention to deceitful spirits and doctrines of demons" (NASB). Paul may have been referring to the prevalent Gnosticism, but his classifying that or some other teaching as *"doctrines of demons"* must make us take notice of the fact that what may be considered as just philosophy or modern thinking or even nationalistic aspirations may indeed be the doctrine of demons. And how do we decide if they are? When we see how they deny the Lordship of Christ and His Kingdom and directly and indirectly oppose the Kingdom's cause, and when we see as a result of these teachings men and women straying from the truth and embracing evil, we know that demonic teaching is at work. And James 3:15 reiterates the existence of "demonic wisdom."

Demons constantly deceive people regarding the person and work of Christ, denying both His divinity and humanity. The inspiration of Scripture, the existence and work of the Holy Spirit, the need for personal salvation through the grace of the Lord, are topics where demonic deception is of such a nature that the "very elect" are led astray. And in many of these areas demons entice people to seek extra and personal revelation.

Let us not be fooled with the packaging of demonic teachings. Though it may be readily discernible when presented as a cult or as an

anti-Christian movement, it may at other times be hidden in the confines of "acceptable Christian norms" and even promoted and prayed about as being teachings from the Word when it might subtly be demonically influenced. Examples here would become odious, but how many evangelical presumptions can be found to have their foundations in God's Word???

How many evangelical presumptions can be found to have their foundations in God's Word?

Cults

Whether we go back in history and look at the teachings of Joseph Smith or investigate the more recent cults like those started (and ended) by Jim Jones or Moses David Berg (founder of the Children of God) or David Koresh, we find them teaching some basic denials of biblical truth. Many cults masquerade as being "Christian," for they acknowledge and promote peripheral biblical teachings while denying the foundations of the faith. We are warned by the apostle John that we should not believe every spirit but should "test" it, and the basis of testing is the Word of God (1 John 4:1-4).

In this book, we can neither list all cults that deny that Jesus is Lord and thus align themselves with demons, nor can we analyze any. But demons and their master strive to usurp God's authority and position and power, and cults that similarly deny the Lord's authority and position and power can be seen as being demonically influenced. Let us *beware* that we do not endeavor to "experience" their teachings, for thereby we fall into the clutches of doctrines of demons.

Many modern ideologies and politically oriented philosophies can be seen to have the same anti-Word-of-God foundation that cults have.

Likewise, many modern ideologies and politically oriented philosophies can be seen to have the same anti-Word-of-God foundation that cults have. Communism and humanism are not commonly classified as demonic, but can we not see the threads of demonic doctrines there—the elevation of "self" (you will become like God, Eve)? And cannot therefore nationalism also be influenced subtly by demonic ideologies? Think!!!

In a world crying for tolerance and acceptance of peoples as they are, to classify some major religions as demonic would raise a hue and cry in some circles. In a brief addendum we deal with false religions separately, but Unger succinctly states the case for why demonic influences can be found in some world religions:

> Satan and his demons will encourage all sorts of errors to keep men from God and His grace. In primitive religions where magic, super-stition, and worship of evil spirits are key factors, demons provide the power to keep men enslaved.[3]

Mental Invasion

The human mind is often one of the chief targets of demons, for here they let the person himself pursue their suggestions and ideas. Seeds of evil, wickedness, lust, and more are planted for man to dwell and build upon so that desire develops and sinful action follows. Demons cannot force a person against his will but can cultivate the thought that brings about the action from the will. John Montgomery says,

> Fallen angels cannot act directly upon the will, but they can act upon the imaginations, thoughts, emotions and desires. When they find a passion alive and active in us, they can play upon these pas-sions and fantasies and so intensify the passion. Evidently they can also inject fantasies and feelings which have no ground in our own character and experience.[4]

Demons cannot force a person against his will but can cultivate the thought.

Demons also control the mind, bringing about certain mental disturbances. This does not imply that *all* mental illnesses are demoni-cally caused, but certainly demonic powers can influence the mind, bringing about depression, guilt, doubt, and fear. Remember the man who brought his son to Jesus in Matthew 17:15? He referred to his son as "moon smitten" ("lunatic" in KJV, "epileptic" in NASB, and "seizures" in NIV). Though the more accurate translations specify physical disorders, it is not unlikely that the boy was mentally disturbed as well. The remark-able thing is that Jesus recognized this as being a condition of demonic

[3] Unger, *Demons*, 150.
[4] John W. Montgomery, ed., *Demon Possession* (Minneapolis: Bethany House, 1976) 337.

63   control, and He rebuked the demon and cured the boy (Matt. 17:18).

Demonic influence can bring about insanity and its accompanying manifestations. The Gadarene demoniac in Luke 8 ran around naked, lived among the tombs, and displayed extraordinary strength. When he was cured, the record says that he was "in his right mind" (Luke 8:35, NASB). This was clearly a case of demonic mental influence!

Suicidal attempts can also be the work of demons. See Mark 9:22.

> By controlling the nervous system a demon can bypass one's own mind and will and directly produce thoughts, words and actions through one's body.[5]

Demonic Assaults on the Body

The classic evidence for this is in the way that Job's body was assaulted by Satan. With a permit from the Lord, Satan "smote Job with sore boils from the sole of his foot to the crown of his head" (Job 2:7, NASB), so much so that Job took a piece of pottery to scratch and relieve himself. The Scripture reference above seems almost like an understatement, for later in the same chapter it says his friends could not even recognize him, and when they did, they wept. Satan surely can afflict our bodies.

The body includes *all* of its parts, for none of the body can be exempt from demonic influence and harassment. That also includes our brains and our whole thinking apparatus. And be aware that demons know in which bodily area we are weak.

We must, at the same time, be very, very careful *not* to ascribe *any* and *every* bodily distress to demonic influence. We should remember that there are situations that are consequential in nature as well as deliberately brought about. The man who develops cancer from unrestricted and willful smoking cannot easily claim that it was demons who brought the cancer cells into his body. And we must avoid seeing every case of illness and disease in the Bible as being demon caused.

We must avoid seeing every case of illness and disease in the Bible as being demon caused.

---

[5] Cottrell, *Demonology*, 20.

Demons 7

Another area to consider is that demonic involvement with our bodies is not limited to sickness and disease. Addictions of various kinds can be demon caused. Many kinds of obsessive behavior are certainly demon oriented.

Jack Cottrell, in his notes on Demonology says, "Control of the body is often a short cut to even greater control of the mind and the will."[6]

Bodily Illness

Scripture cites various incidents where physically ill people were cured when Jesus drove out a demon from them. The operation here is simple to understand: Demons control or take over or possess a human body. They then exercise their will over it. Hence bodily illnesses can be induced.

We are not made aware of how much control the demon had over the dumb man who was brought to Jesus in Matthew 9:32. What is clear is that he was physically dumb, and that Scripture says he had a demon. Any connection between the two? In the next verse we find Jesus casting out the demon, and the result was a return of the dumb man's speech ability. There appears to be an obvious connection between his physical distress and the demon as there is an obvious connection between his physical healing and the removal of his physical problem.

We can see similar connections in the following situations recorded in the Gospels:

1. *Mark 9:17-27*. Here a boy is brought to Jesus with multiple problems: foaming at the mouth (epilepsy?), dumbness, deafness, convulsions, and tendencies for self-injury. Jesus specifically speaks to the demon and indicates the demon inflicted the boy's problem ("You deaf and dumb spirit . . ." Mark 9:25, NASB) and commands the demon to leave. Again, the result is physical healing.

2. *Luke 13:11*. A woman comes to Jesus with a deformity. Jesus says that this is Satan's work (v. 16). He heals her to normalcy.

3. Other incidents of illness and disease are mentioned, but we cannot be certain they were demonically induced. But there is *no* doubt that demons can afflict the body with problems. The progression is from demonic influence and control to bodily affliction. We cannot deduce from this that *all* illnesses are demon oriented, for natural causes are the main reason for the majority of diseases.

---

[6] Ibid., 19.

A medical doctor, Rebecca Brown, **Demons 7**
M.D., in her intriguing book, *He Came to*
Set Captives Free, gives us a biological perspec-
tive concerning demonically influenced diseases:

> Demons tear apart a physical body on the molecular level. They do
> this in such a way that devastating damage can be done to the vari-
> ous organs without altering the appearance of the cellular structures
> under our microscopes. The damage they do usually requires treat-
> ment with physical medicines, nutrition, etc., but the physician can
> know *only* by direct revelation from the Lord, what is really wrong
> with such a patient and what treatment to use. . . . I am *not* advo-
> cating treating a patient without all the appropriate diagnostic tests,
> but every physician, whether he will admit it or not, sees an uncom-
> fortable number of cases in which all the diagnostics do not give the
> answer as to what is wrong with the patient. . . .[7]

Addictions and Obsessions

Often what seems to be mere physical addiction can be demon
oriented. We should avoid seeing a demon behind every bad habit, but
when desire becomes obsessive and compulsive we should at least
consider the possibility of demonic powers behind them. And it has
been seen that some particular addictions like alcohol, drugs, sex, are
prime areas for demonic influence.

Demonic Control of Our Spirits

We can define one's spirit as that entity which is the inner man,
that element connecting each of us to the Divine, which gives person-
hood. Therein lies the will and desires. Satan wants to take this over,
and he attempts this through his demons.

This level of demonic control is far greater than just temptation
and influence (see next section). The words of Jesus in John 8:4 indicate this state: "You are of your father the devil, and you want to do the
desires of your father . . ." (NASB, italics mine). When demons control
our wills and desires, then our very spirits are directed by them.

**When demons control our wills and desires,
then our very spirits are directed by them.**

[7] Rebecca Brown, M.D., *He Came to Set Captives Free* (New Kensington, PA: Whitaker House, 1992) 247.

Demons 7

But how does this happen? How can a person allow himself to come to this stage? And what tactics does the demon world apply to bring a person to this depth of involvement?

CHAPTER 8

DEMONIC POSSESSION
INTRUDERS AND SQUATTERS
IN UNWANTED PLACES

What is demon possession and is it possible? Unger defines demon possession as ". . . a condition in which one or more evil spirits or demons inhabit the body of a human being and can take complete control of their victim at will."[1] And, yes, it is possible. It has been discredited and dismissed as mere mental conditions, hallucinations, symbolism of evil, etc., but the mention of demoniacs and being demonized is clearly seen in the New Testament, especially the Gospels.

(**Important note:** We discuss the terminology used to describe demonic "possession" in another section, for we believe possession implies ownership, and Satan cannot really own anything.)

The term, "demon possessed" is derived from the Greek word *diamonizomai* which is translated in the King James Version as "possessed" (Matt. 4:24). In the Gospels there are numerous accounts of people being under the control of "evil spirits" or unclean spirits" or having "demons" in them. We find Jesus on several occasions "casting" out demons, logically implying that the demons were resident somewhere and were being dislodged from their "dwellings." The casting out was, in all cases, a driving out of the demons from human beings (Matt. 8:16,28-34; 12:22-29, *Note v. 28*; 9:32-34; 17:14-20; Mark 1:21-28,32; 7:25-30; Luke 8:2; 11:14; 13:10-21). There are about twelve such cases where Jesus drove out or cast out or expelled demons from people. In addition He commanded His chosen disciples to drive out demons and authorized them to do so (Matt. 10:1,7-8). When He sent out the seventy, they came back rejoicing that even demons "are subject to us in Your name" (Luke 10:17, NASB). Certainly, the driving out of demons was part of the overall ministry of Jesus and His disciples.

---

[1] Unger, *Demons,* 102.

The book of Acts records both cases of demon possession and of driving out of demons by the apostles. In Samaria, Philip drove out demons with some specifically mentioned results. "For in the case of many who had unclean spirits, they were coming *out of them* shouting with a loud voice . . ." (Acts 8:7, NASB). And Paul actually commands a spirit to come out of a girl to whom the spirit had given divination powers (Acts 16:18). Again, in Ephesus Paul's miraculous works included evil spirits leaving those they had afflicted (Acts 19:12).

While the Gospels and the Book of Acts validate the case for demon possession, there is not a natural corollary that *all* ministries of the gospel should involve driving out demons. Rather, it is indicative to us that demons can and do possess humans and that we should be aware of this activity of the demonic world. Deliverance of persons from demonic control is not a mandate akin to the Great Commission (Matt. 28:19,20), nor is it part of that great commandment itself. Proclaiming the Gospel is and will always be the core of mission and evangelism and therefore a central and vital part of confronting demons. Truthfulness to the Word of God is essential to any kind of dealing with demons, particularly when it comes to deliverance for those who are tormented by demonic power.

An interesting controversy regarding casting out of demons is whether it is through a "truth encounter" or a "power encounter." By truth encounter is meant the presentation of truth to the possessed, allowing them to free themselves of demonic control, while a power encounter involves other persons using authority in the Name of Christ to demand/command the ouster of demons from a person. Needless to say that Jesus' confrontations involved definite power encounters as He, with His authority as the Son of God, commanded demons to come out of persons.

Jesus' confrontations involved definite power encounters as He commanded demons to come out.

Kreeft categorizes demonic influence on men into three levels: temptation, oppression, and possession.[2] He goes on to say that tempta-

---

[2] Kreeft, *Angels,* 115.

tions occur to all people, while oppression happens in the form of some deep, demon-inspired ". . . great sorrow of spirit or

Demons 8

great external tragedies . . ."[3] Possession is of a much more serious nature and is indicative of great demonic control *to those who allow it to happen.* When we open doors to the demonic world, beware of possession.

The progression of demonic control and possession may not be as sharply distinguished as Kreeft suggests, but we can certainly see degrees of influence by demons with some persons just under obsessive temptations while others are under the full control of demonic spirits.

Ed Murphy analyzes King Saul's demonic involvement at great length in his major work, *The Handbook for Spiritual Warfare.* He traces Saul's "slide to disobedience" and then cites three stages of his demonization. Stage One has Saul getting mildly involved and his demonization is limited to "an evil spirit" troubling him (1 Sam. 16:14). Scripture indicates that this evil spirit had Divine permission and was probably allowed to trouble Saul to test him. Stage Two finds King Saul increasing in his demonization, even trying to kill both Jonathan and David (1 Sam. 9–17; 20:30ff.). And then there is the final Stage Three, with Saul now indulging in occult practices and consulting the medium woman at Endor (1 Sam. 28:7ff.).[4]

We may or may not agree with Murphy's analysis of Saul's condition but a few "facts" do appear clearly. *One,* Saul is involved with evil spirits as he is filled with self-pride, power consciousness, and jealousy. Such focus on self naturally took away Saul's dependence on the God who allowed him to become Israel's first king. *Two,* King Saul goes deeper and deeper into his obsession to get rid of David and certainly goes to the ultimate of seeking demonic guidance. *Three,* this shows us that even those who did or do belong to the Lord can let themselves get under demonic influence.

Focus on self naturally took away Saul's dependence on the God who allowed him to become king.

Similarly, it is possible to start with seemingly innocuous contacts with demonic influence, but that will only serve to open the door to further involvement. Demonic control is mostly the person allowing

---

[3] Ibid.
[4] Dr. Ed Murphy, *The Handbook for Spiritual Warfare* (Nashville: Thomas Nelson, 1996) 253.

such things to happen, either in a deliberate, conscious manner like those who practice witchcraft or belong to the Church of Satan, and the likes, or through the avenues of obsessive and paralyzing sinfulness. Sin and the evil one and his demons are naturally intrinsically bound to each other. Sin, deliberate and stubborn sin, can invite demonic control into a person's life. The next, rather obvious, stage is demonic possession where a person thinks and acts through the "management" within him.

There are those who question the whole matter of demonic possession, saying it is not possible. Others will restrict it to those who live by gross sinfulness, saying that just ordinary folk do not get demon possessed. Yet others say it is something alien to the Christian life and Christians are out of the demon-possession situation altogether. (I have included an addendum dealing with Christians and demonic activity.)

In the case of Cain, in the Bible, just before he deliberately murdered his brother Abel out of jealous strife, the Lord God tells him that "sin is crouching at your door" (Gen. 4:7). It is generally agreed that the Hebrew word used for "crouching" has Babylonian antecedents, being a word commonly used to refer to a demon waiting to enter a building or other place to harass those inside. Regardless of whether we believe that the language used is clearly indicative of demons waiting to enter Cain, or just symbolic of sin waiting to dominate Cain, what is clear is that Cain was in line for some form of subordination. Cain was ripe for being influenced by forces other than that of his own volition. Cain seems to have validated this by going on to murdering his own brother.

How does demonic possession occur? Are there warning signs and signals which could help a person avoid such a tragic spiritual occurrence with its eternal significance? And, what symptoms or indications are there to show a person is under demonic control?

The manner and method of demon possession is very nicely outlined by J. Stafford Wright, a British writer:

> One would surmise that the place of possession by an evil spirit (to use inadequate spatial terms) would be the spirit of man, which is the gateway to the spiritual world. This should be under the control of the Holy Spirit when it has been made alive with the new life of God. But if it is not used by its rightful Occupier, it may be used by another. It is also a control-centre for the whole of man's being. If it is merely empty, the being of man will either be unorganized or organized around some inadequate center. Unpleasant complexes may develop as a natural consequence, producing mental and phys-

ical symptoms. Possession by a demon might intensify these symptoms, and may also produce a flood of super-normal effects.[5] **Demons 8**

The above quote by Stafford Wright has in it answers to those who write off the possibility of demonic possession and control as mere psychological or psychiatric phenomena. The psychological and the psychiatric *can both be under the control of demonic power.*

At this point, we must be acutely aware of the problems with terminology and semantics. Words like influence, control, domination, possession etc., may have sharp definitional characteristics when dictionary meanings are applied. However, when dealing with the spiritual subject of being affected by the evil realm, many of these terms overlap each other and distinctions between the categories are vague. We personally feel that we must be more focused on the main issue here, which is that the demonic world does its best to interfere in the human realm, with the main aim of the evil one which is to tempt, take over, and dominate the Lord God's highest form of creation. In some cases, meaning in the lives of some people, they, the demons, can make little headway and are stopped when their tempting begins. In others they influence thought patterns and then decisions, thus making the person much more under demonic control. In yet other persons they hold domineering sway, as they have found avenues to "enter" into the lives of these persons. Let us beware making light of "first degree" demonic power over a person and not dismiss it as mere influence. *Any* kind of demonic relationship with a person is indicative of Satanic footholds in their life as well as an introduction to even more intense activity to follow.

Any kind of demonic relationship with a person is indicative of Satanic footholds and an introduction to even more intense activity to follow.

What follows is an attempt to explain demonic activity in a person's life by creating levels or degrees of involvement. The terminology used is arbitrary though some scholars make sharp divisions of the same. We can, however, talk legitimately of the progression of demonic control over a person's being, starting with "simple influence" and moving on to "total control." It is in this context we use the threefold categorization below.

[5] J. Stafford Wright, *Mind, Man and the Spirits* (Exeter, England: The Paternoster Press, 1968) 111.

Demons 8

There is yet another important consideration that helps us understand "demonic possession" in clearer terms and thus enables us to come to firm and redeeming grips over such situations. Demons are spirit beings and are *therefore not spatial*. The occupation of "space" by demons would mean that there are some "spaces" the omnipresence of God cannot be!!! And that is not a possibility even in the remotest sense. So we must understand any kind of demonic occupation or habitation or possession more in terms of specific, or better said, "specialized" control over persons or objects. Nevertheless, and therefore, our conceptuality of this should never permit us to underestimate the "residential mannerisms" of demonization of a person. The control exercised over a "demon possessed" person is totally akin to that of somebody or something living within that person.

In general, we must remind ourselves that demonic possession is not an overnight activity. It is not limited to peoples living under the banners of non-Christian religions and in seeming situations of superstition and spiritual ignorance. Possession can occur among the highly educated and the modern and among those living in highly developed nations and in "sophisticated" environments. It can happen to those who *let it happen*. Often this can be unintentional though not always unaware, for road signs are there indicating the possibility of demonic involvement.

Demonic possession is not an overnight activity and is not limited to non-Christian peoples.

Clinton Arnold sees a continuum of demonic influence which he diagrams in a straight line. It starts with being tempted, then becoming a regular giving in to demonic temptation, which in turn makes a person "devoured" or "taken as captive" or "taken as plunder," which leads finally to being demonized or "having a demon."[6]

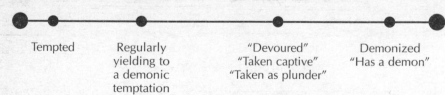

| Tempted | Regularly yielding to a demonic temptation | "Devoured" "Taken captive" "Taken as plunder" | Demonized "Has a demon" |

We see three stages, or progressions, leading to possession. There are no strict and sharply delineated rules or guidelines or indi-

---

[6] Clinton E. Arnold, *Three Crucial Questions about Spiritual Warfare* (Grand Rapids: Baker, 1997) 101.

cations, but these can help us see how a person can get into the awful domination **Demons 8** by demonic forces. Kreeft, as mentioned above, suggests that first there is temptation, which leads to oppression and then possession. We would look at it in terms of Demonic Influence, Demonic Domination, and Demon Possession. These can also be looked at in terms of degrees of demonic control.

Demonic Influence

When a person is prompted and motivated to indulge in evil, we say he is tempted. But when he feels a compulsion to do so, an inner movement which takes away his reasoning and his natural resistance, you can be almost sure that he is undergoing demonic influence. Demonic influence is often behind a lot of irrational behavior such as uncontrollable anger or limitless physical indulgences in various areas (food, sex, etc.).

Demonic influence is often behind uncontrollable anger or physical indulgences.

Demonic Domination

We use the word "domination" here in a specific way to distinguish demonic activity that falls short of full demonic control. We would say that demonic domination includes direct and partial control over certain areas of a person's life and body. Particular spheres of a person's personality and particular parts of his body come under Satan's domination, even though other areas of his life are considered absolutely normal and even very spiritual. In many cases of obsessive and addictive behavior, demonic domination is the key. Again, words of caution must be spoken! Addiction and obsession are also often mere unbalanced mental activities. Yet we must be aware of how demons dominate people to follow, without limits, paths of evil and self-destruction.

Demon Possession

Sometimes the word "demonization" is used as a generic term for any kind of demonic involvement, while at other times it specifies demonic possession. We would rather the word be used to distinguish between domination and total control, but seeing the accepted connotation, we will let the word refer to all kinds of demonic activity in a person. On the other hand, the word "possession" may imply owner-

Demons 8

ship, but where demons are concerned, complete ownership of a creation of God is not permissible to the evil one. Satan could not "own" Job in any way. Satan is only a usurper after all, and all his powers are merely permitted. So, rather, demon possession implies total control or total domination. Just like a person may still belong to a given family by virtue of a blood relationship, yet he or she might be diametrically opposite to all that family stands and lives for, having come under the influence and domination of some other ideology or person promoting some other ideology. Nevertheless, demon possession does involve internal habitation and control while demonic influence and demonization are externally generated. Perhaps a key phrase to understand demon possession could be "demonic residents."

Complete ownership of a creation of God is not permissible to the evil one, but domination is.

The preacher was avidly Pentecostal, but he preached a straight gospel message. In our land of multireligious societies, where Christianity is a minuscule minority, the preacher declared that Jesus was Lord of all and the Savior of the world. With great yet truthful redundancy, he hammered the theme home, that there is no other god who could save except the One who hung on the cross, Jesus the Christ. His techniques could be classified as gimmicks, for he had the crowd singing one simple little chorus again and again and again, till you began to feel somewhat trancelike. But the refrain (and this formed the core of his own proclamation) that we sang repeatedly was, He is the same unchanging Jesus. And I was there, personally there.

I was there, seated on a carpet, for this was an open-air meeting. Right next to where I was, on another carpet, was a Hindu family, very obviously by dress and mannerisms Brahmins. The wife and mother in that group (the group consisted of a father, a mother, and couple of children) was a decent and sedate and well-dressed lady, and I should add, very modestly dressed. But then, all of a sudden, as the song was being repeated again and again, this extremely decent woman got up from where she was seated and ran screaming down the aisle. Right in front of the preacher she joined others who were already there and went into weird dance form. She swept her head around and around till her extremely long hair was loosened and flew around while she danced. Her body went into weird contortions, and her face made frightening grimaces. Her sari was loosening

around her to the point of indecency. What had happened to this woman? Why was she totally unaware of the vulgar scene she was causing in front of hundreds and hundreds of people? Why was her husband merely accepting it all, in spite of the obvious shame to him and the family?

There could be no other explanation than that the woman was "demon possessed," meaning "demon controlled." She had been brought there to be delivered, and the deliverance was just not going to be easy. The demon was not going to leave without a battle and a full scale scenario. The sounds that came from her and the others around were bone chilling.

At the same meeting, I saw a man leap over a tall fence in front of the dais, which would have created some kind of world record in the Olympics high jump event. It was a fearful scene, and through it all the preacher kept announcing God's power over Satan and his angels.

Specially Possessed Objects

Demons not only "invade" and "inhabit" human bodies, which is their prime desire, they also reside in other creatures and in objects of various kinds. Though the casting out of the demons into the nearby grazing swine (Mark 5:13) seems to be an exception, yet the exception does validate the possibility of demons inhabiting other creatures. Non-Christian religions are filled with stories, experiences, and what we would call, from personal experience, evidences of demonic possession of certain trees, mounds, caves, houses, etc. Kreeft in affirming the demonic dream and desire to possess a human also says, "However, demons can manipulate any material vehicles on occasion, including animals."[7]

Edward was a young and dynamic campus minister. I spent a few days with him reaching out to foreign students on the campus. It was a privilege to share in his commitment and dedication, but he had one personal obsession. He was deeply interested in the occult. Edward spent large sums of money acquiring books on the subject of occultism and demonology and such like topics. He treasured his books, some of them being of rare vintage. It was his prized collection, apart from his means of resource on that strange subject. He had them locked away in his private study, where he would retire at night, to delve into the mysteries of evil.

[7] Kreeft, Angels, 123.

Demons 8

> *One night he opened the door of his study and gazed upon his books. He became transfixed at what he saw. Whatever he saw around his books was never ever described by him. The only comment was that what he saw terrified him immensely and froze him into inactivity, until a sudden flash of realization that there was evil around there shook away his entrapment, and he banged the door of his study and fled to his room. He had seen what he would never describe to others and probably could not. He saw the face of evil. Next morning he gathered together his almost priceless collection of occult books and celebrated with a bonfire. He was burning away his money, but he was also burning away his obsession. He got rid of the books, but he also left the campus ministry and went into something else. Was his decision to abandon campus ministry the result of what happened to him? I will never know. But he had looked into the face of "evil."*

Kreeft's succinct statement keeps in mind what has been said earlier, that references to possession and inhabiting, etc., are not spatial, but rather they refer to control and activity. And again, this too is to help demons control human beings and is not an end in itself.

Somehow, dark angels have the power to energize lifeless objects with the goal of enticing people to worship or serve the object instead of the God of heaven. "Transmogrification," more commonly known as "poltergeist" (German for "noisy ghost"), is an uncommon term that refers to strange movements or bizarre changes in inanimate objects, like banging doors or bleeding icons.[8]

(Is there anyone who would deny the possibility of computers being manipulated and possessed by demons?)

> *Brother "Tecson," had done much work in demonology and even had a couple of books credited to him. He was misunderstood by many, but his writings were clearly biblical. He was called one day to pray and cast out the demons that had taken possession of a house. Prior to new ownership the house had been occupied by "hippies" who had conducted strange rites and ceremonies in the building. They had all left, and there were just a couple of people there when the owner called for Tecson to pray for the place to exorcise any evil spirits that were in there.*

[8] Kinnaman, *Angels*, 151.

Demons 8

And "Steven" (a Bible College Student and close friend of mine) wanted to accompany him. Tecson warned "Steven" that if he was sincere and genuine, and had a strong faith in the Lord, and would pray intensively before going, then he could come. Steven did pray, and Steven did go with Tecson. The room that they were let into smelled foul and was very obviously filthy. Only one man was in the room, clearly given to an alternate style of living. He allowed Tecson and Steven to come in. Tecson spoke to the man about Jesus and His cleansing power and explained a little of what He was going to do, and then he began to pray. He prayed specifically that if the house was the dwelling of demonic spirits that they would depart in the name of Jesus. He prayed fervently and with authority. Steven was in a state of subdued fear and decided to open his eyes and look around. What he saw terrified him so much that he almost left the place and ran.

He certainly vowed never to get into such a situation again. When he opened his eyes, Steven had looked straight into the face of the man who was there. Later Steven described it as being a face of intense evil staring back at him. It was not a normal face and yet it was a human face, but it was a face that evoked fear and had Edward trembling. It was a face contorted into terrifying configuration, a face that showed defiance to the prayer of a godly man; a face that did have demonic "shaping." Demon of the house? Demon possession of a place? Would you believe that?

Symptoms

How do we know a person is demon possessed? How do we know that a demon has taken residence in a person and is inhabiting his body? Are there any definite signs to look for or that perhaps automatically manifest themselves?

We must realize that we are dealing with spirit beings, albeit evil spirits. Since they are spirit beings, there are vast differences between humans and "them." This means that we do not look for signs and signals that would be in the natural order of things. This is no "red *cloud* in the morning" sort of sign, nor of the nature of dark clouds before the monsoon. These evil creatures, when in total control of a human being, display themselves in extraordinary and supernatural and evil ways. Realizing this will help us to avoid classifying every illness or disease or even every unexplainable activity as being of demonic origin.

Demons 8

There are, however, some telltale marks of demon possession. These are made manifest *through* the person whom they control. We observe then the way a person behaves and acts and when that behavior and activity is definitely not that of a "normal" human being, then we can look for demonic activity behind it.

There are telltale marks of demon possession.

It must be noted that demon-possessed persons do not always walk around displaying these symptoms, even though in the case of the Gadarene demoniac it appears that the demonic activity in him was almost constantly visible and manifest. Many of these symptoms are seen when demon-possessed people are confronted directly with the claims of Christ and when demons know and feel they are to be dealt with in the Name of Jesus Christ and with His authority and with the power that authority places on His servants.

Psychological Symptoms

1. New or differing personalities. Sometimes this is in the form of the personality of a departed one. At other times it is schizophrenic in nature.
2. Mental disorders, including insanity. Here is where a host of problems arise, for some conclude that all mental disorder is demonic, leading to sharp criticism by unbelievers and others too. At the same time, insanity is a very common tool of demons as they cause the mind to bring about unnatural behavior.
3. Suicidal tendencies and desire for causing harm to others.
4. Obsession with impure thoughts, fantasy, and evil scenarios. Evil in the mind constantly is often a sure indication that demonic activity is at hand.
5. Depression, caused by fear instilled in a person by demons or caused by a lack of confidence and feelings of insecurity, etc.
6. Fear.
7. Depraved mentality.

Physical Symptoms

1. Violence, causing hurt and injury to self and others.
2. Self-mutilation and not feeling the relevant pain that should be there.
3. Unbridled lust, sexual cravings, and extreme sensuousness. A common symptom, which has been clouded over by cultures,

both western and nonwestern, where immorality of the worst kinds have been accepted as modernistic norms.

4. Bad language, cursing, blasphemy. Demons use the most foul and blasphemous language when confronted with the truth of God's Word and when they see their control being taken away.

Demons use the most blasphemous language when they see their control being taken away.

5. Tendency to indecency including nudity, lack of cleanliness and tidiness. Deliberate and shameful exposure of the human body, usually accompanied by evil acts.
6. Foul smells and extremely offensive odors. In keeping with evil being the opposite of good.
7. Specific odors of a cultural nature often associated with religious evil practices.
8. Frothing and foaming at the mouth.
9. Bouts of unconsciousness and appearance of being dead.
10. Feelings of chillness, and general cold and clammy conditions. The "Sanctum Sanctorum" (Holy of Holies) of many Hindu temples demonstrates this.

Supernatural Symptoms

These can also be classified as superhuman, or superphysical evidences. Some common ones are:

1. Superhuman strength. Unger states that this condition is not found in cases of milder demonic influence. "The display of strength through the demonized body is amazing because it is supernatural."[9]
2. Supernatural knowledge and clairvoyance. Neither Satan, nor his angels, are omniscient, for the Lord God alone has this attribute. But demons, having a spirit nature, do have enhanced knowledge. The spirit of "divination" of Acts 16:16 is indicative of this.
3. Speech in totally altered voice. A common expression of this is a woman speaking in a man's voice and vice versa. I have personally been a witness to this.
4. Speaking in languages unknown to the speaker. This is often similar to the miracle of tongues as in the book of Acts, but can be seen clearly as a counterfeit act of demonic origin.

[9] Merrill F. Unger, *What Demons Can Do to Saints* (Secunderabad, India: OM Books, 1991) 145.

Demons 8

Demons, though supernatural beings, and though they are spirits, do leave signposts and landmarks so we could discern their presence and their tactics. Let us be aware of their evil intentions and activities and not be naïve or foolish. Demons *do* torment men.

Reggie stood on the street corner preaching the Word of God with fervor and power. Suddenly he was approached by a man who whispered into his ears. One of the whisperings asked Reggie to stop preaching. Reggie was in no mood to do so, and he was within his legal rights. But then the whisperer scared him by telling him, "I know who you are." Reggie had never seen him before, nor ever come in any kind of contact with him. But the man whispered into his ears certain of Reggie's personal secrets that nobody, just nobody, but Reggie himself, was ever aware of. Reggie's inner secrets were known to a man he had never ever seen before. Could it be anything other than demonic supernatural knowledge?

At the sound of triumph Satan's hosts doth flee.

— Old Hymn

PART THREE

DEALING WITH DEMONS

CHAPTER 9

WHO LET THEM IN?
DOORS TO DEMONISM

How do demons enter men? What channels allow them to become residents in man's personal being? The nature of these questions should immediately alert us to a frightening and sobering fact: *We open the doors to demons. We, intentionally or unintentionally, invite them in!* Even in the case of generational sin, or possible transference, which we deal with a little later, somebody first opens the doors for demonic entrance.

Sinfulness

We can generalize and say that *sin* is the *open* door to demons and that would be true. Satan opened the door to sinfulness. His domain is entered by rebellion against the Living God. The Kingdom of Satan is a kingdom of evil and sinfulness. In Ephesians 2:1-3 the apostle Paul warns against walking in the ways of this world, according to the prince of the power of the air, and in accordance with the lusts of the flesh. The threefold influence of world, flesh, and the devil, keep a man sinning. The devil strives to dominate man's flesh and thereby his whole way of life.

But does every sin usher in the demonic flood that can develop into demonic control and possession? Here again, we cannot and should not permit ourselves to go to irrelevant extremes. We cannot and should not conclude that every sin we commit is letting a demon into our lives. Indeed sin is not just what we do, but who we are, and we are all sinners who have not come up to God's expected standards (Rom. 3:23). And again, we cannot and should not say that it is only "big" sins, and not little ones, that bring about demonic influence. When we sin and sin deliberately, we are promoting in ourselves a weakness that will be exploited by Satan and his followers. We can slowly—perhaps very, very slowly—but surely, be opening the door of

our lives for demons to stick their evil feet in!! Remember 1 John 3:8, which says, ".
. . the one who practices sin is of the devil; for the devil has sinned from the beginning . . ." (NASB).

But are there sins that are more likely than others to open demonic doors? We may not be able to classify sin in such a manner, for a person's involvement with sin, or his "sinfulness" will determine whether he is opening a door to demons or not. But there are some areas of sin that appear to be more "common" when considering demonic influence. Paul lists seventeen works of the flesh in Galatians 5, and sexual immorality heads the list. And so is the case with the listings in 1 Corinthians 6 and Ephesians 5.

Are some sins more likely than others to open demonic doors?

Why does sexual sin figure so prominently in the "works of the flesh," and why is it almost synonymous with demonic activity in the human body?

First, sexual sin, unlike other sinfulness, focuses in on the old sinful nature of man, the "flesh" life. It is a sin of the body, and the emphasis on the body leads to a lessening of the awareness that man is not just body, but body *and* spirit. It was Satan's tempting of Adam and Eve and their consequent fall that led to sex becoming physical only, devoid of its spiritual implications. *Second*, sexual sin is completely self-centered, so much so that Paul said that when a person has an immoral relationship with another person, he or she is sinning against *his own body* (1 Cor. 6:18). And even though the immediate hermeneutic is with connotation to the body being the temple of the living God, yet sexual sin has the characteristic of hurting man where he pleasures the most, in his sexual body. *Third*, sexual sin is a "full body" sinning, for it very decidedly starts in the mind (the desire, the impulse, the fantasy) and goes on to the will (the action, the deed, the happening) and then concludes with the emotions in the body (pleasure, sensations, sensuousness, ecstasy). Satan, then, through leading man into obsessive sexual sin, controls him in mind, will, and body.

Sexual Sin

The varied character of sexual sin not only keeps increasing and magnifying but also is of such limitless and boundaryless nature that it becomes wickedly mind boggling to try to either contemplate all of

Demons 9

But some more prominent sexual sins are listed here.

a. **Lust.** Jesus spoke against it (Matt. 5:28), paralleling it with adultery. Its compulsive nature and its domineering occupation of the mind of man, which when surrendered to, is almost a constant day-long mental activity. All these make it a wide open door to demonic influence.

b. **Fantasy**. Sexual fantasy is similar to lust with perhaps the only difference being in the realm of indescribable imagination and wicked creativity, leading to almost unbelievable scenarios. In order for man to satiate himself sexually, he allows his mind to dwell on and to fantasize on the varied manners of sexual sin. The demons love this, for it makes man's mind their domain.

c. **Immorality**. Whether it is adultery or fornication or other forms of sexual immorality, demons enter in through these sinful acts. We must never forget that Satan used immorality and legitimized it to bring people under his control. A study of the temple prostitution in the worship of Baal and the practice of Devadasis in Hindu temples is ample evidence of demonic influence in immorality.

Satan used immorality and legitimized it to bring people under his control.

d. **Homosexuality**. The much-heralded so-called findings about homosexual genes, which excuse a person's homosexual tendencies, are at the best controversial and at the worst very one-sided assumptions. The findings can be interpreted both pro and con for homosexuality. Dr. Archibald Hart, under whom I had the privilege to study while I was at Fuller, went to great medical and psychological lengths to show us that homosexuality was a "learned" experience.[1]

> We are now witnessing attempts to approve of homosexuality by declaring it is primarily due to brain functions. Thus it is biologically based, not learned behavior. That *some* life-long homosexuals may *occasionally* reveal unusual brain patterns does not prove homosexuality is a biologically determined sexual pattern. It is just as possible that the brain patterns (if they truly exist) are the

---

[1] Dr. Archibald Hart, well-known author and lecturer, was the Dean of Fuller's School of Psychology for several years. The study I did under him was for my D. Min degree, and my reference is from unpublished class lectures.

result of continual, long-term homosexual abuse.[2] **Demons 9**

Murphy also says, "Practicing homosexuals seem more prone to demonization than others who are wrestling with sexual sin. . . ."[3]

The Scriptures constantly teach and reteach that homosexuality is a sin. God does not condemn those who are bound to it, but the activity is sinful. Its binding and fantasizing nature and its obsessive and addictive character are often the work of demons. Homosexuality is often a symptom of demonization.

e. **Autosexuality**. Masturbation, both male and female, is another area of compulsive sexual behavior. Despite the Bible's silence on the matter and the numerous arguments from Christian scholars to defend or condemn the practice, it has been found that very often masturbation has been used as a tool by demonic forces. "There can be a definite demonic dimension to uncontrollable masturbation."[4]

f. **Satanic sex**. Many sexual practices are directly connected with demonic powers and even associated with the worship of Satan and his demons. Sexual ritual abuse is common among adherents of witchcraft, members of the Church of Satan, and other such blatantly demonic institutions. The performance of the black mass is one such occurrence where a nude female is laid on the "altar" and ritual sexual intercourse is indulged in.

Lack of Forgiveness

An unforgiving nature is fertile ground for demons to control and take over, and use to their advantage. The progress from a lack of forgiveness to uncontrollable rage and violence is common and well known. These are all areas that Satanic forces easily dominate and the person is soon under the influence and control of demons.

> To choose not to forgive is to choose to allow someone other than the Lord to control our life. It is to choose to be a victim when Christ wants to set us free. It is also to give ground to the enemy so he can set up a guerrilla base from which to operate in our lives.[5]

---

[2] Murphy, *Handbook*, 551.
[3] Ibid., 534.
[4] Ibid., 151.
[5] Timothy W. Warner, *Spiritual Warfare* (Wheaton, IL.: Crossway Books, 1991) 104.

a. **Animosity**. Hatred is of the devil, for love is of God.

b. **Bitterness**. James talks about bitterness (bitter jealousy—Jas. 3:15, NASB) as being of a wisdom which is earthly, natural, and demonic.

To choose not to forgive is to choose to allow someone other than the Lord to control our life.

c. **Vengeance**. The way of the Lord promotes love and forgiveness not deep-seated bitterness and desire for vengeance. The Lord reserves the right to seek revenge (Rom. 12:20), and so anyone who takes away this privilege from the Lord is opening up demonic doors.

d. **Unabated anger**. Obviously not of God, hence of Satan.

e. **Rage**. The Bible advocates patience, long-suffering, and self-control, all of which are the opposite of rage.

f. **Desire to destroy**. The way of the Lord is to build up, and the way of Satan is to destroy.

Depression

Is depression a sin? We may not conclude this, but we can see how it can be an open door to demonic influence. Depressed people are often prone to impulsive action, and sometimes such actions or activity could be sinful, thus allowing the possibility of demonic entrance.

Desire and Craving for Power

A lust for power is akin to the sin of Satan himself who lusted after the power and position of the Eternal God. In our highly materialistic society we are all aware of how not only does power corrupt, but the yearning for power has led to all kinds of sinfulness. Colossians 2:8 has clear teachings concerning "philosophy and empty deception" (NASB), which is an apt description of a lot of Western capitalistic acumen, with its humanistic base which results in more profit, more money, and more power. But we find such craving for power even in the philosophies of extreme socialism and communism.

A lust for power is akin to the sin of Satan himself who lusted after the power and position of God.

Demons 9

The word "pagan" is in disrepute in this day, and perhaps rightly so. But it aptly describes non-Christian religions and even more aptly can be used in the context of demonic influence. Many of these religions have been almost completely taken over by Satan and are the fertile "breeding" territory for demons as they dominate the adherents of these faiths. Some nonreligious areas of a culture may not be demon oriented, but the religious elements of a non-Christian culture can be highly affected by demonic suggestion, demonic influence, demonic control, and even demonic worship!

The apostle Paul wrote to the Corinthian Christians about Gentile worship. He equates whatever sacrifices that were being offered to the Gentile gods with actually being offered to demons (see 1 Cor. 10:20). And in Romans 1 there is a clear progression from the worship of the One True Sovereign Lord, the Creator of all of creation, to the worship of created things. Thus we see a departure from what God intended towards what man wanted in worship. Paul, in the latter part of the chapter, details the final outcome of this, how this shift in focus from Creator to created led to all kinds of evil and wicked behavior. The shift corrupted what the Lord had instilled in man by creating him in His own image, that desire in man to relate to the supernatural. That divinely given capacity was turned towards self-determined objects of worship—just what Satan aspires for man—that is, to take man away from worshiping the Living God to bowing before created things. Thus we can see how the institution and development of pagan religions is a work of the devil rather than just a social or anthropological phenomenon. (*See the addendum on Pagan religions and demons.*)

I stopped my car to investigate why a crowd had gathered at a nearby road junction. I soon discovered that it was a procession moving to a nearby Hindu shrine. In the center of the procession were two young women who were flaying themselves with neem branches. The neem tree has always been associated with religious connotations and more particularly with demonic influence. The women were not hurting themselves too much, but they kept up a steady dance pace, as they moved towards the shrine, accompanied by relentless and rhythmic drumbeats. They held in their hands, by the legs, two alive, squawking chickens. When they reached the small temple with a huge crowd egging them on, the two girls broke into a form of a ritual dance, going around and around and around

> at a dizzying pace. And then, to my amazed horror and mental distur-
> bance, each girl took the live chicken, plunged its head into her mouth, bit
> the head off and drank the blood. A great cry went up from the crowd and
> the girls who were now very, very obviously in a trance, kept their dance
> going, swallowing the blood, as part of it trickled down from their mouths
> onto their cheeks, and necks and body. This cannot be limited to cultural
> explanations or even to ordinary religious connotations. I believe that only
> the power of the demonic world could cause a person to participate in
> such a literal blood drinking ceremony.

A lot of these religions thrive on superstition, and Satan uses superstition to effectively control the adherents of false religions. Superstition, in a common definition, is the unnatural fear of the unknown and mysterious. This in turn makes the person assign supernatural and divine powers to that same unknown. Superstition is a form of spiritual reality ignorance.

Superstition is a form of spiritual reality ignorance.

Occult Practices

A basic meaning of the word occult is "hidden"; so occultism deals with the hidden side of life. It has its root in the Latin word, *occultus,* which means to cover up or hide. It has the connotation of being something beyond man's normal and natural experiences.

Kurt Koch, whose intense research and insightful writing of demonology had been a boon to those studying the subject, has written an in-depth book on occultic practices (*Christian Counselling and Occultism*) in which he classifies occult practices into three categories, namely, extrasensory perception, extrasensory influence, and extrasensory apparitions.[6] He backs this up with various case studies. However, for our purposes, we will classify occult practices in a more practical manner, even though there might be quite a bit of overlapping between the categories. We will look at occultism under the headings of Occult Institutions, Spiritism, Occult Apparitions, and Entertainment Occult. We will look at how these become open doors to demonization, but

[6] Kurt E. Koch, *Christian Counselling and Occultism* (Grand Rapids: Kregel Resources, 1972) 35.

will not deal with each of the items in **Demons 9**
great detail.

At this point we should note that there is
a great interest in the occult and related subjects. One just needs to
look at the lists of bestsellers in regular bookstores and publishers, and
see the popularity of writers such as Anne Rice and J.K. Rowling. Then
there is the spate of mystery and horror movies, with their either open
or subtle undertones of the occult in them. In addition there is the
growing interest in occult activities with witchcraft even being considered as an alternate way of faith. Are all of these indications of a
Satanic swan song or a result of the spurt making the sinful living both
acceptable and fashionable?

Occult Institutions

Witchcraft and Wizardry

Some people think of witchcraft as an alternate faith and thus
pronounce it as valid. What is often not seen at first is its Satanic and
demonic involvement, and many who get into it for its novelty are soon
under powerful demonic control. A relevant definition of witchcraft is
given by Rick Joyner: "Witchcraft is counterfeit spiritual authority; it is
using a spirit other than the Holy Spirit to dominate, manipulate, or
control others."[7]

> **Many who get into witchcraft for its novelty
> are soon under powerful demonic control.**

Our scope does not permit us to go into witchcraft in detail, but it
has existed for centuries and apart from its non-Christian practices among
various religions, there has also been witchcraft practiced and promoted
in decidedly Christian regions and contexts. Medieval Europe abounded
with witches and wizards who were often used even by monarchy for various purposes. There were both white witches and black witches, the former seemingly using their "skills" for good purposes, like doctors, while
the black witches used their abilities for evil purposes.

In modern times we must be aware of covens that exist in harmless looking communities and of witchcraft practices associated with
the New Age movement. Also, voodooism, so common in the Carib-
bean, obeah (spiders play an important part in obeah practices), were-
wolves, etc., are all variations of witchcraft beliefs.

---

[7] Rick Joyner, *Overcoming Witchcraft* (Charlotte, NC: Morningstar Publications, 1996) 7.

Demons 9

The notorious Salem witchcraft trials should cause us to carefully examine whether accounts of witchcraft are real or just fictional and sensational in nature. But be assured: The devil *does* use witchcraft, and Scripture warns us about it. The Old Testament expressly forbids witchcraft (see Exod. 22:18; Deut. 18:10). And Paul's warnings against "sorcery" in Galatians 5:20 could well be a reference to witchcraft.[8]

Wicca

Is there a difference between witchcraft and Wicca? Without going into much detail, a good definitive explanation is in order.

Wicca is one of the most seductive deceptions that Satan has come up with. It is the contemporary name for the cult of so-called "white" witchcraft or Neo-Paganism, which has been enjoying a renaissance in the United States.

It claims to be a "back to nature" religion which worships the sky and the earth, and thus has attracted many adherents amongst those sympathetic to environmental and ecology issues. . . .

I finally learned in the most graphic fashion imaginable that the difference between witchcraft and Wicca and Satanism is non-existent"[9]

(The above description is by a former Wicca "Priest of the Goddess," William Schnoebelen).

Magic

A common distinction is made between white magic and black magic. The former kind is considered harmless and makes up the milieu of parlor tricks, sleight of hand skills, and a host of "now you see it, now you don't" games used to entertain children and adults. Black magic, on the other hand, involves powers not available to normal man, power from the spirit world. Many religions, particularly animism, use magic in their rituals and ceremonies and the result is domineering fear and superstition among the people who are under the control of the magician or medicine man, etc.

Many religions use magic in their rituals.

[8] A good little booklet detailing the history and practice of witchcraft, though not making spiritual implications, is entitled *A Cauldron of Witches*, authored by Clifford Lindsey Alderman and published in 1973 by Pocket Books, New York.
[9] William Schnoebelen, *Wicca: Satan's Little White Lie* (Ontario, Canada: Chick Publications, 1990) 7.

Divination or soothsaying or fortune telling can be an easy demonic door. In Acts 16:16-18, the apostle Paul commands the evil spirit that empowered the little girl to tell fortunes to come out of her, and the evil spirit did. Man's desire to know the future is manipulated by the demonic world even though demons are not omniscient. But all persons seeking to either know the future in order to plan their own destinies, independent of the Lord God who holds the future in His hands, or those persons playing around with soothsaying and divination are open to demonic influence.

Occult Apparitions

Ghosts and Other "Spirits"

While we pooh-pooh the idea of ghosts, we must be aware of the vastness of the demonic world, and therefore be further aware of their ability to deceive by appearing in varied forms.

Astral Body Experiences

These are claims that a person can actually leave his physical body and travel on an astral plane. A sure occult experience.

Spiritism

Mediums, séances, and the like are the elements involved in spiritistic activities. Here again, it is an effort to know the future, or contact the "spirit world," which is really the demonic world, for God's angels cannot be contacted this way. Spiritism and demonism are in close kinship.

Occultic Entertainment

Table Rapping

I have witnessed "Table Rapping" or as we called it as young boys, "Table Tapping." *The athletic team was out for a tournament and the night before they returned the most spirit-involved boy decided to find out who won the championship, using "table tapping." A coin was produced and the alphabet written, spaced out appropriately in a circle. The boy began his petitioning—a repetition of the plea, "**Any spirit passing by take possession of this coin.**" After a long wait, when the unbelievers were sent away, the coin began to move. **It jerked forward slowly spelling out the answer to questions asked.** I was allowed to put*

*my finger on the coin. **It moved!** I did not push it. And the answers given were right. Eerie, frightening, and real.*

Ouija Board

He was a Bible college student and he narrated this story to me himself. Prior to his becoming a Christian he liked his beer and indulged quite a bit in "games" involving the ouija board. One day when he and his friends were deeply engrossed with their ouija board, strange things began happening. The stereo system came on by itself and the compact discs in the system played loud blaring music. The table began to rattle while there was no breeze or other explainable force for that to happen. No tremors or minor earthquakes. Everything else in the room was steady, but the table shook and beer cans began falling off, while all along without any human intervention the music began playing.

Coincidence? Mere happening by chance? Psychic phenomenon? Or, demonic activity connected with the ouija board? Ouija board fall-out!

Clairvoyance and Clairsentience

Clairvoyance is the ability to know things and predict happenings without a known base for acquiring that knowledge. Similarly clairsentience is the ability to determine the nature of things without using acceptable systems or methods or instruments. Examples are seen in "healers" who diagnose medical illnesses even though they themselves have not had real or proper medical knowledge input.

Hypnosis

There is some value in this medically, but in the hands of unscrupulous exponents it can lead to the mind of the hypnotized person being taken over by demonic spirits.

Transcendental Meditation

Eastern meditation techniques seek to empty a person's mind and thus allow evil intrusions to take place.

Other Possible Doors

Palmistry

Seeking to know the future by "reading" palms is a way of losing dependence on the Lord and no longer entrusting the future to Him. Satan seeks to make us believe that he knows our future and can con-

Satan seeks to make us believe that he knows our future and can control it for us in the way we desire.

Water Divination

A form of clairsentience using "wands" or just forked branches of certain trees to determine where to sink a well and be assured of finding good water. (*I saw it happen. He walked around holding each arm of the forked "twig" in each of his hands, and then all of a sudden it twitched. He was not satisfied and moved around the campus and suddenly the forked twig spun around uncontrollably, going around and around, which under normal circumstances would have called for a twisted arm on the part of the diviner.*)

Telepathy

Transmission of one person's thoughts to another without the use of any communication medium.

Ancestral Sin

This is sometimes referred to as generational sin and is based on the teachings recorded in Exodus 20:5, where the sins of the ancestors led to punishment down to even the third and fourth generations. Another such passage is Jeremiah 32:18. Some would interpret this as being a mere reference to the consequences of sins committed by parents and other ancestors coming down several generations to the descendants. Others believe that the nature of sinning of the ancestors, if related to deliberate turning away from the Living God and the subsequent worship of idols and demonic spirits, then allows the influence created by such evil creatures to be passed on to several generations that follow. It must be pointed out here that the "guilt" of ancestral sin is not imposed on the children that follow, but rather the demonic consequences. It would imply therefore, that if ancestral sin, particularly demonic contact, is "passed on" to succeeding family members, then even children could be demonized. Some would say that this was the reason for Jesus' question directed to the parents of the demoniac in Mark 9:21.

Granted that the precise interpretation of the passage is controversial, many of those who have had confrontation with demonic spirits testify to the existence of demonic transference through generations. Ensign and Howe testify to this:

Since children have not sinned as morally **94** responsible persons at these early years, we have concluded that the evil spirits have been handed down to the children as a consequence of the "Law of Generations" in Exodus 20:5.[10]

Ed Murphy concurs with this:

> In light of this Biblical principal of the law of inheritance of evil, demonic transference or inheritance would *not* appear unlikely. The most obvious possibility would be for occult involvements of parents who rebel against God and join themselves to the no-gods of the spirit world. They usually present not only themselves to the spirits but their progeny also. Studies in non-Christian religions and occultism reveal this transference to be a fact.[11]

A dear Christian friend and brother, a dynamic and effective preacher and scholar of the Word of God, believes that his conflicts with demonic spirits is due to the demonic influences on his father when the whole family were Hindus. And I accept his explanation.

Transference

This differs from generational sin transfer in that it can occur when a demon is being "cast" out. The demon/demons just move from one person to another. Usually this is someone whose faith is weak and who has not been adequately covered with prayer and the protection given by the "full armor of God" (Eph. 6:11-13).

We have a case of transference where the Gadarene demoniac was concerned, though in that case it was transference from a human being to swine and that with the permission of the Lord Jesus Christ (see Mark 5:12-13).

There is one particular belief that some have concerning possible transference which is both not really provable and not seemingly viable. That is the belief that demons are passed on during sexual intercourse from a demonized person to another. This would make the act of intercourse efficacious in passing on spiritual things and such is not possible. If so, then there would be validity to the concept of original

---

[10] Grayson H. Ensign and Edward Howe, *Counseling and Demonization* (Amarillo, TX: Recovery Publications, 1989) 200.
[11] Murphy, *Handbook*, 438.

sin. However, the closeness and intimacy of physical communion, and the nature of **Demons 9** both illicit as well as unnatural sex, when it is coupled with a kinship of mind and spirit, might have the demonic influence from the demonized also affecting the other person.

Pronouncement of Curses

Curses are more than mere pronouncements of negative wishes imposed on somebody. In religions of the East, particularly Hinduism, a curse is considered to be real and effective. People pay priests and others to make curses on their enemies. Often, a childless woman is said to have been curse by someone else close to her. And just as payment is made to invoke a curse by a "holy man" or a priest, so also appeasement is made to break the curse. But are these real?

The Old Testament is fraught with both, blessings and curses. For example, early in Genesis, Noah blesses Shem and Japheth, while cursing Canaan. On the other hand, Paul, in the book of Romans, urges Christians not to curse. "Bless those who persecute you; bless and curse not" (Rom. 12:14, NASB). Evidently cursing is the counterpart of blessing, and if one is efficacious, then so is the other. Derek Prince gives us a simple definition of a curse in his book, *Thou Shall Expel Demons*. He says, "I have compared a curse to a dark shadow over our lives that shuts out part (at least) of God's blessings."[12] And he goes on to say, "Two of the blessings that may be excluded by a curse are physical healing and deliverance from evil spirits."[13]

Paul, in Romans, urges Christians not to curse.

Demonic cursing is when the demonic spirit world is invoked, either through magic or through incantations, sacrifices, and the like, to bring about negative influences and even physical attacks on the individual being cursed. Demons, when given any opportunity to influence or control a person, seize on the curse and inflict their evil powers on the victim. However, we can be assured that this happens to those whose own spiritual lives are not close to the Lord. And also, we can overcome such curses by the power of Him who took our curses on Himself. "Christ redeemed us from the curse of the Law, having become a curse for us—for it is written, "Cursed is every one who hangs on a tree" (Gal. 3:13, NASB).

[12] Prince, *Expel*, 231.
[13] Ibid.

Many Christian psychologists familiar with demonic powers believe that child abuse is indicative of demonic influence and can be an entry point for demons. Ed Murphy categorically (and shockingly) states, "Of the six major doors through which demons attach themselves to the lives of human beings, the door of child abuse is perhaps the most common, most hideous and the most destructive."[14] Explaining this in detail, he shows how Satan knows and uses the baser nature of man, and child abuse is one of the lowest forms of sinning. Satan also knows, he says, that control of a child can lead to control of the adult, and thus through child abuse demonic control can arise. So he says, ". . . millions of abused children do pick up demons, especially if SRA were the context of their abuse."[15] (SRA refers to Satanic Ritual Abuse.)

Child abuse is one of the lowest forms of sinning.

Needless to say, the child abuser, who with almost no exception is also a sexual abuser, is himself demonically controlled or is allowing himself to be demonically dominated. The whole matter of sexual child abuse, whether it is dealing with pedophilic behavior or just child pornography, is a violation of the Lord's norms of sexual conduct and an aberration of the natural sexual instinct. Satan and his forces know this and therefore have very successfully used it to their demonic advantage.

An almost simplified summation, yet one that explains how we open doors to demons, is given by the Basilea Schlink in a little booklet called, *The Unseen World of Angels and Demons*. Mother Schlink says:

> The reality of Satan and his demons is especially evident nowadays in the lives of those who have accepted his offer, choosing to exalt their ego and live a life of unrestrained pleasure by indulging in sex, drugs, and so forth. . . . When people consciously give themselves to Satan or when they come under his power through incantations pastimes: table-turning, fortune-telling, séances, ouija boards, tarot cards and astrology, to list but a few examples—they invite the forces of evil into their lives.[16]

---

[14] Murphy, *Handbook*, 449.
[15] Ibid., 452.
[16] Basilea Schlink, *The Unseen World of Angels and Demons* (Secunderabad, India: OM Books, 1985) 32.

CHAPTER 10

BARRICADE THE GATES
PROTECTION FROM DEMONIC INFLUENCE

A roaring lion looking for prey (1 Pet. 5:8). That's the image portrayed in Scripture of Satan's deepest interest where man is concerned. His aim is to get man into his kingdom, and to accomplish this he does not limit himself in any way. If plain deception does not work, then he adds on to that supernatural expressions, even to the point of afflicting the human body. And to carry out these tasks of his, he uses his demonic cohorts. How does a person combat these forces? What precautions can we take to ward off these evils? Or can we successfully fight against the devil and his demons?

The answer to that last question is an overwhelming and simple, **yes**, we can. Indeed we can. For Christians there is that grand affirmation that "greater is He who is in you than he who is in the world" (1 John 4:4). Similarly, James encourages us, ". . . Resist the devil and he will flee from you" (Jas. 4:7). But what are the steps to be taken, or what are the methods to be used?

Too many manuals on the Christian life give guidance and counseling in carefully outlined and graded stages. Though this is valid where growth is concerned, and steady growth is certainly a deterrent and an obstacle to demonic intentions over us, yet where sin is to be overcome and demons are to be opposed and Satan is to be made to flee, drastic and radical action is necessary. Deliverance is certainly a valid and important function where this is concerned, but *deliverance alone and as an end in itself must never be the ultimate goal.* That is why special meetings and gatherings to drive out demons can be dramatic and sensational, *but there has to be more.* The wagons must be circled. The gates must be barred. The entry points must be posted with sentries. The doors must be locked! And it must begin with a commitment to Jesus, the overcomer of Satan on the cross!

Drastic and radical action is necessary.

This is where it all begins. Yes, we may be forced to "drive" out evil spirits, but the victim or the demon-controlled person **must** be led into a saving and sustaining relationship with the Son of God. Often this is not done. Yet the Gospel warns us about the return of the evil ones to an empty house (Luke 22:24-26).

From creation we are told of the power of Christ over the Evil One (Gen. 3:15). The ministry of Christ on earth was an overcoming ministry as well. In Matthew 12:22-29 and Luke 10:17-19 Jesus declared His power over demons. Further, the plans and agenda of Satan were thwarted and dealt a deadly blow through the victory of the Cross and the empty grave. The power of conquered death and the resurrection are needed to keep the enemy out of our lives.

Coming under the blood of Christ which we access in the obedience of Christian baptism as we bury the old man of sin (demonic influence included) and rise to a new life is foundational in keeping Satan and his forces out of our lives. We should never undermine or underestimate the efficacy of Christian baptism, that burial in water signifying our identity with our Lord's own death, burial, and resurrection (Rom. 6:4). And that significance is gloriously coupled with power over Satan and his works by the writer of the book of Hebrews. "Since then the children share in flesh and blood, He Himself likewise also partook of the same, that through death He might render powerless him who had the power of death, that is, the devil . . ." (Heb. 2:14, NASB).

When we are born of water and the Spirit (John 3:5), the indwelling presence of the Holy Spirit in our lives (Acts 2:38) helps us keep shut the doors to demonic influence. But we must be *aware* of the presence of the Holy Spirit in our lives, and very *conscious* of the fact that He is the **Holy** Spirit. Holiness is demanded of us to deny entrance to demons. I personally like the simple and beautiful affirmation of that great saint of spiritual disciplines, Madame Jeanne Guyon: "Oh, dear one, God has promised that He would come and make His abode with him who does His will. (See John 14:23.) He has promised to dwell in our innermost being—the new Holy of Holies place."[1]

We must be very conscious that the Holy Spirit is the *Holy* Spirit.

[1] Madame Jeanne Guyon, *Experiencing God through Prayer*, ed. by Donna C. Arthur (Springdale, PA.: Whitaker House, 1984) 17.

Sin of any kind is the way doors to demons are left ajar. We must be *fully* *cognizant* that it is not just outrageous sin, or despicable and shameful and deliberate sinning that lets demons influence persons. *Any sin* is like a foot in the door for the evil ones to slowly move their deceptive ways into our lives.

Protect Yourselves with Godly Armor

The apostle Paul, in that great and oft repeated and proclaimed passage in Ephesians 6, details what the armor of God is. But his preface to the items of armor is of great importance. The armor is *not* to cast out evil spirits or deliver a person from their power, but the armor is to *prevent* the devil and his schemes and to keep the doors to demonism shut. The armor is to put a stop to the power of demonic agenda over us. True, and gloriously so, we can also use the armor to attack Satanic strongholds, but Paul begins with the prophylactic injunction, "Put on the full armor of God, that you may be able to stand firm against the schemes of the devil" (Eph. 6:11, NASB).[2] The armor of God is to enable us to bolt and bar the doors of our spiritual lives, "for our struggle is not against flesh and blood, but against the rulers, against the powers, against the world forces of this darkness, against the spiritual forces of wickedness in the heavenly places" (Eph. 6:12, NASB).

The armor of God is to put a stop to the power of demonic agenda over us.

1. *The Belt—Truth.* Satan is the father of lies. Truth protects us as we apply it to our daily living. The belt protects our most private body parts (KJV, "girdle") and likewise we seek truth in our innermost being.
2. *The Breastplate—Righteousness.* We are protected when the righteousness of Christ is imputed to us. Galatians 3:27 says we put on Christ in baptism or are clothed with Him, meaning clothed with His righteousness.
3. *The Shoes—Preparation of the Gospel of Peace.* This does not merely refer to putting on our feet the gospel of peace but also being ready or prepared to proclaim that gospel. When we have a passion to share the gospel of peace with others, we will has-

---

[2] I personally like the KJV word for "schemes," namely, "wiles." Its connotation increases my understanding of Satan's cunning. Used in its verb form it translates as "to lure," "to entice." This is Satan's common method to acquire followers.

ten it to them, thus thwarting Satan's schemes. Many of us have unknowingly deprived Satan and his demons of a victim by sharing with them the gospel of peace.

4. *The Shield—Faith.* Protective armor to ward off demonic doubt and demonic procrastination. We act in faith, and we exercise trust and dependence in Him who has already overcome Satan.

5. *The Helmet—Salvation.* Protection for our heads and our minds. A salvation mind-set is needed. When we have schooled ourselves into a salvation mode, we think differently. We recognize we are saved people and thereby, in faith, ward off Satan's attacks.

6. *The Sword (of the Spirit)—The Word of God.* It's the Word of God that reveals to us God's own nature and the nature of His opponent Satan. We use that Word of God aggressively. In any confrontation with the demonic world we must **never fail to use the Word of God!** After all, Jesus, when He was in the wilderness, frustrated Satan's thinking by using the Sword of the Spirit.

Cover Yourself with Prayer and Petition

Though this is the culmination of the armor of God items, yet the nature of prayer and the efficacy of prayer makes a person invincible to the "wiles" of the Evil One. C.S. Lewis, in his classic satire *The Screwtape Letters*, has the Uncle Screwtape admonishing his demon nephew Wormwood regarding his "patient's" prayer life. Wormwood is told to keep the patient *away* from prayer and not just aim to make the patient feel his prayer life is parrotlike, etc. "The best thing, where it is possible, is to keep the patient from the serious intention of praying altogether."[3]

The common and childlike definition of prayer as "talking to God," is woefully inadequate. Prayer is first and foremost getting into the "presence" of God. When we are in His Presence, we are not just in communion with Him, but we are in a protected and sterile environment. Prayer, seen as such for indeed it is such, becomes a powerful weapon in the arsenal of the person seeking to combat the schemes of the devil. Madame Guyon, in the same book cited earlier, emphasizes that prayer is "Experiencing God."

Prayer is first and foremost getting into the "presence" of God.

[3] C.S. Lewis, *The Screwtape Letters* (London: Collins Fontana Books, 1942) 24.

Richard Foster states that the Lord **Demons 10**
taught us, in the model Lord's Prayer, to
deliberately pray to be kept from the Evil One.

> Now with regard to the petition "deliver us from evil"; as much as we
> might like it otherwise, the original text is quite clear that Jesus is urg-
> ing us to pray for rescue not from evil in a generic sense, but from the
> evil one, namely, Satan. I know that does not sit well in our modern
> and postmodern understanding of reality, but it is there nevertheless.[4]

Prayer is a powerful antidote to demonic activity. Missionary
accounts are in abundance where testimonies are made regarding the
power of prayer over demonic elements. When prayer brings us into
the presence and experiencing of God, the demonic world shudders
and trembles. We are with Him and communing with Him who is the
Lord of All Creation, and that includes all of the demonic realm. He
holds their eternal future in His hands and their doom is already written down.

Shelter Yourself in the Fellowship of the Kingdom

Staying with and within the "crowd" is an almost easy way to
keep out of danger. And it works spiritually. Whether it is in the area of
sharing in corporate worship or having "accountability" with others in
the Church or seeking the counsel and guidance from those of "like
similar faith" or uniting with the Kingdom while meeting the Lord at
His Table or joining with believers in united prayer, whatever the fellowship area and sphere may be, we are sheltered when we are with
the Kingdom of God.

In our modern concepts of the Kingdom of God the real meaning and impact of community is either belied or belittled. During
medieval times the church was indeed a refuge and even so in a literal physical sense. We can catch a glimpse of the marvelous mind of
God and gain glorious insight into His grace as we see the tremendous
benefits of being in His Kingdom. Indeed, the concentration of the New
Testament writers in outlining, detailing of purpose and agenda, ana-
lyzing the leadership and life and conduct of the Kingdom of God on
earth, was not just to fulfill their personal expectations or to satisfy their
own spiritual anticipation. They wrote from inspiration the God-
breathed instructions regarding the nature and makeup of the Kingdom

---

[4] Richard J. Foster, *Prayer: Finding the Heart's True Home* (San Francisco: Harper
Collins, 1992) 189.

Demons 10 of God on earth. *And the church was to* **102**
provide the necessary koinonia encour-
agement, empowerment, and sheltering of the
people of God. The community of believers can be the means of Satan
being shut out, *for he has no place within.*

The church was to provide all the needs
of the people of God.

Even though, at the mundane spiritual level, we can see how fellow believers can help us in our quest for spiritual protection, let us not forget the deeper implications of the Spirit of God within the corporate body, enabling us to stand firm against the schemes of the evil one.

Look at the beautiful progression implied in 1 John 1:5-7. John tells us that Christ is light and not darkness. Darkness is of the Evil One, but ". . . God is light, and in Him there is no darkness at all" (1 John 1:5). Then, when we are out of the darkness, we have fellowship with Him who is light (v. 6). When this is a reality, we automatically have fellowship within the Kingdom. ". . . But if we walk in the light as He Himself is in the light we have fellowship with one another, and the blood of Jesus His Son, cleanses us from all sin" (1 John 1:7, NASB). Staying in the Kingdom keeps us in the light, Who is Jesus, and we have fellowship, in the light, with other Kingdom dwellers. What then of the demons? They remain in the darkness, outside the Kingdom.

Is it possible that the kingdom of Satan could be attacked more vigorously by the Kingdom of God and have its gates shattered more easily (Matt. 16:18) and thereby release countless victims from the grip of demons if the Kingdom was less a conglomeration of self-centered individuals and glory-intent congregations, and instead more of a "purpose driven," united, koinonia-built community of the faithful?

We can keep the demons out! It is possible to stand firm as the apostle Paul said. Let us never despair but go forth confidently, knowing that first of all the victory *has been accomplished* by Jesus on the cross, and second that same victory can be claimed and experienced by us, His children, so that indeed we can stand firm. We can keep the demons out!

CHAPTER 11

EVACUATING THE PREMISES
DELIVERANCE AND EXORCISM

An important fact to consider, as we contemplate getting rid of demonic influence, is that man cannot drive out demons or liberate himself or others from their control. God alone can drive out demons, but this is not a matter of despair but triumph, for God uses men to accomplish this task. God empowers His chosen children to be His instruments in this.

This fact must be realized and accepted by anyone who is confronted with the task of deliverance. When we realize that God alone has the power for this, then it keeps us humble, and dependent. *We can only carry out this dangerous and vital ministry in the name and with the power of God Almighty.* Self-dependence, overconfidence in methods, arrogance that can develop from experience, all these can not only make the mission of demon deliverance a failure, but can also lead to possible problems. In the book of Acts we read of seven sons of a certain Jewish priest, named Sceva, who used the name of the Lord Jesus to drive out demons. *But they were not empowered by God to do so.* What followed is devastating, tragic humor. The demon-influenced man pounced onto the seven young men and overpowered them and literally beat them. The demon was vocal, saying, "I recognize Jesus, and I know about Paul, but who are you?" (Acts 19:15, NASB).

> Jesus is the only one able to free people from occult oppression. Psychiatrists, psychologists and theologians at most are only a poor substitute. Satan is a powerful enemy. He has only been defeated once: at the cross on Golgotha where the archenemy was dethroned. If an oppressed person is unwilling to come to Jesus he can hold out no hope of being delivered.[1]

Satan has been defeated once for all by one means.

[1] Kurt E. Koch, *Demonology Past and Present* (Grand Rapids: Kregel, 1973) 148.

Demons 11

does not mean that Jesus, in His encounters with Satan in the wilderness, and with demons, did not overcome them. But the defeat on the Cross was a deathblow to Satan and was the key point in Satan losing out over his control of man through his chief weapon, which is death itself.

Does this imply that only certain Christians can drive out evil spirits and that certain special powers are needed? Is there a special class of ministry termed, "demon deliverance" or "exorcists"?

It is not necessarily a special ministry, for many a missionary has come to a literal place of confrontation with evil spirits and out of necessity has involved himself in helping people be purged of evil spirits' influence. But we can *prepare* and *protect* ourselves in particular ways for this real ministry. We need the preparation and we need the protection so that we can fearlessly stand firm and hence be used by the Lord God to help those who need deliverance and liberation from evil powers.

In this chapter we will look at the *need* for deliverance, the relevant *authority* necessary, the *preparation* for the task, and the *methods* of exorcism. But first, is there a difference between deliverance and exorcism?

The problem here is similar to that with terminology such as "possession," "control," "demonization," etc. Deliverance and exorcism are different only in terms of the degree of demonic control or influence. When a person's whole mind is under demonic influence, and his body becomes the chief tool of demons to show that influence, then the battle to get rid of the demonic influence is more pronounced and acute. We can see this through the analogy of illness. The effort and the medication used to get rid of a common cold is far different and simpler than what is needed to combat some form of cancer. When Jesus' disciples came to Him expressing their own inability to get rid of a certain demonic spirit, Jesus indicated in His reply that their faith was too "little." The reference to this in Matthew 17:19-20 is followed with the marginal note in the NASB that some later manuscripts add, "But this kind does not go out except by prayer and fasting" (Matt. 17:21, NASB). The account in Mark's Gospel affirms this statement (Mark 9:29). We see then that some demonic confrontations need greater spiritual effort than others, efforts involving greater faith, deeper prayer, and the specific spiritual discipline of fasting. It appears that Jesus is saying that demonic deliverance is possible by all His followers, but some kinds of demonic control (possession, for lack of a better word)

need more protracted "exertion." Hence, if there is any distinction between deliverance and exorcism it is only a matter of the degree of Satanic and demonic involvement with a person.

Need for Deliverance

There is, at times, confusion regarding this. On the one hand there are those who make deliverance a very special ministry, leaving out other endeavors such as edification, proclamation, etc. Often these deliverances are attempted or done with much fanfare. On the other hand there are those who ridicule the whole notion of deliverance and even deny demonic influence. However, we must be open to use the general and effective authority given to us as Christians as those who are covered by the efficacious blood of Jesus, to stand firm, resist demonic influences, and pray for the deliverance of those who need it. *Look beyond the addictions and obsessions.* You might have to make the individual realize that his problem is really one of demonic influence and hence needs to be delivered of it. And if you are his or her shepherd or counselor or minister, confront the demon behind the problem and use the power of the Risen Christ to free such a person from the influences plaguing him or her.

Authority for Deliverance

In the first verse of Luke chapter nine, Jesus provides power and authority over demons to His twelve disciples when He sends them out to proclaim His Kingdom: "And He called together, and gave them power and authority over all the demons, and to heal diseases" (Luke 9:1, NASB). The linking of demons and diseases seems to imply that the reference to the diseases dealt with diseases induced by demonic intervention. But what is specifically and clearly mentioned is that the twelve were given authority over demons. They had now delegated authority. They could cast out demons through the authority of Jesus. He alone has the authority to cast out demons, and He alone has the right and privilege to bestow that authority on others. Casting out demons is done by the Lord's servants only through delegated authority.

Casting out demons is done only through delegated authority.

But another significant element is found in the subsequent verses. The twelve were being sent out primarily to "proclaim the Kingdom of

Demons 11

was evangelistic commissioning. This was a sending out to promote the Kingdom and the King. *But the commissioning included power and authority over demons and demonic diseases and the ability to heal.*

Does that mean that *all* evangelism must include the ministries of healing and demonic deliverance? Such a conclusion would make the evangelist and the preacher seek out such situations and focus on demon deliverance, and often when this happens, the proclamation of the kingdom goes a-begging. The clear implication in the passage is that the disciples were sent to proclaim the Kingdom of God and to boldly deal with any medical/physical or spiritual conflict that consequently ensued. And spiritual conflicts there would be, and spiritual conflicts *there are*, when we attack demonic strongholds with the gospel of the Kingdom. The gospel automatically opposes demonic influences. The result is almost inevitable in situations and circumstances, in countries and nations where Satanic forces have dug themselves into the culture, particularly its religion. But the twelve were not to fear this, for they had power over demons and authority to cast them out and abilities to deal with bodily ailments, be they medically or spiritually induced.

Christians then can have delegated authority to deal with demons, but so often, like the twelve, the faith needed is weak, and the spiritual disciplines of prayer and fasting are absent. Yet we can state that Christians need not fear confrontation with demonic forces but to the contrary can boldly and fearlessly challenge their control of men.

Preparation

We should always be prepared to face the onslaughts of demons, and this even more so and especially when we arouse and threaten their very being through the proclamation of the Word of God. Christian living is the key to combating the schemes of the Evil One and his followers. But this has to go beyond the general good living and church attendance and acts of love and charity which we consider Christian Living. When we know the activities of demons are all around us and when we are in conflict with them, perhaps even combating them in order to save a person spiritually, then accentuated Christian living and decided preparation for the possible clash with demons must be undertaken. The difference is as between the general "Be Prepared" motto of the Boy Scouts and the honing given to those

troops going into guerrilla warfare. And this preparation is founded in the Word # Demons 11
of God, developed through our prayer life, encouraged by the saints around us, and fine-tuned by confident actions against the demonic world.

1. *The Word of God.* Demonic activity may be known to everyone in a general way, since the world is aware of some form of evil that exists. But it is the Word of God that specifies *who* demons are, *where* they come from, *how* they operate, and so forth. Therefore, there is no substitute for knowing what the Lord says, not only about demons, but also about ourselves and our world.

It is the Word of God that specifies who demons are, where they come from, and how they operate.

Another need for being rooted and grounded in the Word of God is that the nature of God's Word is the diametric opposite of who and what Satan is. Satan is called the Father of Lies, meaning the origin of all that is false and untrue. By contrast God's Word is Truth, and truth sets free, while falsehood enslaves.

2. *Prayer.* Specific prayer for spiritual conflict and demonic confrontation must be made. Remember Jesus' word to those of His disciples who were unable to cast out a certain demon. He actually told them that prayer and fasting was needed (Mark 9:29). (Some manuscripts leave out fasting but many also do include it.) Now this was not an indictment against the apostles for *not* praying but rather an injunction for *specific* prayer for being able to deliver someone from demonic power. Steep yourself in prayer prior to any demonic encounters. Indeed, let prayer cover you at all times.

As we increase in holiness, we can ward off demonic scheming to pull us astray.

3. *Holiness and Spiritual Disciplines.* Holiness is not an option. In 1 Peter 1:16 we are commanded to be holy. ". . . You shall be holy, for I am holy" (NASB). Holiness is the antidote to sin and a means of withstanding temptations. They will come, but as we increase in holiness, our withstanding quotient rises, and we can apply that to ward off demonic scheming to pull us astray. And holiness is no magic, for it is developed in us as we stay close to the Word of God, commune with Him in prayer, and exercise our spirits in the disciplines of fasting, simplicity, silence, soli-

Demons 11

tude, etc. Let us not forget that at one time Jesus clearly mentioned fasting and prayer as a means to confront and get rid of demonic spirits (Mark 9:29).

4. *Encouragement and Protection from the Kingdom.* It is fanciful in modern times to just belong to the Kingdom and be Christians "at large." But the New Testament validates the need for local churches and congregations to be places of security and refuge for the new as well as old believers. Hence Paul's letters were specifically directed toward churches, loaded with instructions to help the brethren grow in the faith and increase in their holiness. Paul warned the elders of local churches, enclaves in the larger Kingdom of God on earth, to guard the flock entrusted to them. In meeting with the elders of Ephesus in Acts 20, Paul spoke of wolves coming into the church to disturb the sheep. So elders are to protect the flock entrusted to them. The nature and purpose of the church includes nurturing, encouraging, securing, and establishing believers thus making it more difficult for demons to enslave them.

5. *Confident Activity.* Call this exercise if you wish, but when we anticipate dealing with demons, let us start with confidence in areas where their influence might be detected. Fear has no place in demon deliverance. Let us willingly pray for those who are demonically influenced. Let us boldly confront those whose lives are indicative of demonic control. We must not shy away from standing up to culturally justified activities which are certainly demonic invasions of national psyches, activities such as homosexuality, multiple marriages, consensual adultery, pornography, and the like. The Joneses might do it, but Christians need to confront those Joneses and deal with the demons that influence them!!

Fear has no place in demon deliverance.

Exorcism

Earlier we mentioned that there is no special difference between deliverance and exorcism. Exorcism is a form or deliverance. Why then are we separating it here?

I personally feel that exorcism is more of a planned and prepared event of deliverance. Deliverance can occur anywhere and at anytime. But where exorcism is concerned, it is like a special event! You know

Make it a time of witness and testimony.
Let it be a power encounter where *you* are in
control. Let it be exposure of the power of Christ being triumphant over
evil forces. Exorcism can tell the world that we have an Omnipotent
Lord and a Savior who overcame and overcomes demonic elements
regardless of their own strength and abilities. It is showing all of creation that *Jesus is Lord!*

Exorcism can tell the world that we have an Omnipotent Lord—showing all that Jesus is Lord!

Hence I believe, and therefore suggest, that exorcisms take the
following structure. Remember, that the preparation and authority and
other factors needed to deliver a person from demons are the same
here. But here the deliverance becomes a "media" event, the media
being exposing God's power to all on earth and to "principalities and
powers in heavenly places." It is a proclamation that Jesus is both Lord
and Christ!!!

1. *Make exorcism a Kingdom-related activity.* Get the Church involved. Get the brethren to prepare for it by united prayer and
   fasting and supplications. Not all the church may be actually
   present at an exorcism, but let the church be included in it. Why?

   In places we call "mission fields," there is usually a history,
   often an ancient and horrific history, of demonic manipulation,
   control, and subjugation. But now new life is available for those
   who were steeped in evil. Let that new life begin with a bang,
   with the celebration of Jesus over Satan. Let the praises to the
   King of kings shake the rafters of demonic dwellings. Let all the
   world know that the kingdoms of this world are becoming the
   Kingdoms of our Lord and Christ. A church-related exorcism will
   show the difference between the kingdoms, the Kingdom of our
   Lord and God and the defeated kingdom of Satan.

2. *Let the exorcism be a public event whenever possible.* Many
   times, in mission situations, culture demands a private exorcism.
   We do not need to, or seek to, violate cultural norms that are
   basically harmless, but there are times when we can endeavor to
   change culture if it brings glory to the Lord God.

   Now the nature of exorcising an evil spirit is such that there
   are possible dangers and setbacks. Transference is one of them.
   Failure is another. (There can be failed exorcisms due to reasons

of sin, ill preparation of the deliverer, arrogant, selfish, and vainglorious attitudes, etc.) However, and this might sound strange, if the body of Christ is filled with love for each other and especially the victim of demonic control, and if the body of Christ unitedly seeks the deliverance, then the body of Christ needs have nothing to fear. And all individuals who are wary, or nervous, or fearful, need not get into the public deliverance service. *Be sure to warn the curious and inquisitive, those who seek sensation and excitement, and those who are skeptical and doubtful, that they have no place in an exorcism service. Be selective.*

3. *Prepare for the exorcism.* Follow Jesus' injunctions and encourage and practice prayer and fasting. Let the whole church join in this in decency and order focusing on its necessity and its efficacy where demon deliverance is concerned. Neil Anderson suggests a retreat for this purpose of all church leaders.

Follow Jesus' injunctions and encourage and practice prayer and fasting.

The victim should be helped to prepare for his or her deliverance. This must include having an attitude of humility and subjection to the power and will of God. Then there should be a confession of all sin. It need not be done at the exorcism time, but it should be complete and sincere. Generally people out of embarrassment refrain from divulging some sins, but if the counselor or preacher is truly a man of God, then such confession of sin need not be embarrassing. The man of God should stress the victory of Christ over *all* sin to enable the demonized person to rejoice in it rather than abstain from confession. Further, the demonized person should be taught the way of salvation, and the exorcism should be simultaneous with faith declared through the obedience of Christian baptism.

The demonized person should be taught the way of salvation.

4. *Plan a service of exorcism.* This is not a display of worship abilities but a form of power encounter. There is a fine line between a hoopla-type program and one that would honor God and exalt His Name. *Do not cross that line for the sake of publicity and vainglory. **Do not take glory away from the Lord.*** Remember *we* do

not cast out demons; the Lord does it through His victory over Satan on the Cross. Keep the right perspective in this.

What should be included and focused on in such a service?

First of course is praise. Praise in favor of the Lord's triumph over evil and evil powers. Songs and hymns exalting the Lord's Name and His power and His Glory. Remember the words of that old hymn, "Onward Christian Soldiers," that gloriously declares, "At the sound of triumph Satan's hosts doth flee." But let not the praise be performance oriented but rather dedicated to the victory of Jesus and the defeat of Satan.

Let the praise be dedicated to the victory of Jesus and the defeat of Satan.

Second, prayer should abound. Prayer to the Lord for protection acknowledging the indwelling gift of the Holy Spirit. Prayer for the Church, for their security as well as their faithfulness and love. Prayer for the demonized person—prayer of forgiveness, prayer for deliverance, prayer for continuing spiritual cleanness. Prayer only and always in the Name of Jesus. At the Name of Jesus, Satan's hosts tremble. Use it effectively in your prayer sessions.

Third, let there be proclamation. Preach the Word. Preach boldly and confidently. Tell the old, old story of victory over evil, victory over sin, and victory over death. Let all those who hear be assured that the war is really over and was fought on Calvary. Preach with power, for the Word of God is alive and sharp and incisive. The Word opposes Satanic lies. The Word exposes demonic intent as truth is proclaimed. The Word sustained Jesus in the wilderness and thwarted Satan's plans of temptation.

Fourth, let there be an actual deliverance event. If possible and culturally acceptable, lay hands on the person. If others are prepared spiritually, then allow them to join in. Insist on quiet and closed eyes. This is not an easy matter, for demons resist being expelled, as in the case of the Gerasene demoniac. But let this all be done in decency and in order. *This is not a demonic gala. This is serious business, and a person's whole life is at stake.*

Should demons be commanded to leave a person? Will the demon leave quietly, or would we know it happened? The authority to drive out demons is Christ's alone though He dele-

Demons 11

gates this authority to His disciples and that does include us. But we are not ever taught in Scripture that we ourselves should command demons to leave or rebuke them by name. How then do we get this to occur? We pray *for* the person to be healed. We focus on the person's need for deliverance. Though this seems like a minor issue, there is more at stake here. Our interest is *not* in who or what the demon is. Our interest is in the salvation of that person for whom Jesus died. We concentrate on the person *not* the demon.

The authority to drive out demons is Christ's alone.

This has another logical perspective. By not rebuking or publicly commanding the exit of demons, we are not giving them unnecessary publicity. Our emphasis is on what Christ has done. So often the work of Christ in gaining us the victory over demonic forces is seen as an adjunct while the main event is allowing the demon to get all the attention. Reverse this and let Christ be emphasized and the demon forced, through His victory and the power of His Name, to depart from its victim.

Fifth, let there be closing praise and focused prayer for the delivered. Let expressions of acceptance, love, fellowship be demonstrated. Let the community know that the Kingdom of God is alive and well and victorious, and that the King of the Kingdom can overcome any opposition.

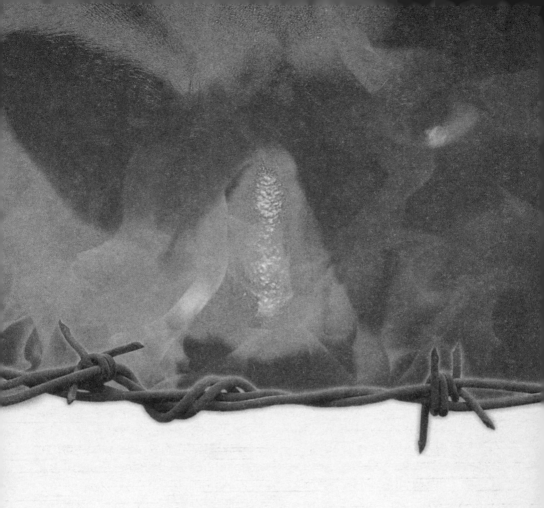

ADDENDA

ADDENDUM ONE
PAGAN RELIGIONS AND DEMONS

> *All night long the drums beat steadily in a trance-inducing rhythm. There was something going on at the nearby Hindu shrine. Devotees spent the whole night there, some with heads circling while their bodies swayed. Many of them were totally unaware of what was taking place in front of them. The gods were being invoked, whether to appease them or seek empowerment, I did not know. What I did know was that when I peeped into the shrine, the sanctum sanctorum was in deep darkness, the deity whose form was not visible to me coated with the offerings of ghee (clarified butter) and oil and with the powders of various other elements. It was strange and it was frightening. What was going on? Not many knew. Satan did though. He was using fear to bolster superstition. He was using tradition to continue gaining, through the religion, allegiance to himself.*

More than one billion people make up the population of my home country, India. Of these, just over 2% at present are Christians. Over 70% are Hindus, followed by Muslims, Buddhists, Jains, Sikhs, Animists, etc., though certainly not in that order. But can we classify all those 70% of the population who are Hindus as belonging to a demonic religion? Can we say they are all in some way or the other demonically influenced? And what about the Muslims and Buddhists and others? All demon oriented?

Look at China with its even larger population than India. Way over one billion people, and the bulk of them belonging to a present-day amalgam of Buddhism, spirit-worship, Confucianism, and the Communist brand of atheism? Do all of them belong to the demonic realm through virtue of their faith?

And what about the vast millions of Islam, all claiming to worship *one* God, whose name is Allah? What about the animists with their original monotheistic concepts?

115   As a teacher of world religions as well as cul- **One**
tural anthropology, and also crossculturalism and
crosscultural communication, an emphasis is made in the
classroom to analyze a culture and to see where and how common
ground could be found in order to convey a message, particularly the
gospel, meaningfully. Religion is an integral part of culture, and indeed
in many situations it shapes the rest of culture. But if these religions are
under the control of Satan and his demons, can *any* common ground
be found?

If these religions are under the control of Satan and his demons, can *any* common ground be found?

In my World Religions classes I define religion as the aspect of
one's experience in which one attempts to live harmoniously with the
power or powers he believes are controlling the world, and I am
indebted to Josh McDowell for that definition.[1] When religions acknowledge that that power or those powers are other than the Living
God, then we have a false religion. In the broadest sense, any religion
that leaves out the saving work of Christ is of the Evil One. That is, the
Evil One, through his chief operation, deceives the world into believing that Christ is *not* the only way to God, and also that man can find
his *own* way to salvation and fulfilled living. The Word of God makes
it clear that these are lies, and in reality there is *no* other way to God
the Father. But does that create a blanket condemnation of *all* non-
Christian religions, declaring that they are all demon dominated?

Please note and remember, that this is not a defense of non-
Christian beliefs and neither is it any kind of compromising accommo-
dation of these religions. In this section we will see how Satan *has*
taken charge of non-Christian faiths, and how we should react to them,
particularly with the aim of bringing the adherents of these faiths to a
saving knowledge of the Lord Jesus Christ.

While we focus, sometimes too much, on the strange, fearful,
and even weird functions of demons, we fail to be acutely conscious
that the main thrust of Satan and his forces is deception. Remember
one of his titles: The Father of Lies (John 8:44). And in the beginning of
time, Eve excused herself by referring to the methodology of Satan saying, ". . . the serpent deceived me . . ." (Gen. 3:13, NASB).

That being the nature and character of Satan and his followers, it
can be expected that, wherever the Church has failed to spread the Good

---

[1] McDowell and Stewart, *Understanding*, 10.

One News of the Kingdom, there evil will triumph; and the greatest of all evils is the denial of the Living Sovereign Lord. That in turn gives rise to false religions, false worship, false allegiances and false promises concerning man's destiny. In Hinduism, the concept of *Maya*, though difficult to fully comprehend and define, says that what we see and experience and live is not true reality but illusion—illusion due to blinded eyes and spiritual ignorance. That same concept can be applied to the "delusion" created by Satan in promoting the false religions of the world. And indeed he has, for he made our ancestors focus on themselves as becoming gods. And from then on man has wanted "godhood," and we see this in different ways and diverse manners. Man, according to Romans 1, turned from the worship of the Creator to worship of the created thing, that which man can control. Man shapes his idols and calls them his gods, but he chooses their form and content. Man, even in the spirit world of animistic religions, "manipulates" the "spirits," now appeasing them, now invoking their powers to man's benefit, and then placating them with man-made offerings. The bottom line of Satan is, "You can be like god. You are god."

This then is the ethic behind non-Christian religions. Whether the worship is polytheistic with its multitude of deities or monotheistic with a focus on an all-pervading deity, when that focus and emphasis is away from the Creator Lord of the Universe, then Satan is in charge. And he delegates man to be in charge of himself, diverting man from his needed dependence on the Lord.

So, are we concluding that all other religions are demon-controlled? What we are concluding is that the Evil One and his evil ones have their input, their domination, their influence, their invoking, over *any* religion that denies the worship of the Lord God and His Son Jesus.

We evaluate religions in the context of either Eternal Good or Deceptive Evil, but without the bigoted condemnation of the individual believers.

Is this not being bigoted and prejudicial? Does this not call for anti-everybody-else except our own brothers in the faith? Not so, for first this is a matter of life and death, eternal life and eternal death. Then, validated Scripture, and also existential validity, says that there is only *one Lord* and salvation is *only* through His Son. And again, though we evaluate religions in the context of either the Eternal Good or the Deceptive Evil, we are doing it *without the bigoted condemnation of the individuals of those faiths.* Jesus displayed love for the Canaanite woman and

117 praised her faith. He did not condemn her, but in his **One**
brief conversation with her He made clear what and
where truth was (Matt. 15:22-28).

Socio-anthropologists have found that often the more primitive a
people, the more likely were they to have ancient monotheistic beliefs.
Even extremely polytheistic Hinduism with its monistic base (contra-
diction of contradictions), has monotheistic elements in its ancient history, though this is mostly not readily acceptable to its radical proponents. Hinduism is an amalgam of the original religion of the Indus
Valley dwellers and the religion brought by the Aryan invaders. The
Aryan invaders were extreme nature worshipers, and hence they
brought with them their belief in a host of nature gods and goddesses.
The original religion of those who were already settled in the Indus valley had traces of monotheism in it.

However, the early monotheism was soon corrupted, and we
believe, and knowing *who* the deceiver is, that Satan diverted man
from being monotheistic to become worshipers of an unqualified,
unknowable, impersonal mono-deity. Then came nature worship and
its polytheism, leading to idolatry and worship of man-made gods! And
the mastermind was Satan. His purpose: to thwart the worship of the
Living God and to take man away from that worship.

Unger, in his book, *Demons in the World Today*, analyzes,
briefly, the Satanic and demonic influence over various individual religions, including Hinduism, Buddhism, Islam, Shintoism, Taoism, etc.
While acknowledging the possibility of some truth in the teachings of
these religions, his summation to this matter of religious pluralism is:

> It is quite obvious that fragments of truth are to be found in the
> prophetic repositories of pluralism. Those whom the apostle called
> to account for preaching "another gospel" are not said to complete-
> ly lack truth. But their message is adulterated and laced with errors,
> violating the essential criterion of the Word concerning the glorious
> Person and all-sufficiency of the finished redemption of Christ
> (1 Timothy 3:16; 1 John 2; 1, 2).[2]

But what then of the demonic side of these religions? How does
Satan control them? What can we see or know of his influence over
these faiths?

Satan the deceiver *keeps* people in blinded ignorance (ignorance
here meaning religious lack of knowledge) of the saving grace of the

---

[2] Unger, *Demons*, 158.

One Lord. Instead he uses magic, superstition, and occultic practices to enslave people. We see this as being very prominent in "primitive religions" as well as in others that are more organized and ordered. The power behind the "manifestations" that make people believe in the magic, etc., are demonic. Consider the following incidents I have seen or had repeated to me by authentic sources:

Satan uses magic, superstition, and occultic practices to enslave people.

Fire walking: *I could not get close to the fire pit. The heat generated from the hot and even blazing coals was too much for me to go close, but I was yet near enough to observe, **very** carefully how the devotees tiptoed over the coals, not a burn or a scar on their soles. Even the clothes they wore, saris down to the ankles, did not catch fire. And every time a devotee made the crossing, the chants and cries rose to a crescendo. Fascinating even to a preacher of the Word of God. Devilishly fascinating.*

Catch the egg: *From the experiences of my own father. The two Muslim "holy men" challenged each other's powers. An egg was produced and they "prayed" over it. Then the egg took off! It flew! It rose, it levitated, and it danced in the air, **out of reach** of the two men. And the chase began. Whoever caught it claimed the greater power. Who did? My father did not know. He knew the egg sailed through the air.*

Who is the thief? *A turkey was stolen from my friend's house. He was my classmate and did indulge in boyhood occultic practices. He and his brother went to the holy man of the local Hindu community and gave him a "betel" leaf, that broad leaf which many people chew as a pastime similar to chewing gum. The holy man chanted and prayed and wiped his hands over the leaf and, presto, the leaf became a TV screen. The event was in Real Player video. The betel leaf showed the action of the thief, how he stealthily entered their yard and stole the bird. When confronted, the thief admitted his crime and returned the bird.*

Taken over by a demon? *I stood before the little Hindu shrine and watched strange happenings. A bell was ringing in frustrating rhythm, ringing nonstop. A devotee stood before the blackened idol, and with hands*

crossed, grasping his ears, he began to chant strange words, or possibly just sounds. Together with this he began going around and around, just in one place, a kind of rotating shuffle. As I watched, he went on and on, his movements becoming faster and faster, almost going at a dizzy pace more and more. Onlookers gathered until eventually, when he could probably not go any faster, with a cry, either of anguish or giddiness, he collapsed onto the floor and his limbs began jerking. White froth oozed from his mouth, mingled with more "strange sounds." What was it? Just physical exhaustion (which it could very well have been)? Dizziness brought on by spinning? Or was it more than that? Was he for that moment and for that time possessed by demonic influence through the gods he sought to worship?

The above validated accounts and experiences (extremely mild in nature, for there are numerous others, much more dramatic and fantastic which could be cited) clearly point to the role and influence of the demonic world in non-Christian religions. As Christians we must have an awareness of this fact and also consider it when we reach out to the adherents with the gospel, and prepare ourselves for possible confrontation with the demonic world when we proclaim the saving truth of Jesus Christ. Faithful proclamation of the Word automatically opposes the lies and deceptions of Satan, and this raises the banners of battle ". . . against the rulers, against the powers, against the world forces of this darkness, against the spiritual forces of wickedness in the heavenly places" (Eph. 6:12, NASB).

Faithful proclamation of the Word automatically opposes the lies and deceptions of Satan.

We can, therefore, put forth three definite axioms and principles to help us properly relate to other religions, *keeping in mind their association with the demonic realm.*

1. There is really only *one* Sovereign Lord and God of this Universe. Satan is a usurper, and though he is "God of this world" (2 Cor. 4:4), yet he is given that role by permission of the *Lord God*. It is not a role that is equal to that of the eternal Alpha and Omega, our Creator and our God! Hence, any other gods or goddesses, whether they exist in the form of idols or other symbols, or just in the mind of man, and even if they are arrayed in the garb of monotheism, they are *really no-*

One

gods. If so, then whatever powers are displayed or privileges bestowed on followers, that has to be the work of the demonic forces of Satan.

The Scriptures reveal that the gods of the nations are *no-gods.* They are not realities in themselves. They are power-less to save their followers. In essence they are demons who manipulate the pagan god systems and actually receive the homage paid to the no-gods (Lev. 17:7; Deut. 32:17; Ps. 106:37, cf. 1 Cor. 10:20-21).[3]

2. Christianity alone truly represents what religion was meant to be, and this is done not through the efforts of its adherents, but rather from the work of Christ and divine self-revelation.[4]

3. While being aware of other religions, we should also con-sciously differentiate between the different religions. Our evaluation of these religions will be, of necessity, primarily negative, but we should still endeavor to see the distinctions that exist. Rommen says, "In the light of the disruptive impact of sin and Satan, all human religious expression will have to be viewed with skepticism. However, one will be ill-advised to simply declare as evil, demonically inspired, or ille-gitimate, every expression of human religiosity."

When there is conversion from a "pagan" religion to Christianity, that of course implies a change of allegiance. Those being converted must be encouraged to make a clean break. "Secret disciples" might help cultural situations and provide physical security, but conversion also involves an open confession (see Rom. 10:8-10) and demonstra-tion that the convert now has a new Lord and Master of his or her life. In this way those demonic forces that influence and empower false reli-gions are rebuked by the new convert. Warner says, "A break with any ungodly spiritual heritage and establishing one's spiritual inheritance based on adoption into God's family ought to be a part of the conver-sion process anywhere."[5]

---

[3] Murphy, *Handbook,* 10.

[4] I am indebted to Edward Rommen for this concept which is part of his synthesis of various articles concerning "A Biblical Theology of World Religions," in the special journal of the Evangelical Missiological Society. (Edward Rommen and Harold Netland, eds., *Evangelical Missiological Society Series Number 8* [Pasadena, CA: Wm. Carey Library, 1995] 246ff.).

[5] Warner, *Spiritual Warfare,* 121.

ADDENDUM TWO
CHRISTIANS AND DEMONS

A constant question asked by concerned Christians is, can a Christian be demon-possessed? We go further back and ask, to what extent can there be contact and conflict between Satan and his demons on one hand and Christians on the other? To answer the latter would of necessity provide an answer to the former question. But in answering these questions and solving the problems that accompany them, we need to consider the nature of both demons and Christians themselves. And we also should go back to the time of creation, and see how Satan *did* influence our Garden of Eden ancestors, Adam and Eve, then.

However, there is another area that needs to be addressed, and that is the surprising naïveté of many Christians. There appears to be a general tendency to underestimate demonic existence, demonic activities, and demonic involvement with Christians. Spiritual reason demands that as Christians we be conscious of the myriads of temptations that assault our thinking processes, and Scripture is full of warnings concerning this. Scripture also assures us that the Lord God, being transcendentally and morally pure and holy, does not tempt anyone. Ergo, temptation then has to be of the Evil One and his agents. So to start out with, Christians, all of them, are items in demonic agendas, destined to be tempted by the devil.

An obedient and faithful Christian is Satan's "thorn in the flesh" and is a bane to demons.

At the same time Christians should have the confidence that they can stand firm against all the "wiles" of the devil (Eph. 6:12, KJV). An obedient and faithful Christian is Satan's "thorn in the flesh" and is a bane to demons. As Unger, who changed his original conceptions that Christians cannot be demon controlled to one of affirming that possibility, says, "He [Satan] also knows and recognizes those who count on their position in Christ and who find and fulfill God's will for

Two their lives. These saints are what the devil fears most, **122** for they constitute the deadliest threat to his plans and ambitions."[1]

As in other parts of this book, we need to be specific with terminology used. One related question therefore would be, what do we mean by possession? In Part III of this book we have spoken concerning demonic influence and demonic possession, and so on. We will reiterate what we said there in this section; but remember, we should not underestimate demonic power; neither should Christians fear it.

Possession implies ownership, and Satan owns, and can own, nothing. The Creator God is the owner of all things, and Satan might have some authority and control over this world of ours being its Prince, but he does not own it. Thus he cannot possess or own human beings. Again, thus, possession is a word not very appropriate for the concept involved. A better word, general no doubt but adequate in many ways, is the word "demonization." The word "demonization" is derived from the Greek word *daimonizomai*, which is translated loosely in the KJV and other early versions as "demon possessed"; many modern versions continue with that translation. However, the idea of possession in terms of ownership is absent in the Greek connotation.

When creation was in its dawn and God's foremost creation, man, was in very close communion with his Creator God and when all things were pure and sinless in the human race, Satan came around seeking to deceive man and thwart God's perfection. Why? Man is the Lord's crown of creation in whom He bestowed His image, and Satan sought to attack where it hurt the most. Man became, and was and still is, the prime focus of the evil forces in our world. Man finds himself the prey which Satan and his forces seek to destroy (1 Pet. 5:8). And he succeeded in deceiving Adam and Eve, *even while they were in intimate fellowship with God, and being provided for and protected in the Eden of the Lord.*

We find later that a man described as "a man after God's own heart" succumbs to temptation, is manipulated by his own thinking to murder, and follows it up with lies. How can this be? Was not King David, the Lord's chosen? Did not David lead a life of uprightness? Though we answer yes to those questions, we can see how Satan tempted and led him on to adultery and murder. We *must* realize that behind the sad story of the Davidic sinning was the hand of the evil one. The Bible makes it clear that the Lord tempts nobody (Jas. 1:13).

---

[1] Unger, *What Demons Can Do*, 18.

123 But again, Satan tempted and influenced David, **Two** *though he was special to the Lord, in communion with* Him, *and even exalted by the Creator Himself.*

The Bible makes it clear that the Lord tempts nobody.

Scripture makes it clear that when men try to live godly lives they will suffer for it (2 Tim. 3:12). Why? Because Satan uses his cunning to make man deviate from the path of holiness and fall into his trap of deception and falsehood. So again, it is the believer that suffers the brunt of Satanic attacks.

We can add on other specific scriptural examples like Simon the sorcerer in Acts 8. He started out as a believer, being part of those baptized through the preaching of the evangelist Philip (Acts 8:13). But evil entered his heart, and he sought to gain miraculous powers through unrighteous and ungodly means. Who tempted him to this? Who assaulted his newfound faith? It had to be the work of the evil one. And so Simon was influenced to do evil *even though he was a Christian.* After Simon's sin the apostle Peter admonishes him to repent, for Simon, though a baptized believer, was so empowered by evil forces that he *lost his faith.* Thus Peter declares, prophetically of course, that Simon was ". . . in the gall of bitterness and in the bondage of iniquity" (Acts 8:23).

Similarly, we can look at the case of Ananias and Sapphira, obedient believers in the church in Jerusalem, who lost their faith and their very lives for allowing demonic temptation to prompt them to sin against the Living Lord. The apostle Peter addresses Ananias with these words, "Ananias, why has Satan filled your heart to lie to the Holy Spirit . . . ?" (Acts 5:3, NASB). Not only did Satan fill Ananias's heart, Satan also influenced Ananias to lie to the Holy Spirit, who was *already in Ananias's heart.*

We conclude therefore that it is possible for demons to influence, oppress, and control Christians.

Demons Can Influence Christians

We must never ever forget that Satan's main, and in some ways most effective, tool and weapon is deception. Deception formed the core of his attack on Adam and Eve. Scriptures abound where Satan is referred to as a deceiver, a liar, a usurper, a schemer, etc. Ephesians 6:11 warns us against the "schemes" of the devil. He is cunning and the KJV word "wiles" is an apt description of his modus operandi.

Two   But what area of man's psyche does Satan most **124** concentrate on to deceive him? It is that area in which man feels the image-of-God impulse to worship what is beyond him. Romans 1 makes it clear that in this area of man's being he fell to worshiping the created things rather than the Creator Himself. Behind it we can see Satan's hand, for he used material things to lead astray Adam and Eve.

In the book of James we read of demonic wisdom (Jas. 3:15). Demonic wisdom might appear logical and philosophical, but beneath it all we should look for the seeds of deception. Hence, we should not treat lightly areas of deception such as false teaching, false religions, cults, wrong doctrine, etc. In all of these and more, we find the mind of the Christian being demonized, and Scripture does make reference to it. In 2 Corinthians 11:3 Paul warns Christians in Corinth about having their minds corrupted by Satanic influence. "But I am afraid, lest as the serpent deceived by his craftiness, your minds should be led astray from the simplicity and purity of devotion to Christ" (NASB). Paul makes a direct analogy between how Satan turned away or corrupted Eve's mind and how Christians could have their minds turned away or corrupted.

Demonic wisdom might appear logical, but beneath it all we should look for the seeds of deception.

Corruption of the mind of a Spirit-filled Christian can only be accomplished by demonic invasion. The corruption that comes from Beelzebub, the Prince of Decay, is implanted in the mind. "Mind corruption" in a Christian is a very serious thing, and a Christian who is under this kind of satanic attack is not helped by being told "he cannot have a demon."[2]

Unger explains how even seemingly minor wrong doctrine can be demonically influenced.

But many demons are nice, refined, religious and "good" in a self-righteous sense. They are perfectly at home in a religion that rejects the gospel of salvation by faith and substitutes the devil's false gospel of salvation by works and extols human goodness as procuring acceptance before God (cf. 1 Tim. 4:1-2).[3]

[2] H.A. Maxwell Whyte, *A Manual on Exorcism* (Springdale, PA: Whitaker House, 1974) 41.
[3] Unger, *What Demons Can Do*, 116.

125 Christians must be aware of how demons can alter **Two** their thinking so that they give in to false teachings. The process is alarmingly simple. An interpolation, or a decidedly wrong interpretation, or an omission to please the crowd, or an addition to create popularity, whatever it is, you can assume rather correctly that such is demonically influenced.

Christians must be aware of how demons can alter their thinking so that they give in to false teachings.

Christians must be aware of how demons can alter their thinking so that they give in to false teachings.

Let us not forget that one of Satan's tactics involves false signs and wonders so much so the very elect can be fooled. "For false Christs and false prophets will arise and will show great signs and wonders, so as to mislead, if possible, even the elect" (Matt. 24:24, NASB). Some of these are being performed on television screens, on public platforms, and on computer monitors. False miracles, false tongues, and false deliverances.

False Miracles

The proliferation today of miracle workers and miracle doers is seemingly an indication of the accelerated work of Satan. But how do we know if a work is of Satan or not? In a country like India, we are aware, and have seen signs and wonders that were definitely *not* of the Lord God, and equally definitely were of the devil. How else can we explain mounds of sweets appearing at a click of the fingers? (Happens to one particular "god-man" constantly.) But what about those who perform signs and wonders with the Bible flashed about?

One sure test to evaluate such miracles, particularly "miraculous healings," is to determine if *any part of the Word of God is denied or rejected or grossly misinterpreted*. "The first test in discovering whether a miracle is of God involves God's Word. God will not work a miracle in support of a teaching that opposes his holy Word."[4]

One sure test to evaluate miracles is to determine if any part of the Word of God is denied or rejected.

We need not have to look far afield for a demonstration of such miracles. Turn the television on and see the "healed" convulse and roll on the stage or have the healer scream like a banshee or burst into sounds unheard of before, and you would know that it cannot be of God. We should consequently be aware of demonic forces behind it,

[4] Edward N. Gross, *Miracles, Demons and Spiritual Warfare* (Grand Rapids: Baker, 1990) 78.

Two for when God's Word is deliberately violated, that vio- **126** lation has to be motivated by demonic powers.

Other such miracles are widely publicized including special knowledge, flashes of insight, visions, dreams, and such like. It is surprising how many prominent "Christian leaders" have claimed extrabiblical knowledge and insight.

False Tongues

The problem of tongues has been around for centuries, or rather, the problem whether speaking in tongues is of God or not is an almost perennial problem. Here we cannot elaborate on this subject beyond seeing if any demonic influence can possibly cause Christians to burst forth into speaking strange sounds or languages. Scripture explains the experience of glossolalia as speaking in another language and always with a purpose in mind, particularly that of proclaiming His Word. Whether tongues are valid today or not is an issue for another area of investigation, but experience shows that it can be used by demons.

False Deliverance

This might sound strange, for we are aware of how a house divided against itself cannot stand, but false deliverance occurs when false preachers, false deliverers, and spiritually oriented fakes participate in and claim deliverance from demons. Scripture warns us of the return of demonic spirits to the same "dwelling," and often false deliverance eventually leads to enhanced demonic control.

Unger refers to demonic influence as being a mild form of demonization. But even if the terminology points to just a casual bout with demonic forces, Christians need to be on guard against demonic schemes and plans that he uses to influence them further.

Demons Can Oppress Christians

Unger would refer to this as stronger forms of demonic influence, but the emphasis is on the word "oppress." Demonic oppression comes in various forms. Christians become subject to all kinds of sinful practices and these in turn lead to obsessive behavior, addictions, and compulsive activity.

One of the most common examples of this is the addictive nature of pornography. Where porn is considered by many as a personal choice experience and harms no other person, it cannot be either totally condemned or considered evil. The fallacies of this view are many,

127 the foremost being that pornography may not harm the **Two**
viewer (stated just theoretically), but it certainly vic-
timizes those who are often forced into performances to provide the viewers with their "entertainment." But is this of demons? As
mentioned in an earlier section, the whole matter of child abuse being
of demons is a valid example here; for a child, porn in all its filthiness
and perverted nature can only be of demonic influence.

When any habit is compulsive and *the compulsion destroys a
Christian's desire to be holy and promotes guilt that in turn hurts his
relationship with Christ and other Christians, then that compulsion has
to be of the Evil One.* Here again we revert to Satan's main weapon,
deception, and his main goal to thwart God's agenda and thereby to
prevent people coming to the Lord. Addiction and obsession cause
Christians to deviate from fulfilling the Lord's agenda for their lives, and
this then is a kind of demonic oppression.

When any compulsive habit hurts a Christian's relationship with Christ and other Christians, that compulsion has to be of the Evil One.

Pornography at its simplest invades a person with guilt whereas
Christ came to take away our guilt. Porn is so addictive that time and
money and mental activity spent on it takes away from using that time
and giving that money and involving one's brain for the things of God.
And at its worst pornography leads to crime, particularly violence and
inhuman and indecent treatment of other human beings who are, like
Christians, also created in the image of God. And can any person, perhaps limiting that to men, claim and prove that the magnetic pull of
pornography has never affected them?

While pornography is a good example of demonic oppression
through compulsion, addiction, and obsession, there are others with
the same magnetic attractions. This would include drugs, alcohol,
compulsive acquisition of material things, among others.

But oppression goes much further than just addictive behavior.
Oppression is seen in Christians who have suicidal tendencies despite
having tasted the Lord's acceptance and forgiveness. Chronic depression, which is often a sign of suicidal tendencies, is sometimes a clear
symptom of demonic oppression. And other mind-involving disturbances or diseases can be the result of demonic oppression such as
split personalities (with an evil, immoral, obnoxious personality being
one of them), insanity, and related "illnesses." But here we caution that

Two we do not diagnose mental situations caused by chemical imbalance, hereditary causes, and the like, as being demonic oppression. Related to the mind are other situations such as inability to discern the truth of God's Word, being prone to blasphemy and filthy speech, a constant negative attitude that spreads out to other believers, and so forth.

Demonic oppression almost always displays itself in violence. Uncontrollable rage and tendencies to cause harm to others, particularly loved ones, are indicative of possible demonic oppression. This of course includes harming one's own body and usually doing so in a way that blood is very evident. This is a common occurrence with false religious teachers and leaders who are obviously under demonic control.

Many diseases can be attributed to demonic control, for as we have seen in other sections, demons do attack the body. With the Lord's permission, Satan attacked and oppressed Job's body with vile, painful, and despicable diseases.

Demons can pass from one level of involvement to another in a believer's life.

Note that we are talking about demonic oppression, which implies that demons can pass from one level of involvement to another in a believer's life. However, we must never forget that it is *we* who open the doors to demonic influence and oppression. We are in charge and we choose to allow these things to happen.

Demons Can Control Christians

This is where the controversy exists and continues. And this is where terminology plays a vital role. We do not use the term "demon possession," for as said earlier, Satan owns nothing. He cannot possess what is not given to him. He became Prince of this world by being given permission to be so. His tenure as Prince of this world is limited, and his end is destined. Meanwhile he strives to control and hold sway over his most prized prey, the saints of God.

How can this be when the Holy Spirit indwells Christians who are obedient believers (Acts 2:38)? To understand this better we should understand what it means to have the Holy Spirit dwell in us. And in this, spiritual logic and reason should guide us.

The Holy Spirit is Spirit. He is a Person but a Divine Spirit Person. He does not occupy space. He cannot be termed as being spatial. Similarly, we read in Scripture of being "filled" with the fullness of

129 God (Eph. 3:20). And in the same chapter Paul talks **Two**
about Christ "dwelling" in our hearts through faith
(Eph. 3:17). And many other passages use similar language.
Now nobody would insist that this is literal or spatial or such like. To
best understand these Scriptures we must take them as being figurative,
and in the cited cases they are metaphorical. But the meaning and
intent behind this spatial language is the concept of control and dominion and authority. And when the Holy Spirit "indwells" us, He controls
and dominates us, or He should control us and have authority over us.

Yet Paul says that within himself two natures exist. The Holy
Spirit strives to have His nature supersede ours so that our human (originally earthly) nature be conformed to His nature. But this coexistence
is conflicting. Our residual carnal nature wars against the new imputed nature of the Holy Spirit. Paul's anguish concerning this is poignant-
ly recorded in Romans 7, where he refers to himself as a "wretched
man." And in Galatians 5:17 Paul articulates the dilemma further. "For
the sinful nature desires what is contrary to the Spirit, and the Spirit
what is contrary to the sinful nature. They are in conflict with each
other, so that you do not do what you want" (NIV).

Our residual carnal nature wars against the new imputed nature of the Holy Spirit.

The clear inferences and deductions and, to me, conclusions are
that we are not spatially invaded by demons just as the Holy Spirit does
not spatially occupy our flesh-and-blood body. But even as the Holy
Spirit works in us to control our natural corrupt natures (or spirits), so
does that nature rebel and prompt us to sin. Sin is of the devil. Sin is
what demons want us to indulge in. Hence, the conflict goes on *within the confines of one person, a Christian person.* Therefore we say that
Christians can be controlled by demons. And if you like the word "possess" so be it, but I do not believe that demons could own us.

> The Bible clearly conceives of the possibility that a Christian may
> allow an evil force to have a controlling and dominating influence in
> his or her life. The apostle Paul admonishes the believers in Rome,
> "Do not let sin reign in your mortal body so that you obey its evil
> desires" (Rom. 6:12). Paul viewed sin as an incredibly powerful evil
> force that once held believers in slavery and apart from God. This
> evil power does not vanish when one becomes a Christian.[5]

---

[5] Arnold, *Three Crucial Questions,* 89.

Two   We must therefore be alert and on guard. We   **130** need God's armor. We need to stand firm. We need to resist. We need to battle against all temptations and evil desires. We need to realize who our real enemy is.

And how do we know a Christian is under the control and domination of demonic forces and hence demonized?

Here again we must remember that Satan's chief weapon is deception. Hence the demonized Christian would advocate deceptive teachings, and legalize deceptive behavior and pursue deceptive goals. These will indicate the extent to which the Christian has given in to the influence of demonic forces. The outward symptoms would be unbridled sin, flagrant violation of Scripture, despicable and ungodly behavior, and justification of an evil lifestyle.

In addition there can be at times the various physical manifestations of demonic control cited earlier: supernatural demonstrations of different kinds, direct denial of the Lordship of Christ, and strong opposition and criticism of the Kingdom of God.

In our multireligious land and culture we see Christians deliberately compromising their faith with those of false religions, compromising the gospel's plain teachings, refraining from proclaiming God's Word when it is necessary to do so, and even worshiping and bowing before the idolatrous symbols of these false faiths. Can we not see demonic control behind all of this?

What Can Be Done?

Throughout the New Testament we are taught how to withstand such demonic invasions. The injunctions are simple, but they must be strictly and sincerely and prayerfully carried out in our daily living. And this can only happen when we are conscious of who the enemy is.

1. Stay close to the Lord at all times. James clearly admonishes us in this (Jas. 4:7). Let the Word of God dwell in you. Let prayer be your watchword. Walk in the ways of the Spirit and deny thereby the way of the flesh.
2. Close any doors that might let demons in. Avoid areas of weakness.
3. In every way resist the devil with the armor of God.
4. Stay secure within the protective community of the Kingdom of God.
5. Focus on your strength and resources in Christ.
6. Have a mind-set of victory.

ADDENDUM THREE

AN INQUIRY INTO THE SUBJECT OF TERRITORIAL SPIRITS AND STRATEGIC-LEVEL SPIRITUAL WARFARE

What are territorial spirits and why is there so much interest in the subject today? One possible reason is the general interest in demons and demonology, some of that interest being serious in intent, from a spiritual as well as nonspiritual and academic perspective. In the same vein, interest in demons and extraterrestrial beings, as well as supernatural creatures, has greatly increased as evidenced by the numerous movies, both with human actors and with animated cartoon characters, that promote the conflict between the forces of good and the forces of evil. Similarly, the obsession of both young and old with books such as the Harry Potter series indicates that people are, at present at least, displaying a sharp curiosity about the realm of evil. However, even though these are possible indications, they are so only in a remote kind of a way. The interest in the subject of territorial spirits stems from the recent concentration of literature dealing with spiritual warfare, with overcoming demonic influence over both institutions and geographical areas. Noted Christian authors from various streams of theology have focused on the subject with an almost fanatical zeal.

There is an assumption drawn from Hebrews 2:5 that the Lord has put this present world under the rulership of angelic beings. The verse says, "For He did not subject to angels the world to come, concerning which we are speaking . . ." (NASB). The supposition is that, since it says the world to come is *not* under angelic rulers, we can presume that this world is under their rule. However, regardless of the interpretation of this verse, we cannot deduce from it that specific geographical areas and countries and nations are under the authority of certain fallen angels, and that those angels are of certain rank.

We know that Satan strives to be like God as well as to usurp His place and authority. But Satan is not like God, and therefore he is not omnipresent. Hence, Satan cannot be at several places at the same time. Naturally, and logically, he uses his demonic forces to carry out

Three his assigned tasks. The issue is not whether demons operate over definite areas or have tasks related to exact nations or other geopolitical entities, but whether these are ruling spirits who need to be discerned and determined by name, rank, authority, etc., and then, through warfare techniques, driven out before the Lord's Church can gain a foothold and become a moving and growing spiritual enterprise.

But what is meant by the term, "territorial spirits"? A clear, unambiguous definition is not given by the proponents of territorial spirits. Demons are classified as per their powers and given authorities, by their abilities and functions, and a host of other distinctives. But the term "territorial" refers mostly to a geographical area, so from a literary viewpoint, territorial spirits are spirits that are confined to a particular geographical territory. However, that kind of explanation does not do justice to the whole concept and context of territorial spirits. In analysis, territorial spirits not only have geographical boundaries and related assigned functions, but they can also be geopolitical in nature. In this way they affect national attitudes and behavior, political institutions, nationalistic psyche, as well as having other jurisdictions such as geographical topography, i.e., mountains, lakes, and rivers, and also objects such as buildings and idols under their command. Peter Wagner, the acknowledged specialist in the subject, divides demons into three categories: "ground-level, occult-level and strategic-level."[1]

Peter Wagner divides demons into three categories.

Chuck Lowe, questioning such categorization, defines the term "territorial spirits" in an almost negative way:

> At first blush the term seems self-explanatory: these are demons who rule over specific geographical regions. They are "geographically located", exercise authority within "assigned areas", and have "geographical limits" for their power.[2]

Terminology

In keeping with the assumption of territorial spirits, a new terminology has developed, and this terminology has been made more popular and put into common usage through the use of acronyms.

[1] C. Peter Wagner, ed. *Engaging the Enemy: How to Fight and Defeat Territorial Spirits* (Ventura, CA: Regal Books, 1991) 20.
[2] Chuck Lowe, *Territorial Spirits and World Evangelisation* (Seven Oaks, Kent, Great Britain: OMF/Mentor, 1998) 18.

Territorial Spirits A definition is given above, **Three**
but territorial spirits are also sometimes referred to
as Strategic-Level Spirits.

Spiritual Warfare Literally this should mean, and it does mean
so, any kind of resistance and aggression between man and the demonic world. It has come to mean much more. Today the term "spiritual
warfare" implies a special ministry, focusing on deliverance of demonized persons from demons, exorcism, spiritual "mapping," etc.

Spiritual Mapping This term was coined by George Otis Jr., who
was president of an organization called the Sentinel Group. Otis col-
laborated with Peter Wagner in many ways, and he defines spiritual
mapping as, "superimposing our understanding of forces and events in
the spiritual domain onto places and circumstances in the material
world."[3] The extreme form of spiritual mapping involves a literal "mapping" of a specified geographical area, delineating sections by drawing
lines, making graphs, specifying corridors of action, etc.

SWN—Spiritual Warfare Network As its name implies, this is
a network group of persons and institutions involved in spiritual warfare analysis and promotion.

SLWS—Strategic-Level Spiritual Warfare This is Peter Wagner's
forte and *pièce de résistance* of his emphasis on the necessity and reality of spiritual warfare as a ministry. This involves military-like terminology and strategy. It imputes a battle scenario to the conflict between
the demonic world and the people of God. It has a basic threefold
approach: "(1) Discern the territorial spirits assigned to the city, (2) deal
with the corporate sin of a city or an area, and (3) engage in aggressive
"warfare prayer" against the territorial spirits."[4]

Exponents of SLWS believe that ordinary opposition to the
demonic world is not enough. A war atmosphere is needed, including
specific prayer focused on demonic control over areas, personal prayer
walks around the affected areas, authoritative cleansing programs and
services, and aggressive driving out of demons.

Warfare Prayer Those who believe that Christians should
engage territorial spirits in warfare, also advocate warfare prayer.
Warfare prayer goes beyond "ordinary" prayer, and is a form of aggression against the enemy. It is going on the offensive rather than defend-
ing oneself. It involves confronting demons, challenging them by

---

[3] This definition by Otis is quoted in *Three Crucial Questions about Spiritual Warfare*
by Clinton E. Arnold, and published by Baker Books in 1997.
[4] Arnold, *Three Crucial Questions*, 146.

Three name, and praying with power and authority to get
them out of a territory. Again, Peter Wagner is the
guru of warfare prayer, and some of his assertions and
those of his colleagues are quoted by Chuck Lowe:

> . . . those who practice SLSW are "able to free the cities and
> nations of the world for the powers of darkness in order to ready
> them for spiritual harvest. . . . Our prayers will release regions from
> the influence of these powers for a season while we go in and har-
> vest. . . .
>
> The prayer of a human being can alter history by releasing
> legions of angels into the earth. SLSW helped to bring down the
> Berlin Wall, open Albania to the gospel, depose Manuel Noriega,
> lower the crime rate of Los Angeles during the 1984 Olympics,
> revive the economy of Argentina, and break the power of the
> demons over Japan.[5]

Territorial Spirits in Scripture

Does the Bible validate the teachings of those who practice
SLWS? Is there a "Thus saith the Lord," for some of the concepts con-
veyed by the proponents of SLWS? Are there examples, or other support, found in the Bible to preach and teach concerning territorial
demons and SLWS? The passage which most readily comes to mind,
and the favorite Scripture for the advocates of "territorial spirits," is
found in the book of Daniel. Daniel is confronted by an interpreting
angel (Gabriel?) and told that he was delayed in coming to help Daniel
because the "Prince of the Kingdom of Persia" was resisting him, and
that Michael, the Archangel of God, came to help him overcome the
Prince of Persia (Dan. 10:13-16).

Later in the same chapter the angel tells Daniel that he must
leave him and go and fight again with the Prince of Persia, and then
with the Prince of Greece as well. "Do you understand why I came to
you? But I shall now return to fight against the prince of Persia; so I am
going forth, and behold, the prince of Greece is about to come" (Dan.
10:20, NASB).

In the passages cited from Daniel one key point is the use of the
word "Prince." This term is used to refer to whoever was opposing the
angel who was to help Daniel, and the same word is used to refer to

---

[5] Lowe, *Territorial Spirits*, 24. Lowe not only quotes Wagner, but also SLWS promot-
ers, Dawson and Otis.

135 Michael the Archangel of God. The conclusion **Three**
therefore is that since Michael is referred to as a
prince and is an angelic being, then the prince of Persia
must also be an angelic being, albeit an evil one.

There seems to be an almost overwhelming consensus among
Bible scholars that the Princes of Persia and Greece are references to
demonic beings who had authority and power to act in those nations.
Though this is probably a good hermeneutic of the passages referred to
in Daniel, there are some valid questions involved here. Were the
"princes," being demonic powers, territorial spirits? Were they limited
by geographical boundaries, or did they have those powers and authority over national identities? What happened when the kingdoms were
wiped out and abolished? And if the two kingdoms were in conflict
with each other, did the demons promote the kingdoms they "controlled" and consequently oppose each other? Is the whole concept of
territorial spirits and SLSW and warfare prayer dependent only on the
Daniel passages?

What happened when the kingdoms were wiped out, and did the demons oppose each other?

We have already seen elsewhere that terminology is of importance in trying to understand the realm and work and functions of
demons. And the term, "territorial spirits" of necessity limits the work
and functions of these princes to the geographical territories of Persia
and Greece. It is valid to assume that when a nation or geographical
entity lost its identity, then these demonic powers shifted to other "territories." Assuming that, then the demonic forces in authority and power
over the old Soviet Union were completely redistributed when that great
nation was split up into a number of smaller nations or territories.
Possible, yes, but that involves the quick change of demonic hierarchy.
So the question is not whether the princes of Persia and Greece were
working in the territories of Persia and Greece, but rather, *does that
imply a total territorial hierarchy of all demonic forces, or a complete
"mapping" out of the world into areas assigned to specific demons?*

The answers may never be conclusive, but it is valid to pose the
above questions to those who use the Daniel passages to create the
elaborate SLWS scheme.

But are there not other passages that warrant the concept of territorial spirits? The Old Testament often does refer to the gods of the
nations as being demonic. And demons are the powers behind idolatry

Three (Lev. 17:7; Deut. 32:17; Ps. 106:36; etc.). There are
also passages from which we can very reasonably
assume that demonic powers were behind the worship of
strange gods (1 Kgs. 14:23; 2 Kgs. 1:2; Isa. 24:21-22; etc.). But nowhere
in the Old Testament is there any clear indication that demonic powers
had territorial authority and ruling tutelage over nations. Demons did
influence and use nations, as in the case of many of the Canaanite gods
who were certainly under demonic influence, but other than the book
of Daniel, we do not find reference to demonic forces holding complete,
assigned, and authorized sway over specific areas or nations.

Nowhere in the NT is there reference to the type of rulers deduced from the book of Daniel.

The New Testament mentions conflicts with demonic spirits and
forces in the ministry of Christ, as well as in the ministries of the Apostles
as recorded in the book of Acts. But nowhere is there direct and clear
reference to the type of territorial spirit rulers as deduced from the book
of Daniel. Demons, in the New Testament, are seen as spirits that concentrate on individual men, oppressing and controlling them. The book
of Revelation has a passage that refers to the dwelling place of Satan.
We read about the church in Pergamum, a city "where Satan lives."

> I know where you live—where Satan has his throne. Yet you remain
> true to my name. You did not renounce your faith in me, even in the
> days of Antipas, my faithful witness, who was put to death in your
> city—where Satan lives (Rev. 2:13-14, NASB).

To put that passage in the perspective of territorial spirit advocates and those who promote SLWS, Satan, like the Prince of Persia and
the Prince of Greece, is the authority and power over Pergamum. But
that is positively not the case, for Satan is not limited to staying in one
place, even though he is not omnipresent. When the Lord God confronted him in the councils of heaven, he declared that he had been
". . . roaming through the earth and going back and forth in it" (Job 1:7,
NASB). So, to limit Satan to a geographical area is not in keeping with
Satan's nature and task goal which is to deceive mankind and turn man
away from the Living God. And logically, if Satan is limited, or was
limited, to Pergamum, then the rest of the world would have been
free of his evil influence, and that is not so. The reference to Satan's
throne probably alludes to the fact that Pergamum was the official
center of Emperor Worship. Again, in Revelation, there is the mention
of Babylon attracting demons and evil spirits (Rev. 18:2), but that could

137 hardly be seen as implying territorial demonic Three rulers.

The early Church has left little or no records that pertain to the type of spiritual warfare being endorsed today, nor is there any substantial reference to any demonic elements that closely resemble the modern concept of territorial spirits.

A conclusion based on Scripture alone would state that, apart from the reference in Daniel to the Princes of Persia and Greece, there is really nothing else of real impact to support the concept of territorial spirits, who have absolute authority and power over both geographical areas and national entities. The Princes of Persia and Greece, demonic forces evidently, were there for the cause of opposing, at that time, the work of the Lord, and this could have direct implication where the life and work of Daniel himself was concerned. Further, the Daniel passages, though they might clearly imply demonic forces, even they do not sufficiently substantiate the whole theory and theories behind SLSW and its other related emphases.

Spiritual Warfare

While we question the theories and assumptions of those who preach Strategic-Level Spiritual Warfare (SLSW), we cannot lower our guard and pretend that all is well with the world. There *is* a war going on, manifest on earth with man and his soul as the choice prize, and being acted and fought out in the heavenly realms, a cosmic battle between the forces of good and evil. The Apostle Paul makes that clear when warning us to be aware that ". . . our struggle is not against flesh and blood, but against the rulers, against the powers, against the world forces of the darkness, against the spiritual forces of wickedness in the heavenly places" (Eph. 6:12, NASB). Our seemingly innocent problems in the Church by which we endeavor to put down wrong doctrine and schisms and divisions and so on, have their counterpart in the heavenly struggle. We must be conscious of who the real enemy is. Behind the earthly battles against immorality and addictions and national prejudices lies the influence of the world of evil.

A war is going on with man as the choice prize.

The Ephesians passage does not immediately imply a ranking hierarchy. Yet this is assumed, and the classifications are analyzed and their roles evaluated. Peter Wagner comments on what Mark Bubeck says about this:

Three Mark I. Bubeck sees Satan as the commander-in-chief of the forces of darkness, leading a hierarchical structure of evil spirits. The most powerful are *principalities* or *princes*. Bubeck understands them to have vast power and a certain degree of independence of action. Under them are *powers* "probably more numerous and somewhat less independent and powerful than the princes." Next are the *rulers of darkness* who serve as lower grade officers. Finally come the *wicked spirits* or *demons*.[6]

Wagner and Bubeck have neatly distinguished between the ranks and authority of the fallen angels in a manner bespeaking that of a five-star general. Though the plausibility of demonic ranks is there, yet the sharp military-like analysis of Ephesians 6:12 does not make for good hermeneutics.

Strategic-Level Spiritual Warfare

The strategy of SLSW is at first glance seemingly simple, but it involves much more than mere confrontations with demonic forces. The steps normally used in SLSW explain their tactics. These include (though not in this order necessarily):

a. Discerning the identity of the spirits including their names.
b. Determining their territory and their authority.
c. Mapping out their strongholds and geographical areas.
d. Specific prayer against the spirits, sometimes including prayer walks around cities, etc.
e. Confronting the spirits and binding them, rebuking them, commanding them to leave.
f. Utilizing praise as a weapon against reentry.

But we must strive to avoid the desire to create sensation and glamorize our daily fight with evil. We are in a war, but let us not seek to fight it with media lights glaring nor seek to do it all in prime time!! Therefore, we question some of these chief elements of SLSW:

1. Discerning who the demon/demons are and finding out what territory they rule. Nowhere in Scripture are we asked to find out demonic names. The term "Legion" with connection to the Gerasene demoniac (Mark 5:9) is explained by the demon himself as meaning "many" or "numerous." Though Jesus did ask the name of the demon, *Jesus did not have to since He was God and there-*

C. Peter Wagner, ed., "Territorial Spirits," in *Territorial Spirits* (Secunderabad, India: Ben Publishing, 1991) 48. Quotes of Bubeck are from *The Adversary*, 72, 73.

139 *fore* omniscient. Demanding names and territories **Three**
are not commanded anywhere.

In the case of Daniel we find a good example
of how to deal with conflicts with the demonic world. First, we
must realize that Daniel was, to a certain degree, not fully aware
of the specifics of the confrontation. He never demanded names
or territories. He was given information, without requesting it,
regarding the Princes of Persia and Greece. His methods of opposing evil forces were prayer—constant prayer—and holy living, as
we find from Daniel 1. Nowhere in the book of Daniel or elsewhere in the Bible is there any injunction given to us to discern
names, ranks, territories, etc. of demonic beings.

Daniel's methods were prayer and holy living.

2. Spiritual mapping is at best a very earthly enterprise, for given
   the supernatural nature of demonic beings, locating them with
   well-defined boundaries seems futile.
3. We are not given authority to "bind" demons or "evict" them
   from certain territories. Jesus gave the seventy the authority "over
   all the power of the enemy" (Luke 10:19). Interestingly, in the
   very next verse, verse 20, He forbids them to "rejoice" over the
   utilization of this authority, something that a lot of SLSW advocates forget. And more importantly, this authority was to drive
   out demons from individuals, not geographical areas. All Jesus'
   teaching to us concerning confronting demonic powers deals
   with bringing individuals to His saving grace and freeing them
   from evil powers.
4. Sometimes SLSW seems almost consorting with demonic forces
   —talk to them, demand their names, bargain with them to leave,
   command and rebuke them, and so on. We have the security
   and support and authority of Him who is far above all the forces
   of evil, and our attitude should be one of victory already gained,
   gained through the Cross and the Resurrection of Jesus. We stand
   firm as Paul admonishes us to *withstand demonic attacks not to
   attack them.* They have already been attacked and defeated!!

Our attitude should be one of victory already gained.

5. Warfare prayer seems to indicate that there are levels of prayer
   and certain levels evoke certain responses. We are commanded
   to pray, to pray without ceasing, to pray fervently, but prayer is
   not commanding spirits to leave cities and nations.

6. The whole ethic and enterprise of Strategic-Level **140**
Spiritual Warfare is human-oriented. We plan,
we strategize, we attack, we pray, we throw out. On
the other hand in that classic and oft-repeated teaching by Paul
in Ephesians 6, we are told that we are to be "strong in the Lord"
and "in the strength of His might" (6:10). The armor and protection is of and from the Lord, hence the "armor of God." We overcome in His name, and with His power, with His authority, and
we leave the strategy and the battle up to Him, for we know in
His Name we shall prevail!!!

Clinton Arnold gives us a few helps in this whole matter of SLSW.
Without elaborating on them I cite them below:

- Some biblical passages sound a note of caution. See Jude 8,
  2 Peter 2:10-11.
- We do not find Jesus, Peter, John, James, or Paul ever attempting
  to take on a territorial spirit.
- We do not have the right to tell a spirit to leave if it has an open
  invitation to stay. (When a people or a nation indulge in evil and
  sin is a norm, then demonic forces move in as by the invitation
  of sin being pursued.)
- Paul's power encounters do not illustrate taking authority over
  territorial spirits. Acts 13:6-12 and Acts 16:16-18 do not advocate or imply SLSW.
- Paul's ministry in Ephesus does not illustrate the binding of a territorial spirit.
- Ephesians 3:10 is not a mandate to serve notice to the territorial
  spirits. (I personally like this Scripture for it shows how the
  Church itself reveals the wisdom of God to demonic forces.)[7]

Conclusions

We do not stand in condemnation regarding either the theories
behind territorial and tutelary spirits nor do we brutally oppose SLSW.
We declare that demons, due to their lack of omnipresence qualities
are limited to certain areas, but whether they remain there permanently, rule over those areas, have authority over the people there, and have
complete jurisdictional powers, is a matter of both interpretation and
speculation. On the other hand we are certain of some clearly taught
biblical facts and principles:

[7] Arnold, *Three Crucial Questions*, 165. Note: The main points are Arnold's and the
comments are mine.

141 1. Satan and his demons were decisively overcome
on the Cross by the Son of God. He is a *defeated* enemy.

2. Sin of all kinds is an open door for demons to enter and to infiltrate systems and people.
3. Christians are asked to stand firm and to resist the devil.
4. Prayer is directed to the Lord God, and He provides, in answer
to our prayer, the protection and security and boldness and
strength we need when we are confronted by evil forces.
5. The Church is the Lord's agency on earth to bring people into His
Kingdom, and the gospel is the "power unto salvation." The
proclamation of God's Word, faithfully and sincerely, is always a
blow to demonic forces.

The proclamation of God's Word
is always a blow to demonic forces.

6. Our concentration, therefore, should be on bringing individuals
into the Kingdom.
7. Similarly, if individuals are demonically influenced and controlled, our full attention should be given to the individual rather
than to territories and institutions.
8. In the name of Jesus, we *will* overcome any demonic forces that
abound in the world.

DEMONOLOGY
BIBLIOGRAPHY

Alderman, Clifford Lindsey. *A Cauldron of Witches.* New York: Pocket Books, 1971.

Alexander, William M. *Demonic Possession in the New Testament.* Edinburgh, Scotland: T & T Clark, 1902.

Anderson, Neil T. *The Bondage Breaker.* Eugene, OR: Harvest House, 1993.

Arnold, Clinton E. *Three Crucial Questions about Spiritual Warfare.* Grand Rapids: Baker, 1997.

Barnhouse, Donald Grey. *The Invisible War: The Panorama of the Continuing Conflict between Good and Evil.* Grand Rapids: Zondervan, 1965.

Becot, David W. *A Dictionary of Early Christian Beliefs.* Peabody, MA: Hendrickson, 1998.

Brown, Rebecca, M.D. *He Came to Set the Captives Free.* New Kensington, PA: Whitaker House, 1992.

Bubeck, Mark I. *The Adversary: The Christian versus Demonic Activity.* Chicago: Moody Press, 1975.

Cottrell, Jack. *Demonology* (Unpublished Class Notes). Cincinnati, OH: Cincinnati Bible Seminary, 1999.

Demaray, Donald. *Listen to Luther.* Wheaton, IL: Victor Books, 1989.

Dickason, C. Fred. *Angels, Elect and Evil.* Chicago: Moody Press, 1975.

_____. *Demon Possession and the Christian: A New Perspective.* Chicago: Moody Press, 1987.

Ensign, Grayson H., and Edward Howe. *Counseling and Demonization: The Missing Link.* Amarillo, TX: Recovery Publications, 1989.

Foster, Richard J. *Prayer.* New York: Harper Collins, 1992.

Gross, Edward N. *Miracles, Demons, and Spiritual Warfare.* Grand Rapids: Baker, 1990.

Guyon, Madame Jeanne. *Experiencing God through Prayer.* Springdale, PA: Whitaker House, 1984.

143 Hammond, Frank and Ida Mae. *Pigs in the Parlour.* Impact Christian Books, 1973.

Horrobin, Peter. *Healing Deliverance: 1. The Biblical Basis.* Tonbridge, Trent, England: Sovereign World, 1994.

House, H. Wayne. *Charts of Christian Theology and Doctrine.* Grand Rapids: Zondervan, 1992.

Huegel, F.J. *The Mysery of Iniquity.* Minneapolis: Bethany Fellowship, 1968.

Hunt, Dave. *A Woman Rides the Beast.* Eugene, OR: Harvest House, 1994.

Joachim, Hans Kraus. *Theology of the Psalms.* A Continental Commentary. Translated by Keith Crim. Minneapolis: Fortress Press, 1992.

Joyner, Rick. *Overcoming Witchcraft.* Charlotte, NC: MorningStar Publications, 1997.

Kinnaman, Gary. *Angels Dark and Light.* Secunderabad, India: Ben Publishing, 1994.

Koch, Kurt E. *Christian Counselling and Occultism.* Grand Rapids: Kregel, 1972.

_____. *Demonology Past and Present.* Grand Rapids: Kregel, 1973.

Kreeft, Peter. *Angels and Demons.* San Francisco: Ignatius Press, 1995.

Langton, Edward. *Essentials of Demonology: A Study of Jewish and Christian Doctrine, Its Origin and Development.* London: The Epworth Press, 1949.

Larkin, Clarence. *The Spirit World.* Philadelphia: Self-published, 1921.

Leahey, Fredrick S. *Satan Cast Out: A Study in Biblical Demonology.* Edinburgh, Scotland: The Banner of Truth Trust, 1975.

Lewis, C.S. *The Screwtape Letters.* London and Glasgow: Collins Clear-Type Press, 1942.

Liardon, Roberts. *Haunted Houses, Ghosts and Demons.* Tulsa: Albury Publishing, 1998.

Lightner, Robert. *Angels, Satan and Demons.* Nashville: Word, 1998.

Lindsey, Hal W., and C.C. Carlson. *Satan Is Alive and Well on Planet Earth.* Grand Rapids: Zondervan, 1972.

Ling, Trevor. *The Significance of Satan.* London: SPCK, 1961.

Lowe, Chuck. *Territorial Spirits and World Evangelization.* Kent, UK: OMF/Mentor, 1998.

McDowell, Josh, and Don Stewart. *Understanding the Occult.* San Bernardino, CA: Here's Life Publishers, 1982.

Moreau, Scott. *Essentials of Christian Warfare.* Wheaton, IL: Harold Shaw, 1997.

Morey, Robert. *Satan's Devices*. Eugene, OR: Harvest House, **144**
1993.

Murphy, Ed. *The Handbook for Spiritual Warfare*. Nashville: Thomas
Nelson, 1992.

Peck, Scott M. *People of the Lie: The Hope for Healing Human Evil*.
Nyoric, WY: Simon & Schuster, 1983.

Penn-Lewis, Jessie. *War on the Saints*. Springdale, PA: Whitaker House,
1996.

Pentecost, Dwight J. *Your Adversary the Devil*. Secunderabad, India:
OM Books, 1969.

Phillips, McCandlish. *The Spirit World*. Wheaton, IL: Victor Books,
1970.

Prince, Derek. *Expelling Demons*. Christchurch, NZ: Derek Prince
Ministries, 2001.

_____. *They Shall Expel Demons*. Christchurch, NZ: Derek Prince
Ministries, 1998.

Richards, Larry. *Every Good and Evil Angel in the Bible*. Nashville:
Thomas Nelson, 1998.

_____. *New International Encyclopedia of Bible Words*. Based on
the NIV and NASB. Grand Rapids: Zondervan, 1991.

Schlink, Basilea. *The Unseen World of Angels and Demons*. Secunderabad, India: OM Books, 1985.

Schnoebelen, William. *Wicca: Satan's Little White Lie*. Chino, CA: Chick
Publications, 1990.

Schnoebelen, William and Sharon. *Blood on the Doorposts*. Chino,
CA: Chick Publications, 1994.

Schuetze, John D. *Angels and Demons: Have Wings—Will Travel*. Mil-
waukee, WI: Northwestern Publishing, 1998.

Stegemann, Wolfgang, Bruce Malina, and Gerd Theissen. *The Social
Setting of Jesus and the Gospels*. Minneapolis: Fortress Press, 2002.

Subritzky, Bill. *Demons Defeated*. New Zealand: Dove Ministries, 1985.

Sumrall, Lester. *Demons: The Answer Book*. Springdale, PA: Whitaker
House, 1993.

Unger, Merill F. *Demons in the World Today*. Wheaton, IL: Tyndale
House, 1971.

_____. *What Demons Can Do to Saints*. Secunderabad, India:
OM Books, 1991.

Wagner, Peter. *Territorial Spirits*. Secunderabad, India: Ben Publishing,
1991.

Wallace, William A. *The Elements of Philosophy: A Compendium for
Philosophers and Theologians*. New York: Alba House, 1977.

145 Warner, Timothy M. *Spiritual Warfare: Victory over the Powers of This Dark World.* Wheaton, IL: Crossway Books. 1991.

Warwick, John Montgomery. *Demon Possessions.* Minneapolis: Bethany Fellowship, 1976.

Whyte, Maxwell H.A. *A Manual on Exorcism.* Springdale, PA: Whitaker House, 1974.

Wiersbe, Warren W. *The Strategy of Satan.* Wheaton, IL: Tyndale House, 1979.

The World's Religions. Hertsfordshire, England: Lion Publishing, 1982.

Wright, Stafford J. *Mind, Man and the Spirits.* Exeter, UK: The Paternoster Press, 1991.

117 Schenck, Kenneth L. "A Celebration of the Enthroned Son: The Catena of Hebrews." *Journal of Biblical Literature* 20, no. 3 (2001) 469-485.

Schindler, Amy. "Angels and the AIDS Epidemic: The Resurgent Popularity of Angel Imagery in the United States of America." *Journal of American Culture* 22, no. 3 (Fall 1999) 49-61.

Shea, John. "Angels We Have Heard on Low." *U.S. Catholic* 6, no. 12 (December 1995) 37-38.

Shedd, Charlie W. *Brush of an Angel's Wing.* Carmel, NY: Guideposts, 1994.

Silver, David Jeremy. *A History of Judaism.* New York: Basic Books, 1994.

ten Boom, Corrie. *Marching Orders for the End Battle.* Fort Washington, PA: Christian Literature Crusade, 1969.

van der Hart, Rob. *The Theology of Angels and Devils.* Notre Dame, IN: Fides Publishers, 1972.

Weber, Bruce. "Angels Angels." *New York Times* Magazine (April 25, 1993) 29-30.

Welker, Michael. "Angels in the Biblical Traditions: An Impressive Logic and the Imposing Problem of their Hypercomplex Reality." *Theology Today* 51, no. 3 (October 1994) 367-380.

Westermann, Claus. *God's Angels Need No Wings.* Translated by David Scheidt. Philadelphia: Fortress Press, 1979.

Whyte, Alexander. *The Nature of Angels.* Grand Rapids: Baker, 1976.

Wiederkehr, Macrina. *A Tree Full of Angels: Seeing the Holy in the Ordinary.* San Francisco: HarperSanFrancisco, 1995.

Wink, Walter. *Engaging the Powers: Discernment and Resistance in a World of Domination.* Minneapolis: Fortress Press, 1992.

_____. *Naming the Powers: The Language of Powers in the New Testament.* Philadelphia: Fortress Press, 1984.

_____. *Unmasking the Powers: The Invisible Forces That Determine Human Existence.* Philadelphia: Fortress Press, 1986.

Zlotowitz, Mier. *Bereishis: Genesis: A New Translation with a Commentary Anthologized from Talmudic, Midrashic, and Rabbinic Sources.* Vol. 1a. Brooklyn: Mesorah Publications, 1986.

Marshall, I. Howard. *The Acts of the Apostles*. Reprint, Grand **116**
Rapids: Eerdmans, 1989.

McManus, Dennis. "Angels: Their Importance in Our Lives." *Catholic World* 238, no. 1424 (March 1995) 68-73.

Miller, Patrick D. "Imagining God." *Theology Today* 51, no. 3 (October 1994) 341-344.

Mitchell, Nathan. "Negotiating Rapture: Rumors of Angels." *Worship* 71, no. 4 (July 1997) 350-357.

Moolenburgh, H.C. *Meeting with Angels: One Hundred and One Real-Life Encounters*. New York: Barnes & Noble, 1995.

Morris, Leon. *The Gospel according to Matthew*. Grand Rapids: Eerdmans, 1992.

Mounce, Robert H. *Book of Revelation*. Grand Rapids: Eerdmans, 1977.

Niebuhr, Gustav G. "After a Hiatus of Maybe 300 Years and Much Skepticism, Angels Are Making a Comeback." *Wall Street Journal* (May 12, 1992).

Niebuhr, Reinhold. *The Nature and Destiny of Man*. Vol. 1. New York: Scribner and Sons, 1941.

Noll, Stephen F. "Angels, Heavenly Beings, Angel Christology." *Dictionary of the Later New Testament & Its Development*. Edited by Ralph P. Martin and Peter H. Davids, 44-48. Downers Grove, IL: InterVarsity, 1997.

_____. *Angels of Light, Powers of Darkness: Thinking Biblically about Angels, Satan, & Principalities*. Downers Grove, IL: InterVarsity, 1998.

_____. "Thinking about Angels." In *The Unseen World: Christian Reflections on Angels, Demons and the Heavenly Realm*. Edited by Anthony Lane, 1-27. Grand Rapids: Baker, 1997.

Parente, Pascal P. *The Angels*. St. Meinard, IN: Grail Publications, 1957.

Peterson, Eugene. "Writers and Angels: Witnesses to Transcendence." *Theology Today* 51, no. 3 (October 1994) 394-404.

Ramm, Bernard. "Angels." In *Basic Christian Doctrines*. Edited by Carl F.H. Henry. Reprint, Grand Rapids: Baker, 1971.

Reid, Daniel G. "Angels, Archangels." In *Dictionary of Paul and His Letters*. Edited by Gerald F. Hawthorne and Ralph P. Martin, 20-23. Downers Grove, IL: InterVarsity, 1993.

Rhodes, Ron. *Angels among Us*. Eugene, OR: Harvest House, 1994.

Riordan, William. "The Interaction between Heaven and Earth: An Interview with Brother Donald Mansir, F.S.C." *The Catholic World* 238, no. 1424 (March 1995) 74-79.

115 Gaebelein, A.C. *The Angels of God.* Reprint, Grand Rapids: Baker, 1969.

Graham, Billy. *Angels: God's Secret Agents.* Garden City, NY: Doubleday, 1975.

Grudem, Wayne. *Systematic Theology: An Introduction to Biblical Doctrine.* Grand Rapids: Zondervan, 1994.

Hagner, Donald A. *Matthew 14–28.* Word Biblical Commentary. Vol. 33b. Dallas: Word Books, 1995.

Halberstam, Yitta, and Judith Leventhal. *Small Miracles: Extraordinary Coincidences from Everyday Life.* Avon, MA: Adams Media Corporation, 1997.

Hirsch, Samson Raphael. *The Pentateuch: Genesis.* Rendered into English by Isaac Levy. 2nd ed., revised. Vol. 1. Gateshead, NY: Judaica Press, 1989.

Hodges, Tom, and Robert Owen. "Do you believe angels, that is, some kind of heavenly beings who visit Earth, in fact exist?" A survey conducted and published in *Skeptic* 9, no. 3 (2002) 14.

Hunter, Charles and Frances. *Angels on Assignment.* New Kensington, PA: Whitaker House, 2001.

"In the Bible, They Don't Talk So Much." *New York Times* (April 1997) Arts & Leisure Section.

Jones, Timothy. "Rumors of Angels." *Christianity Today* 37 (April 5, 1993) 18-22.

Kaminer, Wendy. "The Latest Fashion in Irrationality: When the Inner Child Finds a Guardian Angel, Publishers Are in Heaven." *Atlantic Monthly* 278, no. 1 (July 1996) 103-106.

Kinnaman, Gary. *Angels Dark and Light.* Ann Arbor, MI: Servant Publications, 1994.

Levison, John R. "The Prophetic Spirit As an Angel according to Philo." *Harvard Theological Review* 88 (April 1995) 189-207.

Lightner, Robert. *Angels, Satan, and Demons: Invisible Beings That Inhabit the Spiritual World.* Nashville: Word, 1998.

MacArthur, John Jr. *God, Satan, and Angels: Selected Notes, Selected Scriptures.* Edited by Mark Hall. Panorama City, CA: Word of Grace Communications, 1983.

Maly, Eugene. "Genesis." *The Jerome Biblical Commentary.* Edited by Raymond Brown, Joseph Fitzmyer, and Roland E. Murphy. Vol. 1. Englewood Cliffs, NJ: Prentice-Hall, 1968.

Markoe, Merrill. "I Network with Angels." *New Woman* 7, no. 4 (April 1997) 58-61.